Commercial Homes in Tourism

This volume is the first to examine the commercial home from an international perspective, paying attention to the frequently occurring but often neglected forms of commercial accommodation including farmstays, historic houses, and self-catering accommodation. Conceptually, it helps to explain a range of behaviours and practices, for example the importance of setting and the nature of the host–guest exchange. The idea of home provides a conceptual bridge to related themes, for example identity, gender, emotional management and cultural mobilities whose investigation in a commercial home context offers fascinating insights into hospitality, tourism and society.

This book is structured around three themes. The first is dimensions of the commercial home and includes discussion of issues pertaining to forms and characteristics and female entrepreneurship. The second theme considers the commercial home as an investigative lens to examine wider issues of society, hospitality and tourism such as the commercial home as a tool for rural economic development. The third theme, extending the commercial home paradigm, looks at new areas of development, including the Malaysian Muslim home as a site for economic and political action and the use of the home in marketing regional localities.

Commercial Homes in Tourism is the first book to give recognition to this distinct, economically important and expanding form of tourism business by bringing together recent, international research on this common form of commercial tourism accommodation. Given the global nature of the commercial home phenomenon, and owing to the originality of its theoretical contributions and practical insights, this book will be of interest across a broad range of subjects and disciplines interested in the examination of the home phenomenon, including students, academics and business practitioners.

Paul A. Lynch is Reader in Hospitality and Tourism Management at the University of Strathclyde, UK.

Alison J. McIntosh is Associate Professor in Hospitality and Tourism Management at the University of Waikato, New Zealand.

Hazel Tucker is Senior Lecturer in Tourism at the University of Otago, New Zealand.

Routledge Critical Studies in Tourism, Business and Management
Series editors:
Professor Tim Coles, *University of Exeter, UK* and
Professor C. Michael Hall, *University of Canterbury, New Zealand*

This ground-breaking monograph series deals directly with theoretical and conceptual issues at the interface between business, management and tourism studies. It incorporates research-generated, highly specialised cutting-edge studies of new and emergent themes, such as knowledge management and innovation, that affect the future business and management of tourism. The books in this series are conceptually challenging, empirically rigorous, creative and, above all, capable of driving current thinking and unfolding debate in the business and management of tourism. This monograph series will appeal to researchers, academics and practitioners in the fields of tourism, business and management, and the social sciences.

Published titles:

Commercial Homes in Tourism
An international perspective
Edited by Paul A. Lynch, Alison J. McIntosh and Hazel Tucker

Forthcoming titles:

Sustainable Marketing of Cultural and Heritage Tourism
Deepak Chhabra

The *Routledge Critical Studies in Tourism, Business and Management* monograph series builds on core concepts explored in the corresponding **Routledge International Studies of Tourism, Business and Management** book series.
Series editors:
Professor Tim Coles, *University of Exeter, UK* and
Professor C. Michael Hall, *University of Canterbury, New Zealand*

Books in the series offer upper-level undergraduates and master's students comprehensive, thought-provoking yet accessible books that combine essential theory and international best practice on issues in the business and management of tourism, such as HRM, entrepreneurship, service-quality management, leadership, CSR, strategy, operations, branding and marketing.

Published titles:

International Business and Tourism
Global issues, contemporary interactions
Edited by Tim Coles and C. Michael Hall

Commercial Homes in Tourism

An international perspective

Edited by
Paul A. Lynch, Alison J. McIntosh
and Hazel Tucker

Routledge
Taylor & Francis Group

LONDON AND NEW YORK

First published 2009
by Routledge
2 Park Square, Milton Park, Abingdon, Oxon OX14 4RN

Simultaneously published in the USA and Canada
by Routledge
270 Madison Avenue, New York, NY 10016

Routledge is an imprint of the Taylor & Francis Group, an Informa business

© 2009 Editorial selection and matter, Paul A. Lynch, Alison J. McIntosh
and Hazel Tucker; individual chapters, the contributors

Typeset in Times New Roman by
Taylor & Francis Books
Printed and bound in Great Britain by
MPG Books Ltd, Bodmin

British Library Cataloguing in Publication Data
A catalogue record for this book is available from the British Library

Library of Congress Cataloguing in Publication Data
Commercial homes : an international perspective / edited by Paul Lynch,
Alison J. McIntosh, and Hazel Tucker.
    p. cm.
  Includes bibliographical references.
  1. Hospitality industry. 2. Bed and breakfast accommodations.
3. Boardinghouses. I. Lynch, Paul, 1959– II. McIntosh, Alison J., 1971–
III. Tucker, Hazel, 1965–
  TX911.C6124 2009
  338.4′791–dc22
                                        2008040958

ISBN 978-0-415-47018-6 (hbk)
ISBN 978-0-203-88031-9 (ebk)

Contents

Figures

Tables

Contributors

Anne Benmore is a Senior Lecturer in Human Resource Management/Organisation Studies, at Bournemouth University, UK. She has a first degree from the University of Bath and a MA in Human Resource Management from Bournemouth University. Anne is currently working toward a PhD thesis, again at the University of Bath. Her research involves investigating how emotional labour is experienced in small establishments in the hospitality industry (specifically, small hotels). Anne has taught HR-related subjects at undergraduate and postgraduate level for many years. She has developed a particular module, Emotion in Business, which is popular amongst UK and international Master's students at Bournemouth University. Anne is a Member of the Chartered Institute of Personnel and Development.

Barbara A. Carmichael is a Professor in the Department of Geography and Environmental Studies at Wilfrid Laurier University, Waterloo, Ontario, Canada. She has an MBA from Durham University Business School, UK and a PhD from the University of Victoria. She is also the Associate Director of the NeXt Research Centre (Nascent Entrepreneurship and the Exploitation of Technology) in the School of Business and Economics at Wilfrid Laurier University. Her research interests are in skier-choice behaviour, special events, casino impacts, rural tourism, market segmentation, and resident attitudes towards tourism and tourism entrepreneurship. She is a member of the editorial board for *Tourism Geographies* and has published papers in the *Journal of Travel Research*, the *Journal of Travel and Tourism Marketing*, *Tourism Management*, *Tourism Review International* and the *Journal of Vacation Marketing*. She is a former Chair of the Recreation, Tourism and Sport Specialty Group of the Association of American Geographers.

Philip J. Goulding is a Senior Lecturer in Tourism Management in the Centre for International Tourism Research (CITouR), Faculty of Organisation and Management, Sheffield Hallam University, UK. He completed a PhD at the Department of Hospitality and Tourism Management, University of Strathclyde. Philip was previously Senior Lecturer in Tourism at Napier

University. He was variously responsible for undergraduate and postgraduate programmes in tourism and hospitality management and active in teaching, educational development and consultancy in tourism and local economic development, destination management and policy. As a research focus, temporality in tourism synthesises each of these interests. On this theme, Philip has contributed to various conferences, books and journals. He was awarded prizes for best research papers at IHTVC (2005) and Anatolia (2006) research conferences. Philip's publications and research interests are linked to the role, implications and evolution of temporality and temporal change in tourism businesses and destinations, in local economic development and tourism policy. He has a long record of academic development and leadership in tourism and hospitality education in the UK.

C. Michael Hall is Professor of Marketing in the Department of Management, University of Canterbury, New Zealand and Docent, Department of Geography, University of Oulu, Finland. Co-editor of *Current Issues in Tourism*, he has written widely in the tourism field with current research focusing on global environmental change, regional development, servicescapes, gastronomy and tourism policy.

Candice Harris is a Senior Lecturer in Management in the Faculty of Business at AUT University Auckland, New Zealand. Her research interests include gender and diversity issues in tourism and management, human-resource management, and qualitative and critical approaches to research. She is a Deputy Director of the Centre for Work and Labour Market Studies based at AUT University and a member of the New Zealand Tourism Research Institute. Candice has also recently participated in research teams from the New Zealand Centre for Small and Medium Enterprise (SME) Research based at Massey University.

Gayle Jennings is Associate Professor of Tourism Management, Department of Tourism, Leisure, Hotel and Sport Management, Griffith University, Gold Coast Campus, Australia. Her research agenda focuses on quality tourism experiences as well as the use of qualitative methodologies. She has sole authored and edited a number of books, and written book chapters and journal articles across a range of topics relating to theoretical paradigms that inform research processes, water-based tourism and quality tourism experiences.

Elisabeth Kastenholz is a German citizen living in Portugal. She holds a Degree in Tourism Management and Planning, a Master's Degree in Business Administration and a Doctoral Degree in Tourism, and works as Professor of Marketing and Tourism at the University of Aveiro. Her research interests include rural, nature and sustainable tourism, tourism destination marketing and consumer behaviour in tourism. She is at present the coordinator of the undergraduate programme in tourism at the University of Aveiro.

Brian King is Professor and Head of the School of Hospitality, Tourism and Marketing at Victoria University, Australia. The University won the Australian Tourism Award in the Education and Training category in 2000 and in 2005. Brian has occupied management roles in the tour operations, resorts and airline sectors. He is author/co-author of several books including *Creating Island Resorts, Case Studies in Tourism and Hospitality Marketing* and *Asia-Pacific Tourism: Regional Planning, Co-operation and Development*. He is Joint Editor-in-Chief of the journal *Tourism, Culture and Communication* and holds editorial board positions with a range of leading refereed journals.

Lucia Laurincikova is managing the activities of the Institute for Minority Entrepreneurship at the Dublin Institute of Technology, Ireland. Lucia's principal research interests lie in exploring minority entrepreneurship, including socially disadvantaged and marginalised groups such as ethnic, female, disabled, travellers, gay, grey (over 50 years old), socio-economically disadvantaged and Gaeltacht entrepreneurs. She is currently undertaking her PhD studies at Dublin Institute of Technology where she is focusing on mapping out minority entrepreneurship in Ireland and the ways of engendering minority entrepreneurship. She is also involved in Ireland's Network of Teachers and Researchers of Entrepreneurship.

Paul A. Lynch is Reader in Hospitality and Tourism Management in the Department of Hospitality and Tourism Management, University of Strathclyde, Glasgow, UK. His main research interests are commercial homes, lifestyle entrepreneurs, networks and networking, social enterprises, critical hospitality and highly qualitative research methods. Paul has published in the fields of entrepreneurship, hospitality, human-resource management, leisure, sociology, service sector and tourism. He is co-editor of *Hospitality: A Social Lens*. He is a Visiting Professor at the University of Stenden, Netherlands.

Kelley A. McClinchey is a PhD Candidate at Wilfrid Laurier University, Waterloo, Ontario, Canada in the Department of Geography and Environmental Studies. Her research interests include rural tourism, tourist image, sustainable rural systems and culinary and event tourism and tourism entrepreneurship.

Alison J. McIntosh is Associate Professor at the Department of Tourism and Hospitality Management, University of Waikato, New Zealand. Her main research interests are in tourists' experiences of heritage and culture, the subjective, personal and spiritual nature of tourism and hospitality experiences, and qualitative and critical approaches to tourism research. Alison has published in leading journals such as *Annals of Tourism Research, Journal of Travel Research, Tourism Management* and *Journal of Sustainable Tourism*.

Gianna Moscardo has been a member of the academic staff of the School of Business, James Cook University since February 2002. Before then she was a Principal Research Fellow and project leader in tourism research in the Cooperative Research Centres for Reef and Rainforest, Townsville, Queensland for eight years, managing a series of research and extension activities aimed at enhancing the sustainability of tourism activities in Northern Australia. Her qualifications in applied psychology and sociology support her research interests in understanding how tourists make decisions and evaluate their travel experiences and how communities and organisations perceive, plan for, and manage tourism and tourists. She was recently elected to the World Tourism Organization's International Academy for the Study of Tourism Scholars.

Ziene Mottiar is a Tourism Economics lecturer in the School of Hospitality Management and Tourism, Dublin Institute of Technology, Ireland. Ziene has a range of research interests, in particular in the areas of tourism firms, regional development and entrepreneurship. She has publications in a variety of journals including *Journal of Sustainable Tourism*, *Journal of Vacation Marketing and Leisure Studies* and forthcoming articles in *Journal of Sustainable Tourism* and *Current Issues in Tourism*. In addition she has written a number of book chapters in the area of small tourism firms. She is currently involved in research in the areas of minority entrepreneurship, lifestyle entrepreneurs, tourism-destination development and tourism multinationals.

Kevin D. O'Gorman completed his PhD in the Department of Hospitality and Tourism Management, University of Strathclyde, Glasgow, UK. His research interests are concerned with the history and philosophy of hospitality and his PhD research is an analysis of ancient, classical and mediaeval texts both in their original languages and modern commentaries on them, to discover the origins of hospitality.

Patricia Sloane-White is an Assistant Professor of Anthropology at the University of Delaware, USA. She conducted anthropological fieldwork on Malay entrepreneurship and the Islamic economy in Kuala Lumpur, Malaysia from 1993 to 1994, and earned a DPhil in Social Anthropology from Oxford University in 1996. She conducted further research in Malaysia from 1996 to 1998 on the Malay middle class, on gender and on Islamic corporate culture. She is the author of the book *Islam, Modernity and Entrepreneurship among the Malays* and various articles on contemporary social life and social change in Malaysia.

Marion Sparrer is Lecturer at the University School of Tourism/University of A Coruña, Spain. She holds a Master's degree in Economics and Quality in Tourism (University of A Coruña) and a PhD in Geography (University of Santiago de Compostela). Her main research interest lies in the fields of tourism geography, rural tourism and development, tourism and gender, and tourism planning.

Daniela Stehlik was appointed as inaugural Professor in Stronger Communities at Curtin University of Technology and Director, Alcoa Research Centre for Stronger Communities, Australia in December 2003. She is one of Australia's leading social scientists working at the intersections of resiliency, human-service practice and social cohesion focussing on families and communities in regional/rural Australia. She has published widely in Australia and internationally, and regularly presents her work at national and international conferences.

Hazel Tucker is Senior Lecturer in the Department of Tourism at the University of Otago, New Zealand. She has a PhD in Social Anthropology from Durham University, UK, and has conducted extensive fieldwork into tourism and social change in central Turkey. She is author of *Living with Tourism* (Routledge, 2003) and co-editor of *Tourism and Post-colonialism* (Routledge, 2004). She has also published on heritage construction and interpretation, host–guest relationships in tourism, and tourist experiences and performances in the package tour sector of New Zealand.

Leanne White is Lecturer in Marketing at Victoria University in Melbourne, Australia. She has taught Marketing, Public Relations, Communications and Australian Studies at universities since 1988. Leanne has also worked in the areas of public relations, research and policy in government and higher education. Her research interests include advertising, national identity, commercial nationalism, Australian popular culture and the Olympic movement. Leanne's MA research thesis (1995) was entitled 'Commercial Nationalism: Images of Australia in Television Advertising'. Her doctoral thesis, which examines manifestations of official and commercial nationalism at the Sydney 2000 Olympic Games, is currently being completed.

Foreword

This study of small hospitality enterprises is a welcome development in a new field of study, opened up in part by the study of hospitality as a social phenomenon. All over the world, and throughout history, societies have developed norms and values relating to the treatment of strangers and visitors from outside of the community. Academics from a number of fields have increasingly looked to these traditional approaches to hospitality as a way of better informing the study of the contemporary world. For those researching the commercial activities of the 'hospitality industry' the study of hospitality from an array of social-science perspectives has better informed the study of the relationship between guests and hosts, and the potential for 'turning customers into friends'. For other academics, working within the social sciences, hospitality has enabled the study of guest and host relations as a metaphor for the relationships between communities and those who come from outside that community. This book, though informed by a number of different social sciences, is firmly located in the study of commercial hospitality services within the context of small firms.

In particular, the text explores the commercial hospitality being offered in domestic settings – the commercial home of the title. Those offering accommodation services in the form of small hotels, bed and breakfast establishments, guesthouses, farmstay settings and a number of other establishments where owners are frequently sharing their domestic premises with fee-paying guests. They are, in effect, businesses which overlap the domestic and commercial domains of hospitality. These businesses engage in commercial activities on a range of levels, from the occasional paying guest in the more popular times of year, to businesses which attract and host customers throughout the year, and where earnings from commercial activities represent a substantial part of total household income. Given the variations of the relationships between the commercial and domestic settings, and between hosts and guests, the commercial home enterprise provides a fascinating arena for study. This book makes a welcome contribution to our understanding of these relationships.

The linkage between the commercial home and hospitality is not an accidental one. The sector is dominated by micro-firms often based on owner management with few, if any, employees outside of family members. For many, the hotel, guesthouse or bed and breakfast establishment is their first and only business venture. Many decide to offer commercial-accommodation services because there are perceived to be low barriers to entry. Those with large enough domestic dwellings can offer out spare bedrooms to paying guests, and in many locations, the cost of buying a commercial property is not very much greater than the cost of buying a domestic dwelling. Most importantly, many would-be entrepreneurs enter the accommodation-services sector assuming that the skills sets for commercial operations are largely similar to those used when offering accommodation to family and friends. Naivety about the commercial dimensions of offering these services to paying guests is frequently a feature of these owner-managers' approaches, and as a consequence, there is evidence of quite high levels of churn in ownership in this strand of the accommodation sector.

The exploration of the commercial element of the commercial home provides, therefore, a rich seam for researchers. The origins, business motives, prior experiences, perceptions, training of owner managers, survival rates and churn in ownership are all interesting avenues for research. Certainly, one strand of analysis describes these businesses as being run by 'lifestyle' entrepreneurs. That is, business run for not purely entrepreneurial motives. Some enter the business so as to live in a particular location, or to have more personal control, or as a form of semi-retirement. As a consequence, research into the skill sets developed and strategies pursued in the functional aspects of managing commercial hospitality as a service through approaches to marketing, customer care, service quality, training and development, cost control, accounting practices, and so on, is insightful. The fact that these micro-firms represent such a high proportion of the potential supply of accommodation-services provision make them interesting to those concerned with hospitality and tourism, as well as to those studying entrepreneurialism and small-firm management.

Whilst the study of the commercial dimensions of the commercial aspects of the commercial home yields a host of interesting and fascinating issues to be studied, the home element also suggests some rich veins for exploration. Fundamentally, the relationship between the commercial and domestic is potentially of great interest. For example, the extent to which the domestic is impacted by the commercial and vice versa will be of interest to a number of different social scientists. The management of physical space between family-member hosts and paying guests impacts on both family members and guests. For guests, there may be the perceived attraction of staying with a 'real' family in a domestic setting, but the reality is of 'private' areas exclusively for family members and guest areas which have been depersonalised to make the accommodation look more like professional hotel areas. Research into these differing perceptions of hosts' relationship with guests, and guests' varied expectations of their relationship with hosts, has the potential to yield some valuable insights.

In addition, the commercial home can represent gendered spaces and domains in the hosting role. The management of the delivery of this array of service experiences can reveal much about gender roles, and expectations and roles in the wider society. Research into how these gender roles are played, and by whom, in different settings can reflect expectations of appropriate roles and behaviours, as well as power and status displayed in different commercial home settings. An associated, but separate, theme might relate to the gender of the chief entrepreneur and the relationship between the commercial home as an entrepreneurial activity. To what extent is the property a home with a few paying guests, or is it largely a commercial site with private accommodation attached, and is there any relationship between these issues and the gender of the entrepreneur?

This book makes a unique contribution to our understanding of this significant but grossly under-researched aspect of the entrepreneurship and hospitality and tourism-service provision. It benefits from a multidisciplinary approach with different authors writing from an impressive array of perspectives. It also benefits from an international authorship which confirms the global nature of the phenomenon. The domestic setting was the original location for commercial guests, as hotels and dedicated commercial accommodation only emerged when there were increased numbers of travellers. Even today, remote rarely visited sites will largely rely on small, commercial home provision. Hotels only begin to appear when the site becomes less remote and the volume of visitors increase. The sad irony is that whilst hotels are the subject of much research, this aspect of the accommodation sector is grossly under-researched and misunderstood. This book makes a welcome and stimulating contribution to understanding service provided in commercial homes. Without doubt it will stimulate a revision of thinking, increased research activity and many follow-up texts.

Conrad Lashley
Professor/Director of the Centre for Leisure Retailing
Nottingham Business School
Nottingham Trent University

Preface

The genesis of this book was in the post-prandial phase of hospitality sitting around a table at a hotel's outdoor restaurant in July 2005 that overlooked a sparkling cobalt-blue Adriatic sea; the occasion was the farewell dinner of the first Critical Tourism Studies Conference in Dubrovnik, Croatia. Whilst our colleagues boogied on the veranda, we tangoed with the work we had each been doing covering New Zealand boutique accommodation and bed and breakfasts, Turkish cave homes and Scottish commercial homes. We identified similarities in terms of our small accommodation focus and our largely qualitative approaches, and enriching differences in our emerging narrative interpretations, ideologies and viewpoints, such as gendered perspectives. We saw potential value in a larger academic community drawn from a range of disciplines to explore this highly complex and socially significant phenomenon in further depth, and questioned the further qualitative insights which might emerge if viewed through different cultural lenses. So, from this conversation, the idea for this book arose, a book intended to be multidisciplinary and international in its scope. We received over 40 expressions of interest to our call for contributors, testimony to the significance of commercial home accommodation as an area of investigation. We are delighted with the range of contributors and the subjects and disciplines represented: anthropology, economics, entrepreneurship, environmental studies, geography, hospitality, management, marketing and tourism; with hindsight, we feel we might have attracted submissions from an even broader range of disciplines and with greater geographical scope had we better understood the limitations of the distribution networks we employed.

In conceiving of this book we sought to counterpoint the idea of small commercial accommodation as downsized versions of hotels, hence the uniqueness of the concept signalled by the 'commercial home'. As the book progressed we grew ever more confident in the power of the commercial home concept as a means to explore major issues of cross-disciplinary relevance, for example gender, marginalisation, the ethic of hospitality, social discourses, meanings of home, the private and the public domain, the personal emotions and significances of a 'home'; authenticity and performance, entrepreneurship, lifestyle and economic development. The book also made us realise that commercial homes merit study in their own right and we would like to see focused modules developed in the programmes we teach, as well as the concept entering into common parlance and ways of thinking in relation to economic development policy. Therefore, our vision regarding the potential of the commercial home concept is considerable and we hope that readers will be similarly inspired to help realise our ambitions.

Paul A. Lynch, Alison J. McIntosh and Hazel Tucker

Acknowledgements

Paul: My sincere thanks: to colleagues and my employer, the University of Strathclyde, in providing the time, space and encouragement to undertake and complete this book project (I know it's not RAE-able but I think it's very worthwhile); to all the Routledge people for making this project happen; to the series editors for having faith; to my friends and significant others for their companionship, support and understanding; to my mum and (from a distance) my dad; to my children, Brendan and Joe, for being the sunshines of my life. I would also like to thank Elsevier for permission to reproduce parts of Paul A. Lynch (2005) 'Commercial home enterprise and host: a United Kindom perspective', *International Journal of Hospitality Management*, 24(4): 533–553, and Paul A. Lynch and D. MacWhannell (2000) 'Home and commercialised hospitalty', in C. Lashley and A. Morrison (eds) *In Search of Hospitality Theoretical Perspectives and Debates*, Oxford: Butterworth-Heinemann, pp. 100–114, in Chapter 1.

Alison: I would like to thank a number of individuals who have aided me in the completion of this book. Thank you to my colleagues at the University of Waikato – Anne, Asad, Charlie, Chris, Christine, Greg, Jenny, Leonie, Maria, Naomi, Tim and the WMS Research Office – for their support and encouragement, and for allowing me the time and funds to make this project possible. Thank you also to C. Michael Hall for bringing this publishing opportunity to my attention, and to Paul, Hazel and Candice for their friendship, collaboration and engaging conversations over many a cuppa. Special thanks also go to my friends and family for always being there for me and providing their unconditional love and support during periods of writing both in the UK and New Zealand.

Hazel: I extend sincere thanks to the Department of Tourism at the University of Otago for providing the support, time and funds to allow me to complete this project. Helen Dunn's and Diana Evans' help in the final manuscript preparation was especially appreciated. Thank you also to my colleagues for their encouragement and support, particularly Michael Hall who always urged me to publish! I owe special thanks to my nearest and dearest: to Rob and Liam (aka Virgil, driver of Thunderbird 2); and to mum and dad for always being there and for always being fantastic.

1   Introduction

Paul A. Lynch, Alison J. McIntosh and Hazel Tucker

Emergence of the commercial-home paradigm

The hotel has been the dominant paradigm that has long determined, and served as, a commercial accommodation role model. Its counterpoint, the private home, is often represented as the antithesis to the hotel (Douglas 1991; Ritzer 1993). Recently, however, the commercial home enterprise has been proposed as a distinctive alternative to both the hotel and the private home whilst simultaneously acknowledging hotel and private home influences (Lynch 2003; 2005a; 2005b; 2005c; Lynch and MacWhannell 2000). As such, the commercial home constitutes a fusion of the commercial, social and private domains of hospitality proposed by Lashley (2000a: 5): commercial, i.e. 'the provision of hospitality as an economic activity'; social, i.e. 'the social settings in which hospitality and acts of hospitableness take place together with the impacts of social forces'; private, i.e. 'issues associated with both the provision of the "trinity" [food, beverage, accommodation] in the home as well as considering the impact of host and guest relationships'. The commercial home paradigm has thus emerged to challenge the primacy of the hotel paradigm and gives recognition and greater prominence to one of the most frequently occurring forms of commercial accommodation, including homestays, bed and breakfasts, farmstays, self-catering accommodation, guesthouses and small family hotels.

Small commercial accommodation has typically been studied through three lenses of entrepreneurship. The first lens is that of the small business or small firm where the size of the organisation is usually the main distinguishing feature (Ateljevic 2007; Carr 2007; Thomas 1998). This approach is helpful in being sensitive to the scale of the operation and its individual features rather than assuming it is a smaller version of a larger organisation and uncritically applying concepts derived from the study of the larger organisations. Problems with the small business approach include sector differences and various views on the concepts of 'small' or 'micro' (Morrison 1998a; Morrison and Conway 2007; Peacock 1993; Thomas 1998). The second lens is that of the family business where the family ownership is the main distinguishing feature and therefore can shed light on the significance to the

running of the organisation of the people element through making prominent family goals, life cycles and interrelationships (Getz and Carlsen 2000;
Getz, Carlsen and Morrison 2004). Such an approach is not size-sensitive
and gives prominence to the family unit. The third lens employed is that of
the lifestyle entrepreneur (Ateljevic and Doorne 2000; Morrison et al. 2001;
Di Domenico 2003). The importance of this approach is in rejecting the
primacy of the profit-making motivation and giving recognition to the significance of owner values and life aspirations in determining economic performance of the commercial operation. However, empirical evidence regarding
the actuality and realisation of desired lifestyle as opposed to a discourse of
lifestyle (whether the discourse is created by respondents or researchers is not
always clear) is largely missing from the hospitality and tourism literature.
All three approaches are influenced by organisational studies undertaken
outside of the hospitality sector and seek to provide a comparatively large-scale
discourse to explain types of mainly small commercially oriented organisations.
In effect, they have been 'imported' and imposed upon the study of small
commercial hosting accommodation.

A newer, fourth, lens is thus that of the commercial home enterprise; in its
origin, specific to the study of small accommodation enterprises viewed from
a hospitality perspective. This lens is influenced by reflection upon the
strengths and limitations of the preceding lenses, as well as consideration of
previous studies within hospitality and tourism that have sought to capture
the essential features of small accommodation enterprises. A number of
terms have been employed by researchers to describe small accommodation
enterprises so that their quintessential dimensions are captured: 'parahotel
business' (Schwaniger 1989), 'supplementary accommodation sector' (Seekings 1989), 'boutique accommodation' (Morrison et al. 1996), 'specialist
accommodation' (Pearce and Moscardo 1992), 'quasi hotels' (Slattery 2002)
or 'homestay' (Lynch 2000a) to name a few. Such descriptors attempt to
provide an umbrella term for small commercial lodgings that either seem to
aspire to copy hotel-type accommodation or to describe a form of accommodation letting that serves as counterpoint to a typically hotel benchmark.
However, there is a lack of agreement regarding the types of accommodation
being described and the descriptors largely emphasise the functionality of the
lodging without necessarily conveying any deeper sense of its nature. The
emergence of the commercial home paradigm is empirically grounded in forms
of small commercial accommodation and unifies conceptual characteristics,
notably that of the home.

Definition, concepts and types

A commercial home enterprise is where the home or a home construct is
used for the purpose of generating income through accommodation letting.
A detailed definition, description and discussion of the commercial home
enterprise is found in Lynch (2005c: 534–5), who developed the concept of

Table 1.1 Broad characteristics of commercial home enterprises derived from meta-analysis

	Smallest commercial home unit, e.g. host commercial home unit, family	Medium-sized, e.g. guest house	Largest commercial home unit, e.g. hotel
Number of bedrooms	1–2 rooms for guests		15 rooms for guests
Room-occupancy levels	Lowest		Highest
Host perception of commercial home	Private home	Commercial home enterprise	Business enterprise
Entrepreneurial orientation of host	Least entrepreneurial		Most entrepreneurial
Economic dependency on hosting income	Low economic dependency		High economic dependency
Most common primary host gender	Female	Female/Male	Male
Degree of partner involvement	Least partner involvement		Most partner involvement
Family-participation level	Family involvement		Family run
Higher education frequency	Lowest frequency with higher education		Highest-frequency with higher education
Host-training orientation	Lowest		Highest
Host engagement with home	Greatest engagement		Least engagement
Home–host relationship	Home as reflection of self highest		Home as reflection of self lowest
Product commodification	Least		Highest

Source: Lynch 2005c: 550.

the 'Commercial home' to refer to types of accommodation where visitors or guests pay to stay in private homes, where interaction takes place with a host and/or family usually living upon the premises and with whom public space is, to varying degrees, shared. 'Commercial home' therefore embraces a range of accommodation types including some (small) hotels, bed and breakfasts (B&Bs) and host family accommodation, which simultaneously span private, commercial and social settings. The terms 'hotels' and 'B&Bs' are used synonymously for accommodation such as guesthouses, boarding houses, lodging houses (Walton 1978), and therefore should also be included as commercial home establishments. Not only the physical description and attributes are important, but also the associations: private homes, interaction with host/family who live on the premises, sharing of space that thereby becomes 'public'. The associations are linked by the concept of the home which is identified as a powerful physical, cultural, emotional and temporal construct (Lynch 2005a). It is the home concept that distinguishes commercial homes from other forms of accommodation such as those hotels where the host's private home is not on the premises, and where the boundaries distinguishing public space, which is open to staff and visitors, from private space, which is open to staff only, are relatively distinct. In the commercial home, the host and/or family do not need to live on the premises all the time. For instance, self-catering cottages may share the fact of being a private home but not that of a host/family living continuously on the same premises. The visitor may nevertheless be very conscious of the presence of the host family through, for example, furnishings, locked cupboards, choice of reading material and music, or the presence of notices, say, on operating the boiler. The important feature in such cases is the presence of the host in absentia, i.e. evidence of the emotional engagement (Lynch 2000a) or personal expression of the host (Lynch 2005c: 535).

In the original study which gave rise to the commercial home concept (Lynch 2003), accommodation identified as commercial homes had no more than 11 letting bedrooms, with most having between 3 and 6 bedrooms; it was found that the home element diminished whilst the business element became more accentuated as the amount of letting accommodation increased. In effect, increasing commodification of the accommodation arises in conjunction with both increasing number of letting bedrooms and greater throughput of guests. This dimension of accommodation size, whilst not definitively fixed, distinguishes the commercial home from other studies that have adopted higher numbers of bedrooms in an attempt to capture a distinctive accommodation type, for example specialist accommodation (Morrison et al. 1996). The key characteristics of the commercial home as outlined by Lynch (2005c: 550) are summarised in Table 1.1.

Reference to a commercial home enterprise is helpful in drawing attention to a distinctive fusion of concepts (Figure 1.1), i.e. importance of host/family, host/guest sharing of space, host emotional engagement with the property, the importance of the home setting, the host involvement in the product construction, the commercial nature of the activity, the small size of the accommodation, and, implicitly, issues of (often) family ownership and the concept of the lifestyle entrepreneur. Recognising the home dimension renders the issue of gender as highly significant, as is the use of personal social networks for business purposes. Personal goals of the owner-manager may lead to distinctive conceptions of success and failure. The owner-manager's personal values are important in determining the house rules of conduct and these may have a significant effect upon the nature of the guest's stay, as indeed the host characteristics and hosting style are highly influential on guests' experiences (Tucker and Lynch 2004). Likewise, the stage in the family life cycle, for example the presence of children, or family events, such as divorce or bereavement, will be significant factors determining the nature of the guest's stay.

Commercial homes differ according to the degree of host/guest separation:

1 Commercialised hospitality within the private home where the owners live on the premises and public space is shared by visitors and the owner's family – this category may be subdivided by the degree of integration of the visitor with the family and their activities, for example, private house bed and breakfasts, host families.
2 Commercialised hospitality where the owner lives on the premises and the unit is also the family home but where public space for the visitor is

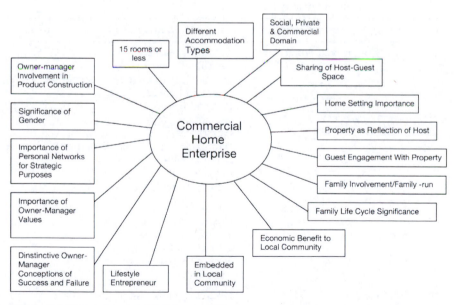

Figure 1.1 The commercial home enterprise.
Source: Lynch, 2005c: 549.

separated from that of the family, for example, small hotels, town houses, guesthouses and some bed and breakfasts.
3   Self-catering where the home owners live off the premises ... [and] the home is usually a second home.

(Lynch and MacWhannell 2000: 104–5)

Commercial home enterprises in tourism have also been classified as being of three broad types, which are outlined in Table 1.2: the Traditional Commercial Homes, Virtual Reality Commercial Homes and 'Backdrop' Homes (Lynch and MacWhannell 2000). Of the three types, traditional commercial homes is the type which has, to date, been most extensively researched.

Traditional commercial homes

The traditional commercial home is the main focus of this book and its main characteristics have been outlined in Table 1.1. Virtual reality enterprises and backdrop homes are also important to describe briefly, as these two types assist in highlighting the graduated nature of the commercial home concept, not only within a category as seen in the above typology of host–guest separation, but also across categories.

Table 1.2 Commercial home types

Categories of Commercial Homes	Examples of Types of Commercial Homes
Traditional Commercial Homes	Cultural homestays Host families Self-catering properties (ex-second homes/ second homes) Bed and breakfasts Farmhouse stays Guesthouses 'Monarch of the Glen' properties Small family-run hotels Religious retreats Writers' retreats
Virtual-reality Commercial Homes	Boutique hotels Country-house hotels Town-house hotels Commercial self-catering Serviced apartments Timeshares
'Backdrop' Homes	Houses used as visitor attractions

Source: Adapted from Lynch 2005a: 39.

Virtual reality commercial homes

The issue of significance here is the borrowing and developing of the home concept purely for commercial advantage (what Wood (1994: 14) refers to as 'pseudo-accommodation'). Such tourism enterprises largely present a different set of issues to traditional commercial home enterprises as described above. There are two main types of virtual reality commercial homes. First, serviced enterprises, for example boutique hotels, country house hotels and town house hotels, are concerned with reproduction of the image and presentation of a (high socio-economic group) home product as well as the high level of personal service. Second are forms of accommodation offering no or limited service concerned with reproduction of the image and presentation of a home product, for example self-catering accommodation that is bought or built to operate solely on a commercial basis. A key absentee in both types is the sense of personal ownership and reflection of the host's identity. As a consequence of the home dimension, particular issues arise in respect of management and staff development and marketing strategies, as well as product design.

'Backdrop' homes

The challenge for these enterprises is in retaining the sense of home whilst successfully managing and promoting commercial activity. Ownership patterns in respect of houses used as visitor attractions may also create unusual challenges owing to, for example, a family living on the premises, or ownership being vested in a committee. 'Backdrop' homes often have strong voluntarism values mixing with a commercial imperative, such as in some National Trust for Scotland properties (a charitable organisation concerned with the preservation and ownership of properties deemed of cultural importance).

Significance of home setting in hospitality studies

Studies of small commercial accommodation types have largely treated each one in isolation from others with the result that common features and characteristics of general relevance to the hospitality situation are overlooked. The issue of home setting is a case in point. A few prominent authors (Lowe 1988; Pearce 1990; Stringer 1981; Wood 1994) have suggested the importance of the home setting in hospitality product construction. Stringer (1981: 361–363) referred to the location of the bed and breakfast operation as guaranteeing a relatively high intensity of interaction between host and guest; in part, this may be a function of the size of such accommodation units. He observed that such use of the home for the provision of an economic service was relatively rare. Hosts and guests were identified as expecting the provision of a 'homely' atmosphere. He also called for research into the issue of 'the "home" as providing various types of accommodation for work and commerce' (Stringer 1981: 373). Pearce (1990) conducted an investigation of farmstay accommodation in New Zealand. He noted a similarity of his study of farmstays to that of Stringer (1981) being that of 'staying in another person's home' (Pearce 1990: 340), suggestive of both conceptual and emotional similarities. The conceptual framework of analysis employed (i.e. Argyle et al. 1981) included environmental setting interpreted at two levels, in its regional and physical context, and the farm home itself. Pearce had relatively little to say about setting other than as a physical construct. However, he reported hosts as clearly identifying setting as having a key role in visitor management and satisfaction.

Lowe (1988: 200), who studied small hotels in a rural area in Scotland, argued that despite the numerical preponderance of the small family hotel, 'there is a considerable degree of ignorance in terms of understanding what a small hotel means to the owner, his staff, the guests and his family'. Lowe (1988: 209) ascribed near-anthropomorphic status to the 'small hotel' which is run 'as a family first and a business second'. Lowe (1988: 210–211) reported guests who 'considered the hotel to be almost a home from home' and had strong affective relationships with the hotel and an 'almost proprietorial interest'. He perceived the nature of the small hotel environment as dysfunctional from a family perspective, different from 'a well run normal family home of those not working in the hotel business' (Lowe 1988: 211). He also saw the environment as being a prime determinant of the guest product. For example, he reported 'continually being rebuked in calling the dining room the restaurant' (Lowe 1998: 218) and attributed this to the dining room having domestic connotations divorced from monetary transactions. Wood (1994: 6) drew attention to how 'hotels have become increasingly "domesticated"'. Facilities in the hotel room were perceived to emulate a 'home away from home' (Wood 1994: 10), a process of 'pseudo-domestication' (Wood 1994: 14); Wood did not differentiate between types of hotels.

Stringer (1981), Pearce (1990) and Lowe (1988) have all highlighted in different ways the significance of the home setting in the construction of the small commercial accommodation product. Stringer most clearly signalled the importance of the home setting. Lowe focused on the family (home) business setting as a key determinant of the product. Pearce, through reporting his hosts' perspectives, identified its central importance. Wood identified emulation of the home concept. It is significant that across different accommodation types, all of these authors identified, directly or indirectly, this common characteristic of the home. The perspectives of Stringer, Lowe and Pearce fit into the traditional home concept whereas the Wood perspective fits into the virtual reality commercial home type.

Given the preponderance of small commercial accommodation enterprises, consideration of the significance of the term 'home' or the nature of 'domestication' has been surprisingly neglected from hospitality and tourism academic studies. Therefore, with concepts of 'home' being such an integral part of the commercial home product, it is important here to outline some of the key issues relating to the concept of the private home in the wider literature.

Meanings of home

The difficulty in coming to grips with the concept of home is in its rich social, cultural and historical significance (Moore 2000), coupled with the vast multidisciplinary literature on it, including the disciplines of sociology, anthropology, psychology, geography and history. Mallet (2004) provides a useful examination of the dominant and recurring ideas about home repre- sented in this literature, discussing how home is variously related to house, family, haven, self, gender and mobility. The idea of home as haven is very much premised on the distinction between the inside and outside world (Wardhaugh 1999). In this view, home is a space free from public scrutiny, political engagements and non-familial relationships. It is a space of security, intimacy and regeneration (Allan and Crow 1989).

It is argued by Rybczynski (1986), however, that it was specifically seven- teenth-century bourgeois ideas about privacy, domesticity, intimacy and comfort that emerged as the organising principles for the design and use of domestic spaces in Europe. This was further compounded by the separation of home and work brought about by the industrial revolution. Hence, when discussing 'commercial homes', we should be careful not to associate home and house uncritically. Indeed, we must be aware that, reflecting its specific northern European cultural origin, the concept of the commercial home has a tendency to already privilege the relationship between house and home. Hence, the attempt of this book to attract different cultural perspectives and a deliberate inclusion of chapters that raise questions regarding the nature of home, for example association of home with boat (Jennings' chapter), mon- astery (O'Gorman and Lynch's chapter), village (Tucker's chapter), and sur- rounding countryside (Hall's chapter), as well as contesting the construction of the commercial and the private as a priori dichotomous concepts (Sloane- White's chapter). Further, simple associations of the house with immobility and strangers as mobile have also been questioned in relation to the commercial home (Lynch et al. 2007).

There is also a significant literature relating home to issues of place and space (Douglas 1991; Massey 1995; Perkins and Thorns 1999). Douglas (1991), for example, points out that we pose the question 'Where is your home?' not How, Who or When, thus tending always to produce a locali- sable idea of home. Indeed, the origin of the word 'home' in different lan- guages gives rise to subtle variances in meaning and associations. For example, the German word for house, thought of as a building, is imbued with the sense of home, whereas the English term 'home' derives from *ham*, meaning village, estate or town (Hollander 1991). Elsewhere, also, such as Nuakata Island, Papua New Guinea, 'home' means the matrilineal village, or even the island itself, and is not a private physical dwelling (Mallett 2003). Western conceptions of home, however, have tended largely to privilege a physical structure such as a house (Bowlby et al. 1997; Giddens 1984), with the emphasis being on the home-house as main provider of personal and familial security in an increasingly alienating world (Dupuis and Thorns 1996; Madigan et al. 1990).

Some authors have argued for home to be viewed as a 'socio-spatial system' that represents the fusion of the physical house together with the social unit of the house*hold* (Douglas 1991; Rapport and Dawson 1998). Relating this to Massey's work (1994), the home is a place that is constituted by particular social relations and, as such, is always contingent and unstable. Indeed, the strong association between home and family is noted by many researchers (Bowlby et al. 1997; Finch and Hayes 1994; Jones 1995, 2000). Some authors have even gone as far as to suggest that the link between home and family is so strong that the two terms are almost interchangeable; without the family a home is only a house (Bernardes 1987; Crow 1989; Gilman 1980). This raises some interesting issues in relation to the concept of the commercial home; can we also say 'commercial family'? Home is associated so prominently with family because it tends to encompass the location and the particular house in which a person lived in childhood, and so it also symbolises the family relationships and life courses enacted within those spaces (Mallett 2004).

Nevertheless, such a strong association between home and family has also been criticised for its privileging of the Western, white, middle-class nuclear family (Bowlby et al. 1997; Wardhaugh 1999). Social anthropology literature suggests that the nuclear family is irrelevant to the meaning of home in many cultural contexts. Cross-cultural notions of kinship mean that, for many people, the extended family is just as important to the sense of identity and home. Moreover, even in Western society, the concept of the nuclear family has become increasingly irrelevant, thus exposing any continued assumptions of such household arrangements as promotion by religious and state institutions of heterosexual 'normality' and its associated gendered roles and relationships (Munro and Madigan 1999).

Home and gender

There exists a wealth of literature on the relationship between gender and home. In particular, feminist critiques of home argue that gender differentiation relating to the meaning of home is inevitable since home is so integrally bound up with identity and self. As Darke (1994) has argued, it is precisely because the home is associated symbolically with ideas of calmness, security, stability and values typically associated with 'privacy' that it is no surprise that the meaning of home is differentiated by gender (Darke 1994). Some early research on gendered meanings of home found that whilst men linked home primarily with status and achievement, women viewed home primarily as a haven (Rainwater 1966; Seeley et al. 1956). Feminist writers, however, have identified home as a site of oppression, exploitation and male domination (Barrett 1980; Comer 1974). This argument goes hand in hand with the 1970s feminist theories which saw a causal relationship between women's confinement to domestic space, as mentioned above, and their lack of access to authority, prestige and cultural values (Buitelaar 1998). A study by Tannen (as cited in Cooper-Marcus 1995) identified gender differences in preferred home location with females preferring locations closer to city centres than male partners, owing to their more restricted mobility. Moreover, it has been recognised that women's own experiences in the home, and particularly the meanings women attach to their work in the home, must not be overlooked since, for many women, their work in the home, and consequently the home itself, is a strong source of identity, pride and satisfaction (Darke 1994). Related to this, also, Di Domenico (2003) and Morrison *et al.* (2001) have drawn attention to the importance of lifestyle entrepreneurs. It is important that we should fully understand such concepts if the study of commercial homes is to be advanced. This book contributes to such understanding by providing insights into the 'entrepreneur' lifestyle and mindset.

Issues of the division of labour in housework are crucial in discussions of the interrelationship between gender and home (Darke 1994) and also, therefore, discussions of the commercial home. Although the home is generally considered a feminine, nurturing space (and hence often symbolically associated with 'mother'), women often lack authority within this space and their emotional and spatial needs are considered secondary (Darke 1994; Munro and Madigan 1999).Women's creation of a commercial business out of the home, then, may afford them a greater sense of status, authority and rights within the home (see the chapters by Mottiar and Laurincikova, Jennings and Stehlik, and also that by Tucker, in this volume). In other words, women's sense of home as a haven for relaxation was already disturbed by their responsibilities of reproductive and domestic labour, and so turning that labour into commercial gain highlights its value and worth.

It is inevitable that women's and men's engagement in some sort of paid work within the home will impact upon family members' experience of home and family relationships (Massey 1996; Phizacklea and Wolkowitz 1995). Some researchers have noted how such 'paid work' for women creates a double burden of work within the home, because they remain primarily responsible for the carrying out of domestic reproductive duties. Hence, commercial work within the home might increase women's experience of home as a site of oppression. Moreover, opening the private home up to commercial entrepreneurial activity is likely to further disturb the meanings and experiences of home that Rybczynski (1986) cited as key to, at least European, associations with home; that is, home as a site of privacy, domesticity, intimacy and comfort. In other words, it is inevitable that the commercial home disrupts the notion of home as haven or refuge, as a private place that people can retreat to and relax in.

Anthropomorphic home

The dramaturgical metaphor of Goffman (1959) has been highly influential in hospitality and tourism analyses, for example MacCannell (1973), Hochschild (1983) and Crang (1997). However, in terms of understanding small commercial accommodation businesses, an alternative and equally powerful conceptual lens is that of the private home. The home literature, as discussed above, focuses on the home setting as an almost distinct and living entity, that is, it brings the background into the foreground. The literature highlights the home meaning(s) as being in the eyes of the householders. Beyond being a functional unit, it becomes an entity with 'whom' a discourse is entered into. The home reflects the householder's personality as well as communicating social expectations. Cooper-Marcus (1995) studied people's relationships with their home, identifying home as a place of self-expression. She drew attention to the psychological importance of the home, how the individual's psychological development is tied up with meaningful emotional relationships, positive or negative, with significant physical environments such as the home. Thus, homes and their contents are identified as a mirror of self, as providing strong statements about the householders. Gurney (1996) identified five different types of ideologies about private home ownership, which Darke and Gurney (2000: 89) later suggested might be helpful in differentiating householder attitudes to hospitality and their expectations of guests. The five types are pragmatists, petty tycoons, conflictual owners, extrinsic owners and lexicowners. Of these, the extrinsic owner is identified as closest to the commercial home host, particularly in the better quality bed-and breakfast establishments. For this type of owner, the home is a means of expression where the guest is indispensable to admire the results. The concept of a possible commercial host personality is of interest, but of greater note is that all types identified above are founded on the nature of the relationship with the home. This is an under-explored area in hospitality and meriting investigation (Sweeney and Lynch 2008). One can envisage practical applications in terms of suitability for commercial hosting through completion of a hosting personality assessment questionnaire; or communication of information on a host's personality might assist guests in selecting commercial homes, given the central importance of the host in the small accommodation experience (Tucker and Lynch 2004). The idea of the home reflecting the householder's personality might suggest guests in commercial homes engage in a process of forensic psychological profiling.

Home behaviours

A number of studies have been conducted from an architectural perspective concerned with the use of buildings, as much as their spatial design. Bernard (1991) reported findings concerning changes in lifestyles and their consequences on the way homes are used. The author argued that it is harder today to differentiate people on the basis of social class than previously. Whilst there was similar social class behaviour regarding the receiving of guests in the living room or dining room, 'marked differences appear in the way guests have access to other areas of the home' (Bernard 1991: 198). An occupational distinction was identified, with people in farming occupations the least likely to receive guests in the living or dining room (Bernard 1991: 198), and the least likely to open their private space to family and friends. Differences were identified regarding the degree of accessibility of the household space according to guest versus family status, occupation, education and age (in respect of guests only). Bernard observed, 'the older the person, the more impregnated he or she is with principles and reception decorum of the former times'. He adds, 'the wish to preserve one's privacy is stronger when the private area of one's home clearly reveals the sedimentary strata of memories and habits' (1991: 199).

Class differences in sociability have been identified by sociologists, such as in Paradise's study (as cited in Bernard 1991), which contrasted the ritualistic character of the modes of sociability among the working class with a more open or more spontaneous character found among the upper and intellectual classes. Bernard concluded:

> Aspirations to abolish the limits of private space reflect the mentality of members of the upper class, whose socio-cultural identity is strongly and sufficiently well established so that they fear no infringement from families and friends. Among the middle or popular classes there is a tendency to be more cautious and more dependent on the opinion of others.
>
> (Bernard 1991: 200)

Bernard's (1991) study provides explanations for 'performance behaviour' associated with the 'identity politics' (in the terminology of Crang 1997) of the 'actors'. Interestingly, gender does not seem to have been explored by Bernard. The class differences identified may also be a function of available space, rather than simply education. The recognition that the layout of the dwelling unit bears a relationship to understanding the behaviour taking place within does not appear to have been given much emphasis in studies on hospitality/tourism settings, with the exception of Whyte (1948).

Public and private space may therefore be perceived as temporal constructs. Attitudes towards private space in commercial homes show evolution, as can be seen in comparing Walton's (1978) accounts of the evolution of Blackpool boarding houses from the mid-nineteenth century to the 1970s, together with more contemporaneous accounts (e.g. Bryson 1996; Medwed 2000). It seems only appropriate that further research should explore such issues if our understanding of hospitality is to be extended. As said above, the idea of home as haven is premised clearly on a distinction between public and private (Wardhaugh 1999). Discussion of the ways in which the construction of private and public spaces is affected in commercial home enterprises takes place in Chapters 4, 5 and 10 of this volume.

The tensions inherent in the commercial home

The term 'commercial home' brings together two arguably antithetical concepts, that of commerce and the home, and it is the inherent tension that exists between the two that captures the essence of this accommodation type and thereby generates a whole set of distinctive social, business, commercial and tourism-related issues. This tension may best be seen in considering the concepts of commerce as embodied in the hotel, and the home being referred to as the private home (see Lynch 2005a discussing Douglas 1991). The hotel, as a larger commercial operation, and the private home may have shared characteristics such as sites for providing hospitality, a sense of welcome, as well as other services. They both have spatial boundaries and therefore compartmentalise space. However, as argued by Lynch (2005a), where the hotel captures the idea of a virtual market, the private home represents a virtual community; where the hotel is asynchronous, i.e. not requiring fair access to goods nor imposing strong behavioural obligations (other than with regard to payment and general social public behavioural norms), the private home is synchronous. That is, it is based on achieving 'fair access to goods' (Lynch 2005a: 45) as well as obligations (types of social control) such as the guests' obligations to conform to hosts' rules (Tucker 2003b). Hospitality in the hotel is concerned with calculable activity in contrast to the gift economy of the private home. The hotel is concerned with efficiency whilst the private home embodies massive redundancies. The hotel's justification is in its pursuit of commercial goals whereas the private home's justification is in its continuance. In the hotel one purchases privacy whereas within the private home there is limited privacy.

At the same time as the term commercial home resides in dichotomous perspectives of the commercial and the non-commercial, public and private, the commercial home itself breaks down and raises questions regarding the validity of such dichotomous classifications (c.f. Lynch et al. 2007). This interrogation of perceptions and understandings is especially relevant in terms of the social ethic of hospitality that is played out within the commercial home. Jacques Derrida (Derrida and Dufourmantelle 2000) refers to broad universal laws of hospitality. However, the reality of the commercial home reveals the idiosyncratic, ethnocentric interpretation of such laws by the hosts as they 'oscillate between commercial and non-commercial interpretations', often giving rise to a non-standardised, unique personally hosted experience (Lynch et al. 2007: 140). Therefore, the commercial home challenges many binary distinctions, for example between: the public hotel and the private home, home and away, commercial and non-commercial, commodification and authenticity, work and home.

About this book

This book is not intended as a comprehensive overview of the commercial home enterprise in tourism. Rather, it provides an array of perspectives on the commercial home that variously confirm the utility of the concept, demonstrating its international relevance and application in different cultural contexts and disciplines. The aim is to enable a meeting ground for the exchange of viewpoints, to confirm aspects of previous research, to elaborate dimensions of the commercial home in greater depth, to reveal new insights into the commercial home, to propose new research directions and critique and, finally, to seek to extend the commercial home paradigm. To achieve these aims the book is structured into three parts. Part I includes Chapters 2 through to 6, which elucidate key dimensions of the commercial home concept. Part II of the book consists of Chapters 7 through to 11, all of which examine the commercial home as a lens through which to investigate wider issues of society, hospitality and tourism. Part III presents four contributions, Chapters 12 through to 15, which extend the commercial home concept into new areas.

Starting Part I is Chapter 2 by Moscardo which considers dimensions of bed and breakfast accommodation in the North Queensland region of Australia and presents a continuum of forms of commercial home accommodation conceptualised within a systems framework. Different forms of commercial home accommodation are distinguished based on the importance or centrality of the accommodation to the overall desired tourist experience. At one end of the continuum, Moscardo positions the commercial home accommodation as standard accommodation that offers primarily a support service for a holiday. At the opposite end of the continuum are those forms of commercial home accommodation that can be considered the attraction in their own right because they offer a specific type of experience (for example, a romantic getaway or spa experience). The pressures on this continuum are also discussed, including motives and expectations of tourists, characteristics and motives of hosts, growing regulation of the sector, characteristics of the region in which it is located, and impacts of the host–guest interaction; each of these pressures exert influence on the overall role that commercial homes play within the wider visitor experience and support the need to consider different forms of the commercial home phenomenon.

Chapter 3 by Mottiar and Laurincikova provides a conceptualisation of the commercial home enterprise based on an entrepreneurial perspective; that is, the focus for conceptualisation is not the owner as host, but as an entrepreneur. Implicit in this perspective is the gendered nature of the entrepreneurship. Specifically, the authors discuss issues faced by female commercial home owners in relation to motivations and barriers to new venture creation using a case study of female bed and breakfast and guesthouse entrepreneurs in Gaeltacht areas (Irish-speaking areas) in Ireland. The authors draw attention to the lifestyle motivations underpinning the nature of the commercial home enterprise, as well as to the gendered role of the work; yet they also allude to the lack of personal gain from the situation. As such, implicit in an analysis of the dimensions of the commercial home enterprise are issues of work–life balance, support networks and the nature of gendered entrepreneurship.

Chapter 4 by Jennings and Stehlik analyses the dimensions of the commercial home in relation to its wider complementary context. Specifically, using a case study of commercial homes in rural Australia, the authors broaden understandings of the commercial home construct beyond commercial private home settings to consideration of commercial private home enterprises embedded within a wider farming, or agri-tourism, context. Examined in this chapter are: key dimensions of the commercialised farm space and place and resultant (re)interpretations of public/private domains; farm life and 'home' sites and sights; the nature of gendered roles and responsibilities; the influence of changing farming practice; and how these collectively influence the lived experiences and discourses of farmstay providers. For example, the chapter discusses the challenge this poses to the traditional discourses associated with the 'family farm' and the conflict in family relationships as a result of the changing roles of women's work, their identities and negotiation of public/private shared space within the farm home as the women move into more public domains. Three emblematic ways to represent such farmstay experiences are presented: tourism experience as family life – 'naturalistic' farm life; creation of the 'ideal' environment – 'still life' farm life; and mediated experiences – 'impressionistic' farm life.

Chapter 5 by Hall positions the commercial home phenomenon as embedded within exurban processes and applies the concept of 'servicescape' to examine the way in which the spaces of the commercial home are produced and consumed. The spaces of home include not only the physical structure of houses and buildings and the rooms within, but also the surrounding gardens and countryside. Drawing on interviews with bed and breakfast operators in the Canterbury region of New Zealand, the chapter examines how these spaces of home potentially create new tensions with respect to understandings of public and private space and its construction. Specifically, the three dimensions of servicescapes – ambient conditions, spatial layout and signs, symbols and artefacts are used to frame discussion of the production and consumption of public and private spaces of home. Importantly, the chapter elucidates the often shared visions of rurality of visitors and their hosts in exurban space which can foster the 'co-creation' of elements of the servicescape. For example, according to Hall, elements of the servicescape are often deliberately used to create conversations and generate successful social interaction between host and guest, and to convey the 'appropriate atmospherics of "home"'.

Chapter 6 by Carmichael and McClinchey examines the physical and human dimensions of the rural setting in the commercial home phenomenon. Specifically, perceptions of the rural landscape and the physical and built environment (including heritage, quaintness, architecture, gardens, interiors and aesthetics) are examined in relation to their influence on the rural tourism experience for both hosts and guests. Human dimensions, including social conformity, use of social rules, role play and dissonance, and social interactions between visitors, local residents and host–guest are also examined, both within the region and at the accommodation itself. Thus, different geographical scales and elements of physical and human dimensions that describe the commercial home setting are considered. These dimensions are presented within a conceptual framework drawing on a case study of bed and breakfast operators and their guests in South-western Ontario, Canada. The authors use the framework to proffer discourse about the complexity of meaning given to the private home, the equally complex meanings and perceptions afforded to that home by guests sharing the space, engaging in a monetary transaction as well as reflecting on the meaning of their own homes, and the importance and meaning of the rural landscape, rural lifestyles and settings for commercial homes.

Chapter 7 by McIntosh and Harris is the first chapter in Part II of the book. This chapter uses the commercial home as an investigative lens to examine wider debates surrounding personal experiences within the context of tourism. Using a case study of commercial home hosts in the Waikato and Auckland regions of New Zealand, the chapter presents the personal narratives of hosts to examine the nature of their personal relationship with their 'commercial' home, the impact of hosting on their personal, private and family life, the impact for other life stakeholders, and the strategies hosts use in order to minimise the impacts on their life from hosting in the home. The authors proffer that a 'hosting discourse' is evident in the relatively homogenous narratives of the hosts they interviewed. In particular, the authors describe a formalised discourse whereby positive reporting was evident; specifically, that there is an emphasis on describing 'nice guests' who cause, if any, only minor problems or irritations, and that hosting is reported to only minimally impact on family and personal life events. As such, the authors advocate the need to examine the personal and subjective narratives of tourism and hospitality from the wider perspective of the life course and events of individuals, and raise the need for researchers to question traditional more formalised approaches to research that perhaps do not necessarily capture the true reality of lived experience or, conversely, pose an official discourse to be reported.

Chapter 8 by Goulding evaluates the commercial home enterprise within the wider perspectives of temporality and seasonality, drawing on a large-scale survey of commercial home operators in Scotland. Different manifestations of temporality are identified in relation to commercial home operation, and the motivations and behaviours associated with seasonal trading examined. The author gives particular attention to 'lifestyle proprietorship' or lifestyle entrepreneurship which purportedly affords temporal flexibility in a commercial home environment and a basis for flexible, independently constructed trading patterns. The author comments on how many commercial home enterprises engage in seasonal trading and often planned short term closure, with many closing for lifestyle business objectives and orientation, including personal lifecycle, well-being and work–life balance motives. As such, the author concludes that the commercial home concept provides a more unifying and explanatory construct than either 'lifestyle business' or 'family business' in shedding insights on temporality from a provider perspective, especially due to its focus on the home environment as a natural retreat from the demands of long periods of intense hosting activity, both in operational and psychological terms.

Chapter 9 by Benmore uses the dual lenses of emotional labour and hospitality to provide a cross-disciplinary framework to understand the complexities of host and guest behaviours in commercial homes. Specifically, the author contends that commercial home owners, as hosts within the hospitality relationship, effectively manage their own and guests' behaviour within their homes through flexible and autonomous use of emotional labour. They do this by adroitly operating within and across the three domains of hospitality: social, private and commercial. Using a case study of small and large hotels in a major UK resort, the author explores how host and guest behaviours are shaped by each party's perceptions of the commercial home as a 'home', and it is proposed that perceptions of the 'home' element influence how guests feel they can and should interact with the host who lives in the home. Benmore discusses how emotional labour was evident in hosts' choice of guest selection as a way to protect the home, in the creation of social rules and standards, home identity created for the business, suppressing disquiet, self-imposed attitudes to hosting and housework, and their 'performance' towards guests. Generally, tailoring the use of emotional labour to protect the home and business appear to conflict with the cultural origins of hospitality traditions and thus merit the need for a wider lens for examination.

Chapter 10 by Tucker discusses the provision of tourism hospitality in the gendered space of the cave houses of Göreme in central Turkey showing the different ways in which the cave houses have been constructed by men and women in their 'commercial home' performances. Specifically, women's identity and associations of 'home' are closely aligned with the domestic space of the house, whereas men's identity and associations of 'home' are more attached to the wider (public) place of the village. Consequently, as the cave houses of Göreme became turned into tourist accommodation establishments (*pansiyons*), the space of the cave *pansiyons* became 'public', and therefore, male space, and men became the main hosts in these commercial homes. As such, through the wider investigative lens of gender, the chapter proffers the need to examine the influence of gender roles, division of labour between men and women, and the gendered meanings associated with 'domestic' and 'private'/ 'public' space and meanings of 'home' in the commercial home phenomenon.

Chapter 11 by Kastenholz and Sparrer uses the commercial home as a lens through which to examine and challenge theoretical assumptions about rural tourism, especially its ability to enhance understanding between local residents and tourists. Specifically, the authors discuss rural tourism in Portugal, Spain and Northern Germany to elucidate different concepts of the 'commercial home' in the rural context in relation to the host–guest relationship that is typically associated with the rural tourism experience. They also discuss the degree to which this relationship extends the home context to further include the guests' integration into the wider rural community. Whilst similarities are found to exist in the nature of the commercial home enterprises in the rural environments they studied, differences encountered are discussed in light of the diverse types and degrees of development of tourism business in each region, shaped by distinct legal, social, political and economic contexts. Kastenholz and Sparrer argue that, except for the particular experiences between hosts and guests, a substantial exchange between rural and urban culture may be questioned, as the integration of the commercial home accommodation into its rural environment is rather modest. Furthermore, the rural commercial home may reinforce illusions about the rural way of life due to staged rural tourism settings.

Chapter 12 by Sloane-White begins Part III of the book by extending the notion of the commercial home into the religious cultural context through an examination of the Muslim notion of the hospitable home in Malaysia. Specifically, the Muslim notion of the hospitable home is based on the Quranic injunction that the Muslim home shall always be open to guests, and that travellers shall never be turned away from food or shelter. However, the chapter explores how the modern Muslim home in middle-class, urban, contemporary Malay life is today used as a site to transact, affirm, exchange and justify new social, economic and entrepreneurial identities. Sloane-White demonstrates that the Malay Muslim idea of 'home' and its imperatives for hosts and guests can be reworked to meet the needs of new economic, political and social roles. It is further suggested that a modern Muslim home can have economic utility in the Malaysian context, but that its utility can be manifested via a traditional cultural idiom. Specifically, the author suggests that not only money exchanged between host and guest defines the nature of the 'commercial home', but in the Malay case, the intangibles of status, social ambition and social control can be transacted as capital in the home, turning it into a site for political dominance and economic intent. As such, Sloane-White proposes that self-interested transactions can be submerged in traditional, ritual and even rural dimensions of 'home' and 'hospitality', thereby extending the commercial home paradigm.

Chapter 13 by O'Gorman and Lynch extends the traditional notion of the commercial home into the wider context of religious tourism to examine the monastic environment as a distinctive form of 'communal' home delivering monastic hospitality to guests. Drawing on research at monasteries in the UK and Europe, the authors examine contemporary monastic hospitality in relation to setting, artifacts, discourse, politics of identity, sequences, social control, space and product. O'Gorman and Lynch conclude that the monastery as commercial home is extremely complex; there are different layers of the commercial home within the monastery and differing layers of hospitality provision. Within the monastic cloister the hospitality that is offered to meet the guest's physical and metaphysical needs is also not a simple concept. The prima-facie purpose of the monastery is not to offer hospitality but rather to house the monks in a community environment so that they can dedicate their lives and live their vocation to the service of God. For example, the separation of the monks from their guests is not an act of inhospitableness, but rather is mandated by the Rule and is necessary for the monastery to function. As such, whilst the authors highlight similarities between a traditional commercial home and the monastic cloister, differences arising from both the communal nature of the institutional home and the philosophical purpose and praxis suggest a further category of 'communal commercial home'.

Chapter 14 by King and White discusses the historical development and diversity of the commercial home in regional Australia, arguing that enterprises which may be considered marginal to the commercial home definition (as commonly understood) also need to be considered alongside the conventional commercial home since they are critical to the emerging destination appeal. Such businesses, the authors argue, reflect a range of lifestyle preferences of both established residents and incomers, and represent a diverse range of resident and visitor interests and target audiences, including straight couples, gays and lesbians, families and retirees, those in search of pampering, gourmands, alternative lifestyle seekers and artists. Local depictions of homeliness in the Australian example reflect the influence of migrant communities (that is, non-indigenous to Australia) in the social, cultural and aesthetic landscape. Such ethnic plurality, the authors suggest, has shaped the development and operation of the commercial home sector in Australia, sometimes conveying nostalgia for forms and settings commonly found in Europe. King and White conclude that future evaluation of the commercial home phenomenon must be firmly positioned within an analysis of its diversity of form, changing tourist demands and fashions, and changing destinations – especially in the context of the influence of domestic and inbound migration and impact on perceptions of traditional 'homeliness'. Such analysis may proffer understanding of businesses extending beyond the commercial home phenomenon.

Chapter 15 by Jennings extends the notion of the commercial home beyond land-based settings to include 'mobile homes' or sailing boats/yachts or motorised boats in water-based settings; specifically, this is done through an analysis of long-term ocean cruisers who go on board as contributing or paying crew. Jennings points out that elements of primary, secondary and/or commercial homes are exhibited in some cruise vessels. She also argues that, individually and collectively, boats as well as harbours may be vicariously and explicitly utilised as home settings and to provide water-based homescapes. As such, commercially oriented and water-based home styles of life may have complementarity with dominant domains of usage identified for land-based commercial homes. In particular, long-term ocean cruisers choose to integrate a commercial home enterprise into their 'style of life' in order to sustain a cruising lifestyle and to gain companionship. Jennings further suggests that, for cruisers, the use of the boat as a commercial space can result in issues related to social construction and performance of identity, home/boat as commercial enterprise, private/public tensions, equality/ inequality, discrimination, marginalisation, gender and observance of rituals, as well as legal and bureaucratic responsibilities. For the guest-crew, issues related to appropriate behaviours and etiquette, opportunities to learn in conducive environments, knowledge and skill match or mismatch to challenges, safety and security issues, gender issues, resource usage, guest-crew expectations and satisfaction, and legal requirements and protocols characterise the nature of the extended 'mobile commercial home' experience.

Chapter 16 provides a conclusion to the book. It analyses the key themes emerging from the contributions, reappraises the commercial home concept in the light of the contributions, and proposes new research directions. As such, it consolidates the knowledge contained within the previous chapters and seeks to build upon this knowledge to move towards a future research agenda into the commercial home phenomenon, as well as the nature and significance of the 'home' and 'home host' for hospitality and tourism more generally.

Conclusions

The commercial home sits at the crossroads of a number of major themes in hospitality and tourism whose examination through the integrative perspective of the commercial home lens potentially brings improved and new understandings to, for example: the nature of family business; lifestyle entrepreneurship; gender; hosts and guests; hospitableness and hospitality; performance; authenticity; commodification; sustainability; seasonality; rurality; peripherality; architectural heritage; networks; community; economic development (Figure 1.1). In consequence, and in line with the multi- and inter-disciplinary nature of hospitality (Lashley et al. 2007), commercial home enterprises provide a disciplinary meeting ground for the examination of important but under-explored dimensions of hospitality, tourism and society.

The study of commercial home enterprises is important on a number of levels: to explore a relatively neglected form of hospitality accommodation (certainly, one reading of commercial home enterprises is that they represent socially marginalised forms of accommodation (Lynch 2005c)); to redress an ongoing bias in the literature towards larger forms of accommodation; and to give recognition to an important social phenomenon that reflects the enduring significance of the home enterprise in contemporary society mirroring the central importance of the private home. This book thus addresses a gap in the literature with regard to the use of the 'private' home for the provision of commercial hospitality, placing a particular focus upon the complexities residing in the interaction of the domestic and the commercial.

Part I
Dimensions of the commercial home

2 Bed and breakfast, homestay and farmstay accommodation

Forms and experiences

Gianna Moscardo

Introduction

The recognition of the commercial home as used in bed and breakfast and farmstays as a separate and distinctive form of tourist accommodation offers opportunities to develop new conceptual approaches to understanding a range of different aspects of tourism. The facets of particular relevance in the present chapter include the role of tourist accommodation in the tourist experience, the host–guest relationship and the nature of tourism development, especially in more rural and peripheral regions. In order to develop these conceptual analyses of the commercial home in tourism it is important to understand the key dimensions and categories of the phenomenon under study. This chapter will argue that tourist accommodation provided in commercial homes incorporates a number of different forms of tourism experience and that understanding the key dimensions that determine these forms is an important prerequisite for the development of more integrated theoretical frameworks.

After a brief review of definitions and presentation of different geographical histories of commercial home accommodation, a case study of tourists using commercial homes for accommodation in the North Queensland region of Australia will be employed to demonstrate the existence of a continuum of forms of commercial home accommodation. Pressures on this continuum will be reviewed before a systems model of the commercial home accommodation phenomenon is presented. This systems model is based on a review of key literature. It will be argued that this system includes a number of tensions and that these tensions differ according to where a particular commercial home is located on the continuum of forms of accommodation. Each form of accommodation is associated with a different set of tensions, giving rise to different challenges and outcomes.

Definitions and history

Lynch (2005b: 530) provides a definition of the term homestay that is most suited to the present discussion. In this definition a homestay 'is a specialist term referring to types of accommodation where tourists or guests pay to stay in private homes, where interaction takes place with a host and/or family usually living upon the premises, and with whom public space, is to a degree, shared'. This definition can therefore be seen as incorporating a number of other terms, including bed and breakfast, guesthouse and farmstay.

Several historical accounts of the use of the commercial home for tourist accommodation note that it has a long history in many countries, but that in the second half of the twentieth century the use of commercial homes for tourist accommodation has varied greatly across different geographical regions (Ames 1999; Kaufman et al. 1996; Lanier 2000; Sakach 2004). More specifically, it has been suggested that in the United Kingdom and Europe there has been a continuing tradition of commercial home use as a budget form of accommodation. In the United States, Canada, Africa, Australia and New Zealand, however, the commercial home has only recently been taken up again as a form of tourist accommodation. In these settings this type of accommodation is typically more expensive than standard forms of accommodation and is seen as an alternative or specialist type of experience (Ames 1999; England Research 2005; Kaufman et al. 1996; Lanier 2000; Lubetkin 1999; McGehee and Kim 2004; Pearce 1990; Sakach 2004). This seems to suggest that there are a number of different forms of tourist experience classified under this single label.

The Far North Queensland case study

The existence of different forms of commercial home accommodation can be illustrated with an example. This case study is based on data collected from a survey of tourists to the Far North Queensland region of Australia and a content analysis of accommodation listings for this region. The region is centred on two coastal tourist centres, Cairns and Port Douglas, offering traditional sun and sea resort-style experiences. These two locations offer a range of traditional hotel, motel and self-contained apartment style accommodation as well as shopping, restaurants and departure points for numerous day tours to the adjacent Great Barrier Reef and Wet Tropics Rainforest areas. The region is one of the most popular destinations in Australia for both domestic and international tourism, although it has faced increasing competition from other coastal regions in recent years (Moscardo et al. 2004). In addition to this increasing competition, the region as a whole has also faced challenges associated with managing the negative impacts of rapid tourism growth (Pearce et al. 1996) and finding ways to spread the tourism benefits to the areas that form the periphery of the region.

The coastal hinterland of the region, the Atherton Tablelands, offers a different tourist experience with cooler conditions associated with a higher elevation and a mixture of rural scenery, small towns and tropical rainforest settings. Searches of various accommodation guides indicate bed and breakfast and farmstays are the dominant form of tourist accommodation accounting for 64 per cent of all the establishments and 44 per cent of all the room stocks in the region. While the average room rate of AUD$145 per couple per night would suggest that these establishments are seeking more affluent guests, this average hides a large range of prices, with the commercial home accommodation in this region including budget options as well as very exclusive product. The main themes in promotional material for these commercial homes are luxury, romantic getaways, access to rainforest environments with a special emphasis on wildlife viewing and bird watching, and opportunities to meet local farmers. The advertising and description of the available establishments suggests that there is a range of commercial home accommodation in this destination, from those offering access to the region's attractions, where the accommodation plays a support role only, those that offer special access for a particular activity such as wildlife viewing, to those in which the accommodation is a central component of the experience on offer.

The visitor data were collected from tourists approached in key transport nodes in the region including airport departure lounges, ferry terminals, visitor centres and bus stations, as well as at rest areas and commonly used stopping points on the main highway accessing the region. A total of 2664 surveys were completed with an overall response rate of 63 per cent. The survey was available in both English and Japanese and collected information on demographics, travel behaviours including the type and location of accommodation used in the region, travel motives, activity participation and places visited in the region.

Table 2.1 provides a breakdown of overall accommodation use in the region by the survey respondents. As can be seen, 6 per cent of the sample stayed at least one night in a bed and breakfast or farmstay which is consistent with figures provided for the entire country by the Bureau of Tourism Research (Hossain 2004). Table 2.1 also provides a breakdown of the other accommodation choices used by those who stayed in a commercial home. This distribution shows that commercial home users tend to choose hostels/lodges and caravan parks more often than non-commercial home users – a

Table 2.1 Patterns of accommodation use

Types of Accommodation	Used for at least one night for whole sample (%)*	Used for at least one night by those who stayed in a commercial home (%)
Hotel/motel/resorts 3 star or more	32	13
Hotel/motel/resorts less than 3 star	28	25
Hostel/lodge/guesthouse	38	50
Caravan park	26	46
Friends and relatives	6	–
Commercial home	6	–

Note: * Numbers total more than 100% because of multiple responses.

finding consistent with that reported for farmstay visitors in Canada (Lang Research 2001). It appears that this group includes both travellers who generally seek more alternative or specialist forms of accommodation and budget conscious tourists.

Table 2.2 provides the results of comparisons between commercial home users and non-users on demographic and travel behaviour variables. Only results that were statistically significant at the $p < 0.05$ level are included in the table. It can be seen here that commercial home users were most likely to be travelling as a couple, more likely to be travelling alone, less likely to be travelling with family, more likely to be female, and more likely to be younger than non-users. In addition, commercial home users in this study were more likely than non-users to have longer stays in the region, to spend less time planning and to have planned less before arriving in the region.

Table 2.2 Demographic and travel behaviour comparisons

Variable	Commercial-home Users (%)	Commercial-home Non-users (%)
Travel Party		
Alone	28	16
Couple	41	43
Family	6	14
Friends	19	21
Tour	2	3
Other	4	3
Gender		
Female	58	50
Male	42	50
Usual place of residence		
Australia	36	45
North America	15	6
UK/Ireland	19	27
Other Europe	19	13
Asia	6	4
Other	5	5
Mean age	35 years	42 years
Mean weeks spent planning this trip	19	26
Planning Approach		
Most planned before departure	5	15
Some planned before departure	27	25
Most planned on arrival	20	23
Made plans day to day	48	37
Days spent in the region		
<6	5	21
6–7	11	15
8–14	28	28
15–30	23	20
>30	33	16

Overall commercial home users were more likely to be international visitors and within that category more likely to be from North America and mainland Europe. Several features of this profile are consistent with data presented for commercial home users in other countries, especially with regard to the travel party (Hossain 2004; Lang Research 2001) and gender (Hossain 2004). The younger age of this group is, however, not consistent with other studies, which typically report commercial home users as older (Hossain 2004; Lang Research 2001; Tourism Queensland 2002). This difference reflects the different profile of visitors to the region as a whole and highlights the importance of recognising not only national differences in the development of the commercial home for tourist accommodation, but also regional variations within countries.

A number of significant differences were also found between commercial home users and non-users in terms of the features they sought in a travel destination (see Table 2.3). Commercial home users were more interested in access to wilderness and undisturbed nature, learning experiences, opportunities to see wildlife they would not normally be able to see, and outdoor adventure activities. These results are consistent with research in other locations (Fennel and Weaver 1997; Hossain 2004; Ingram and Sherwood 2002; Lang Research 2001; Tourism Queensland 2002). They also had higher mean importance scores for shopping and resort areas, but lower means for first class accommodation, high quality restaurants and visiting friends and family.

Commercial home users were also different from non-users in their patterns of activity participation in the region and the locations and attractions visited. In terms of locations the commercial home users were significantly more likely to get to more peripheral sites and to travel further within the destination region. The opposite was generally true of the tourist attractions visited, with commercial home users less likely to visit all attractions except for those located in more peripheral regions or those with a specialist theme

Table 2.3 Mean importance ratings of destination features travel choices

Destination Features	Mean Rating for Commercial-home Users	Mean Rating for Commercial-home Non-Users
Opportunities to visit friends/family	1.5	1.7
Access to wilderness/undisturbed nature	3.3	3.0
Access to resort areas	2.0	1.6
Opportunities to shop	2.0	1.6
Opportunities to increase knowledge	3.0	2.6
Access to wildlife not normally seen	3.2	3.0
Outdoor adventure activities	3.3	2.8
First-class accommodation	1.5	1.9
High-quality restaurants	1.5	1.8

Note: Five-point rating scales from 0 (not at all) to 4 (very important).

Table 2.4 Activity participation

Activity	Commercial-home Users (%)	Commercial-home Non-users (%)
White-water rafting	26	21
Dive trip to the GBR	19	14
Fishing	22	12
Snorkelling	76	54
SCUBA diving	46	30
Long rainforest walks (> 4 hours)	43	28
Bird watching	25	18
Wildlife watching (no tour)	37	24
Rainforest scenic drive	59	47

such as the Royal Flying Doctor Service Visitor Centre (visited by 14 per cent of commercial home users but only 8 per cent of non-users), and the Botanic gardens (visited by 18 per cent of users and 9 per cent of non-users). The pattern of activity participation was consistent with previous results (see Table 2.4). Commercial home users were more likely than non-users to engage in outdoor adventure activities, which is consistent with their importance ratings for these destination features. They were also more likely to visit rainforests and to independently seek wildlife viewing opportunities.

The overall pattern of results, from both the analysis of the promotional material and from the market research, is consistent with the existence of several forms of commercial home accommodation ranging from options catering for tourists simply seeking budget accommodation to support their visit to the region, through commercial homes that provide access to particular natural environments and their wildlife, to more exclusive total experience oriented options catering for more affluent visitors seeking luxury. In addition the case study illustrated the importance of destination region characteristics in influencing the nature of the commercial home accommodation market opportunities.

The continuum of commercial-home accommodation

According to Johns and Lynch (2007) researchers have not usually sought to distinguish sub-categories in tourism services like accommodation and this omission can limit our understanding of the phenomenon. Lynch (2005c) provides one of the few exceptions with an analysis of commercial homes in the United Kingdom that distinguished a number of different types based on a range of characteristics including size, gender of host, entrepreneurial orientation of the host, host training and product commodification. While Lynch's (2005c) analysis was concerned more with the characteristics and perspectives of the commercial home hosts, the themes identified are consistent with those highlighted in the present case study.

The results of the analysis in the previous section support an argument that there are several forms of commercial home accommodation and this conclusion is also supported by the differences in characteristics of the phenomenon in different regions. It is proposed here that one way to distinguish between different forms of commercial home accommodation is to place them along a continuum based on the importance or centrality of the accommodation to the overall desired tourist experience. The use of overall desired tourist experience as the underlying dimension of the continuum is consistent with the data presented in the case study, literature reviewed on defining and describing commercial home accommodation and recent overt recognition of the importance of experience as a core feature of tourism and leisure (Fesenmaier and Gretzel 2004; Smith 2003).

Figure 2.1 provides an overview of the proposed continuum of commercial home accommodation. At the left end of the continuum the commercial home accommodation acts as standard accommodation and offers primarily a support service for a holiday. At this end it is more likely that the commercial home accommodation will be self-catering or guesthouses and more budget in orientation. It is also likely that these options will occur in more remote locations with smaller visitor numbers or high seasonality that may make it difficult for more standard forms of commercial accommodation to be viable. At the opposite end of the continuum are those forms of commercial home accommodation that can be considered as the destination and the central or major focus of the desired tourist experience. Here the commercial home is an attraction in its own right, either because of the history or architecture of the home itself or because it offers a specific type of experience such as a romantic getaway, spa experience or luxurious retreat. Such forms of commercial home accommodation at this end of the continuum are likely to be more expensive and exclusive and can occur in any tourist destination. Between these two extremes are forms of commercial accommodation that provide access and support for specific attractions,

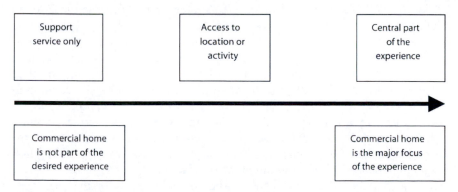

Figure 2.1 Continuum of commercial home accommodation.

such as wildlife viewing, or types of activity, such as nature walks or meeting locals.

Barnett's (2001) analysis of Maori tourist operations in New Zealand provides examples of forms of commercial home accommodation that lie along this spectrum. In this study four homestay businesses were profiled, all with the common theme of having Maori owners and providing guests with exposure to some degree of Maori culture. This exposure varied, however, from a case of providing hospitality consistent with Maori culture in general, through the host taking a special interest in Maori development issues and discussing these with guests, to a situation where guests were invited to participate in Maori cultural activities if they wished, and finishing with a homestay that offered Maori food, traditional fishing and a personal tour to local indigenous communities. Arguably none of these examples are cases where the commercial home is a destination in its own right; rather they fall in order along the middle of the continuum with the increasing importance of the homestay in the tourist experience determining their relative position.

There are several pressures on this continuum. McIntosh and Siggs (2005) and Johnston-Walker (1999) note that the motives and expectations of tourists in general are changing towards a greater desire for personalized experiences and service. These changes put pressure on commercial homes to move towards playing a greater role in the visitor experience. Ingram and Sherwood (2002), however, describe an opposing pressure. In their study of farmers there was a move towards the provision of more budget, self-catering style as farmers saw both the potential for greater returns on investment and to relieve pressures on them and their families as hosts. A third pressure on this continuum is the growing regulation of the sector. In order to respond to problems of quality consistency in commercial home accommodation, a number of associations and grading schemes have been developed. It has been argued that these regulatory systems work against the personalised and authentic nature of the commercial home and also result in hosts having to place a greater emphasis on professional management than personal hosting (Clarke 1999; Gladstone and Morris 2000; Quek 1997; Tourism Queensland 2002).

The location of a particular example of a commercial home accommodation on the continuum is determined by the characteristics of the region in which it is located, the features of the home, the characteristics and motives of the host, and the target tourist market. Where it falls on the continuum also has implications for the type of host–guest interaction expected and the range of facilities and services included in the commercial home experience. The place on the continuum also has implications for the impacts of the commercial home accommodation on its guests, hosts and the destination region in general. The continuum also offers a way to better integrate research findings. Currently many studies provide details of the characteristics of either the hosts or guests for commercial home accommodation in a particular region. These studies produce an array of results which can be difficult to reconcile. By placing the results in the context of the continuum we can begin to build more consistent patterns of connections between key variables.

A systems approach to understanding accommodation in commercial homes

Recently, Farrell and Twining-Ward (2004) and Hall (2005a) have argued that tourism researchers need to take a systems approach in order to improve our understanding of various tourism activities and problems. Hall (1989) and Ngaima (2002) suggest that the rise of systems thinking in management in general is the result of a convergence of trends in a number of disciplines including ecology and sociology. A systems model sets out the main components or elements of a particular phenomenon and the number and type of relationships between these elements (Maani and Cavana 2000). The more detailed the systems model, the better it will be able to be used to identify underlying processes and predict both problems and potential responses to these.

Figure 2.2 presents an initial systems model of commercial home tourist accommodation based on a review of the relevant literature and descriptive models presented by Lynch (2005b) and Evans and Ilbery (1989). Evans and Ilbery (1989) developed a model to describe the factors that were involved in farmers choosing to take up tourist accommodation provision as a form of farm diversification. They suggested that there were three types of strategy that farmers could select in terms of their approach to tourism accommodation – as a secondary source of income to support a hobby farm or a debt-free farm owned by retirees, as a survival strategy for farmers who wished to stay in mainstream agricultural production but required additional income, or as a business expansion or improvement strategy. Evans and Ilbery (1989) argued that the choice of strategy was determined by the characteristics of the farmer, especially their life cycle stage, the farm, and the nature of the external government policy and economic pressures. Aspects of this model were supported by results provided by McGehee and Kim (2004). Lynch (2005c) provided a similar set of factors in his model of motivation for hosts in commercial home accommodation. In this model the external environment offers a set of push factors, while the characteristics of the host and the type of tourist demand create a set of mediating filters that influence the type of commercial home experience offered.

Lynch (2005c) was particularly interested in the implications of these decisions for the resulting type of interaction between hosts and guests. The systems model presented in Figure 2.2 has this host–guest interaction at its centre and it is proposed here that the nature of this interaction is critical in determining the types of impact the commercial home accommodation has on the key actors. Research conducted in New Zealand and Scotland

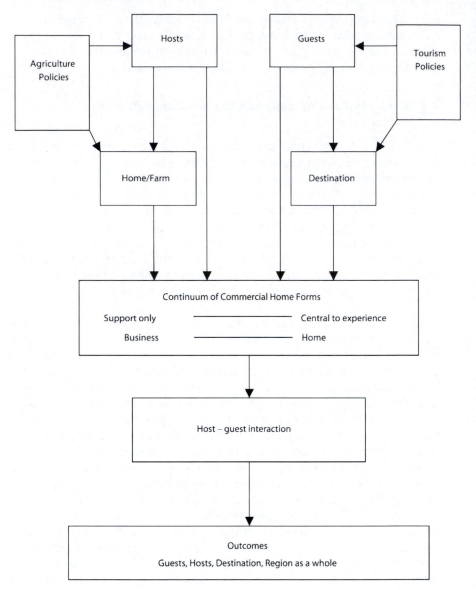

Figure 2.2 An initial-systems model of commercial home accommodation.

suggests that the match between hosts and guests is a critical one that has important implications for the perceived quality of the experience for both parties (Tucker and Lynch 2004). The nature of this interaction depends upon the characteristics of the guests and their expectations together with the characteristics of the hosts and their motivations for offering tourist accommodation. In turn the nature of the home itself and its location and the type of tourism in the destination region influence the interaction both directly and through both the guests and the hosts. In the case of hosts these factors act as constraints on the type of commercial home accommodation experience that can be offered. In the case of the guests these factors influence their expectations of the types of experience on offer and also filter the types of guests in the region.

The available research into the characteristics of commercial home hosts suggest that key variables influencing the type of experience offered include demographics such as age, gender and life cycle stage (Gladstone and Morris 2000; Ilbery et al. 1998; Lynch 1998; McGehee and Kim 2004; Rogerson 2004) and motivations. The major types of motivation that have been identified are economic survival, hobby/social interests, lifestyle support, presentation of culture or region, and the pursuit of growth and profit-oriented business opportunities (Barnett 2001; Evans and Ilbery 1989; Getz and Petersen 2005; Gladstone and Morris 2000; Lynch 1998, 2005c; McGehee and Kim 2004). Lynch (2005c) also argues that actual experiences with guests influence host behaviour. Fewer, but similar, studies have also been conducted on guest profiles, although these have not been linked to choices or outcomes. In the case of guests, motivations include wanting access to a particular location (Fennel and Weaver 1997), budget family holidays (Hossain 2004), support for a specific activity such as hunting or hiking (Clarke 1999), and escape/indulgence (Johnston-Walker 1999).

The home and destination components are included despite a lack of research into these components of the system. In the case of the characteristics of the commercial home itself, the only available research is focused on farms and both Evans and Ilbery (1989) and McGehee and Kim (2004) have demonstrated that the size, location, history of occupation, and type of farm all influence the form of commercial home accommodation offered. Logically it can be argued that characteristics of other types of homes such as architecture, size and history will be important variables. Aspects of destinations have also been neglected in research, although the differences noted across studies conducted in different regions support an argument that characteristics such as the image presented for the destination, the type of activities available in the destination and the profile of other accommodation available in the region will also influence the type of commercial home accommodation offered.

Finally, there are the outcomes of the host–guest interaction. Four key areas of outcomes have been identified in the systems model in Figure 2.2 – impacts on the guests themselves, the hosts, the destination and the region as a whole. A very limited number of studies have been published looking at outcomes for guests and these have focused almost exclusively on satisfaction or perceived service quality (McIntosh and Siggs 2005). Tucker (2003b) looked at the outcomes of the host–guest relationship, particularly in rural settings. Other possible areas to explore could be what guests learn about the destination region and its culture from interacting with commercial home hosts, and the extent to which the personal interaction contributes to a sense of well-being associated with the experience. Pearce (1990) reported that some hosts had formed long-term friendship with their guests, another potential outcome worth exploring. In a similar fashion, research into outcomes for the hosts has also been mostly limited to examinations of financial outcomes and occupancy (see Kaufman et al. 1996; Nuntsu et al. 2004). Lynch (1998, 2005b, 2005c) suggests that there may be impacts on hosts from the guest interactions and having to share their private household spaces. This is further explored in Hall's chapter of this volume.

The third area of potential impacts is on the destination. The destination is presented separately from the region as a whole here so that specific impacts on the tourism of the area can be considered. Again this is a topic that has largely been neglected. At least two topics for research have, however, been identified. Hossain (2004) argues that the nature of the commercial home accommodation available in a region can influence its destination image. This raises the question of the manner in which commercial homes contribute to a total image for a region. Vallen and Rande (1997) reported that hosts are often important sources of information on local attractions and activities for their guests, another area that could be further examined.

The final area to be considered is that of the impacts of developing commercial home accommodation on the region as a whole. The use of private homes for tourist accommodation is often put forward as an option for peripheral and developing regions because of the belief that this form of tourist service provision creates better economic outcomes for regions with a greater share of the tourist dollar kept in the region, more opportunities for locals to participate in tourism employment, less environmental damage because of the use of existing buildings and smaller numbers, and less cultural impact because of the opportunity for hosts and guests to interact in a more balanced fashion (Andrew 1997; Dernoi 1981; Gladstone and Morris 2000; Rogerson 2004). Unfortunately there is limited evidence to support these claims and what is available is contradictory. Some studies support the positive impacts of commercial home accommodation citing enhanced employment opportunities and better incomes (North West Farm Tourism Initiative 2004), and greater use of local produce as benefits (Nummedal and Hall 2006). Others have found the opposite, with Becken et al. (2001) demonstrating high levels of energy consumption per guest for commercial homes in New Zealand, Oldham et al. (2000) reporting limited income for hosts in South Africa, and Shackley (1993) questioning the benefits for local employment in a Namibian study.

Conclusions

In a discussion of the pressures on the commercial home accommodation continuum, a tension within the continuum was noted between market forces encouraging a move towards the home becoming more central to the tourist experience and economic forces encouraging hosts to provide a greater number of more budget options. This is just one tension in the commercial home accommodation system. Stringer (1981), Pearce (1990) and Lynch (1998, 2005b, 2005c) have all noted tensions in the host–guest interaction component of the system. Here the more personal nature of the interaction is seen to constrain guest behaviours in ways that would not occur in traditional accommodation and to impact on the hosts. Other tensions include those between agricultural and tourism policies in terms of the kinds of incentives given to potential hosts by different government programs, tensions between the motives and constraints on hosts and market demands, and tensions between the values of stakeholders and their desired outcomes.

Much of the research that has been published has been concerned with finding ways to encourage and support the further development of commercial home accommodation. In order to determine if these aims are desirable, and if so to achieve these aims, it is important that we understand the whole system and how it differs across different forms of commercial home accommodation. The value of the initial systems model is to begin to integrate the existing research findings in such a way that the nature of the tensions in the system can be acknowledged and analysed. In particular, analysis of the tensions in the system will be important in determining the long-term sustainability of this form of tourist accommodation.

3 Hosts as entrepreneurs

Female commercial home entrepreneurs in Gaeltacht areas in the west of Ireland

Ziene Mottiar and Lucia Laurincikova

Introduction

The commercial home literature, as the phrase implies, concentrates on the home as a place where hospitality is provided for tourists. An important contribution to this literature has been the discussion of what actually defines a commercial home (Lynch and MacWhannell 2000). A clear area of interest has also been in the social interactions that occur within that home between host and guest. This relationship must be examined in the context of the fact that studies such as Stringer (1981) show that gaining an insight into the realities of family life is a key attraction for the visitor. However, the shared use of family space can lead to tensions. Darke and Gurney (2000) describe hospitality in commercial homes as a performance which the host under-takes for the guest. In a similar vein, Dann and Cohen (1991: 163) discuss 'social exchange and the profit motive masquerading behind a phoney front of friendliness'. Mottiar and Tucker (2007) examine the web of power that the host spins in Göreme, Turkey, as the host controls which local businesses 'their' guests visit.

Another area of interest has been the gendered nature of commercial homes. As Lynch (2000b: 106) states, 'hosting in the home is generally perceived as a gendered occupation'. Darke and Gurney (2000: 83) note that 'it remains the case that women's identity is much more closely tied up with the home than men's and [they argue] that the hospitality in the commercial sector offers the services of a surrogate mother or wife'. Dart (2006) considers issues of the blurring boundaries of work and leisure space and argues that many who work at home experience a sense of 'disembeddedness', with a loss of the traditional home space. Similarly, Sullivan (2000: 202) notes that 'some co-residents experience loss of space, which can cause them dissatisfaction and lead to conflict', while Mirchandani (2000: 178) looks at 'two contradictory images which co-exist in individuals' lives – one, that it allows individuals to integrate their work and family lives; and two, that it necessitates the maintenance of a strict division between paid and family work'.

While these discussions have added to our understanding of the commercial home and have developed a literature in this regard, an under-researched area has been that of the entrepreneurial nature of these businesses. It is in this area that this chapter seeks to contribute to our understanding of commercial homes. The focus here is not on the owner as host but as entrepreneur and this chapter seeks to contribute to our knowledge about commercial home owners as entrepreneurs.

The broader context – female and tourism entrepreneurship

The research that follows on commercial home entrepreneurs can be set within the broader female entrepreneurship and tourism entrepreneurship contexts, and it is from these literatures that the research questions have emerged. Two-thirds of entrepreneurial activity worldwide is reported to be by men, in no country are there more female than male entrepreneurs and on average men are twice as likely as women to start up a new business (Fitzsimons and O'Gorman 2007). From a sector perspective, more females engage in consumer-oriented ventures while there are more men in manufacturing (Allen et al. 2007).

Much of the literature is concerned about differences between male andfemale entrepreneurs (for example, Brush 1992; Chell and Baines 1998; DeTienne and Chandler 2007). Rubery (2005: 177) criticises this focus believing that 'the extant literature is dominated by andocentric perspectives which has resulted in women's experiences of starting and growing businesses being overlooked, or compared with those of men, which often has the effect of excluding, subordinating, or marginalising them'. In terms of female entrepreneurs as a distinct group, some of the key issues debated include motivations for entrepreneurship among women (Chu 2000), the issues of a glass ceiling (Simpson and Altman 2000), educational background (Menzies et al. 2004), use of role models (Singh et al. 2006), differences between white and minority women business owners (Smith-Hunter and Boyd 2004), networking (Renzulli et al. 2000), family influences on business (Sullivan and Lewis 2001; Renzulli et al. 2000) and barriers to women achieving their entrepreneurship potential (Brindley 2005; Fielden et al. 2003; Marlow and Patton 2005).

In line with this literature, the research presented in this chapter seeks to focus on such issues in terms of female commercial home entrepreneurs. In particular, it is concerned with motivations and barriers to new venture creation. Helms (1997) believes that women often start a new business for three types of personal gain: personal freedom, security, and/or satisfaction. Buttner and Moore (1997) note a key motivation as the combination of work and family responsibilities and Cromie (1987: 251) supports this by saying that the entrepreneurs he studied saw entrepreneurship as a way of 'meeting simultaneously their own career needs and the needs of their children'. Lynch (1998) investigates the motivation of commercial home entrepreneurs, in particular, and he distinguishes between push factors (such as labour-market conditions and time to spare) and pull factors (such as the opportunity to supplement income, social and psychological benefits and entrepreneurial benefits). An important aspect to consider for female commercial home owners especially is that perhaps they are attracted to this particular business as it is an extension of the traditional female role. Goffee and Scase (1985) note that women who are highly committed to both entrepreneurial ideals and conventional gender roles tend to establish businesses which are extensions of their domestic work.

This chapter seeks to add to the motivations debate by taking a sectoral approach and investigating female entrepreneurs in the commercial home sector. It will add to the limited knowledge that we have about commercial home entrepreneurs by focusing on Gaeltacht areas (Irish-speaking areas) in Ireland. While there are no national statistics available, it is noted that small scale samples have indicated female domination among commercial home owners. In Ireland, Breathnach et al. (1994: 69) note that 'one sector of the tourism industry which is exclusively dominated by women is the bed and breakfast (B&B) sector'. Thus the commercial home sector is an ideal case to study female entrepreneurs.

This chapter will contribute to our limited knowledge regarding motivations among female commercial home entrepreneurs. It will also add to Breathnach et al.'s (1994) work on bed and breakfast owners in Ireland particularly. More specifically, it will fill a gap in the literature by attempting to ascertain whether these entrepreneurs believe that establishing the business has provided them with what they wanted from it. In other words, have the desires or ambitions that motivated them to set up the business in the first place been fulfilled?

A feminist perspective on entrepreneurship focuses on the fact that, just as in the employment market, women are disadvantaged by their gender. In particular, liberal feminist theory highlights discrimination and the lack of access to resources and education as the reasons for relatively low levels of female entrepreneurship. Gundry et al. (2002) and Helms (1997) highlight financial barriers, Weiler and Bernasek (2001) focus on a lack of networks and mentors, while Bruni et al. (2004) view access to information and assistance as explaining factors. Social feminist theory postulates that low female entrepreneurship participation rates can be attributed to social and market structures whereby there is gender division of market and non-market roles, and the traditional role of women in society is as homemakers (Henry and Kennedy 2002). Commercial home entrepreneurs are perhaps a perfect example of female entrepreneurs who fulfil their entrepreneurial ambitions within the restrictions and limitations of a society which divides responsibilities according to gender. Thus, running a bed and breakfast allows these women to conform to social norms and thereby overcome social barriers so that they can be a homemaker based in the home '24/7' whilst also maintaining a job or fulfilling their entrepreneurial ability.

As important as identifying the barriers to commercial home entrepreneurship is, it is equally important to ask if and how these barriers were overcome. A growing area of interest in the tourism literature has been the role of networks, clusters and inter-firm relations (for example, Hall 2004a; Jackson and Murphy 2006; Mottiar and Tucker 2007). Such relations can aid firms in overcoming the difficulties experienced due to their small size. Although Renzulli et al. (2000) found that women tend to have more homogeneous networks than men with respect to kin, which can present a business disadvantage, McGregor and Tweed (2002) highlight the new generation of female business owners who are well networked. As such, they are more likely to have and want mentorship and to have greater expansionist intentions. Lynch (2000b: 109) investigates the issue of networks among host families for English language schools and concludes that his study 'tended to support the finding ... that in the early stage of enterprise development there is a heavy reliance on informal networks of friends, family and social contacts in the neighbourhood'. For the current sample of commercial home entrepreneurs, who can be classified as a minority population due to their gender, first language and location, being part of a network may be particularly important to aid enterprise development and to overcome difficulties that may be experienced.

The key questions addressed are: What barriers to entrepreneurship do these female commercial home entrepreneurs face? How do they overcome these barriers? Are these entrepreneurs part of networks and do they have strong inter-firm relations which help them to overcome difficulties and barriers?

Methodology

The empirical research for this chapter was undertaken in September 2006. The research is concerned with female bed and breakfast and guesthouse entrepreneurs running businesses in Gaeltacht areas in Ireland. This study concentrated on the commercial home female entrepreneurs located in counties Galway, Mayo and Donegal. These counties are located on the Western seaboard of Ireland.

The objective was to include all female-owned bed and breakfasts in these areas in the sample. To do so, names and addresses of entrepreneurs who met the criteria above were attained from a number of websites and national and association brochures for bed and breakfasts and guesthouses. While every effort was made to identify all commercial home owners in the area, it is likely that some have been omitted as they do not advertise nationally. In total, 102 questionnaires were posted to the identified commercial home owner. The questionnaire comprised 23 questions which had a mix of open-ended and closed questions. The closed questions asked respondents to, for example, rank factors or tick relevant boxes as this would provide us with more categorical quantitative data, while open ended questions were used to gain insights into respondents' opinions and their particular 'stories'. The questions dealt with the key research questions noted above: asking about their motivations, whether they had attained what they set out to achieve, the difficulties they experienced in setting up and running their business and how they overcame these difficulties, and the role of networks and government agencies in their development. The questionnaire was piloted over the previous summer to ensure that questions were clear and that the questionnaire was not too long. Some issues were addressed in a number of different questions in order to increase the reliability of the data. In a bid to increase the response rate, stamped self-addressed envelopes were included for the completed questionnaire. In the first instance, 18 questionnaires were returned. Follow-up telephone calls were made and the final response rate was 31. While this is lower than we would have hoped, the sample provides a good geographical range and provides us with representative data to investigate our research questions. It also provides a basis upon which further research with a greater number of respondents can be conducted.

Findings

Profile of entrepreneurs

The age profile of the female commercial homes owners in this sample shows a concentration in the 45–54 age group (43 per cent of survey). It was interesting to note that the largest proportion of commercial homes in the survey were established in the 1980s and 1990s, while only two businesses were established after 2000. The combination of older age profiles and start-up period suggest that commercial homes are becoming less attractive to the younger female entrepreneur in the Gaeltacht area. As one respondent notes: 'I think the bed and breakfast sector is in big decline in Gaeltacht areas. I don't see many young women starting a bed and breakfast. It's a difficult life and no guarantee of wages, no guarantee in holding down a mortgage.' In the main, these businesses were the women's first experience of running a business with only five having had a business before this. Out of those who did not have any previous entrepreneurial experience, 43 per cent had some previous working experience as employees in the hospitality/tourism sector while 57 per cent did not have any previous hospitality/tourism experience before setting up their commercial home. This paints a picture of entrepreneurs with little business experience before their current activity and in the majority of cases, no previous experience working in the hospitality industry.

All of the respondents were listed as the main proprietor of their establishment in their promotional literature. According to Sullivan and Lewis (2001), co-residents' role in home-based businesses is common as the boundaries between home and work space are often blurred (Dart 2006). This was the case with these entrepreneurs, with 77 per cent of the businesses receiving active family assistance. In most cases, it was husband and children who helped with managing and running of the business on a day-to-day basis.

What are the key motivations for establishing a commercial home enterprise?

One of the primary research questions posed in this study concerns the motivations these women had to start their commercial home business. Table 3.1 shows the main motivations among the sample. The second column shows what percentage of those entrepreneurs in each motivation category believed that they had achieved what they set out to in this regard.

The biggest motivation among this group was to supplement family income combined with family responsibilities of raising children. As one entrepreneur stated: 'I decided to stay at home when my first child was born. It was a means for earning some extra money that was needed.' Another commented, 'I was a traditional mum who wanted to rear my children myself and saw this as a method of supplementing our income.' It is important to note that while income is an extremely important factor, these entrepreneurs see their income from this business as a way of supplementing the family income or contributing to the household income. The objective is to add finances to the family or household rather than for the business as an entity to gain profits, as is likely to be the case with other entrepreneurs. This shows the primary focus on the household rather than the business and, again, reflects the entwined nature of home and work for a commercial home entrepreneur. It also reflects Goffee and Scase's (1985) description of a conventional female entrepreneur who plays a traditional female role and has low commitment to traditional business goals.

The motivations outlined by these respondents display an emphasis on lifestyle issues; for example, 73 per cent wanted a more family-friendly job, 70 per cent were motivated by meeting interesting people, 47 per cent wanted a better work–life balance, and 40 per cent set up the business in order to

Table 3.1 Key motivations for commercial home entrepreneurs

Motivation	Motivation (%)	Percentage who fulfilled these motivations
To supplement the family income	83	88
So I can look after the children while I work	80	100
A more family-friendly job	73	95
To meet interesting people	70	86
A higher income	63	74
We needed more money for the household	57	94
It allows me to contribute to the household income	53	100
A better work–life balance	47	71
To stay in this area	40	100
A better lifestyle	37	82
More freedom	30	89
I wanted something to do with my spare time	30	89

stay in the area. This is similar to Lynch's (1998: 331) findings which noted that 'the primary motivations for hosting are concerned with psychological "feel good" and educational factors arising from hosting'. In the literature, there has been a debate about whether commercial home entrepreneurs are an example of lifestyle entrepreneurs (Lynch 2005c; Morrison et al. 1999). It is clear that lifestyle issues are very important motivations in terms of these entrepreneurs and, while income is important, many lifestyle issues are highlighted as key motivators. As Lynch (2005c: 25) states, 'it would be worthwhile exploring the working realities of commercial home hosts in order to determine just what sort of lifestyle is being achieved'.

Have these entrepreneurs achieved what they hoped for?

It must be noted that these female entrepreneurs are 'survivors', as most have been in business for more than ten years. So while more than 70 per cent of respondents in each category of motivation believed that they have attained their target (see Table 3.1), it must not be forgotten that an unidentified number of commercial homes have ceased to exist (and are therefore not part of this sample) and in most cases those could be said to have failed to achieve even minimum targets. So, what follows is an analysis of the more successful commercial home entrepreneurs in these areas.

In terms of income, it is interesting to note that those seeking to supplement the family income, attain more money for the household or contribute to the household income have relatively high levels of achievement rates (88 per cent, 94 per cent and 100 per cent respectively). However, only 74 per cent believed that they had achieved a higher income. This subtle difference indicates that success is more apparent in term of the household, as there is now greater income, rather than in terms of the business or individual who, in 25 per cent of cases, did not achieve a higher income as they wanted.

The second key motivator was related to looking after children and having a more family friendly job. More than 95 per cent of respondents believed that they had achieved this by setting up the commercial home enterprise. Again, it is important to be aware of the nuances of this point as only 71 per cent of those who wanted a better work–life balance felt that they had achieved it. This may reflect the fact that while the entrepreneurs could better balance work and family responsibilities this was 'difficult, especially when children were young as, with a very heavy work load, I had to have time for everything'. Another entrepreneur commented: 'I managed to balance both, though it's not easy. Also I found that some of my children resented the invasion of guests'. Another respondent noted the fact that 'you are never away from your work'.

So, whilst these women had achieved the objective of being able to look after their children, this has not necessarily been easy from the individual entrepreneur's point of view, and work–life balance is still an issue in many cases. These responses reflect the discussion regarding the issue of work and leisure space for home workers as discussed by Dart (2006), Mirchandani (2000) and Sullivan and Lewis (2001). It is also notable that entrepreneurship in this sector binds women to traditional roles as they continue to be the primary carers for children and now also run a business. Furthermore, the personal characteristics and day-to-day activities that this type of entrepreneurial activity requires are those which are most often ascribed to women – cooking, cleaning, caring for others and providing hospitality. These entrepreneurs now do this for their families and guests. This mirrors Sullivan and Lewis's (2001) argument that female home-based work can compound gender inequity by reinforcing their greater responsibilities for childcare and the management of the family.

So, while it seems that the majority of entrepreneurs did fulfil their key motivations from a household and family perspective, from a personal or business perspective, success in fulfilling motivations is less evident.

What are the barriers to becoming a commercial home entrepreneur?

When asked about the biggest barrier to becoming an entrepreneur, answers varied greatly as they depended on different personal and business circumstances at the time of starting up a new venture. While for some, financial viability, re-organising home to facilitate guests, financing and standards compliance were the biggest barriers to overcome at the start, for others, these barriers were more of a personal nature. Lack of self-confidence, lack of experience and the 'mental barrier' of letting strangers into one's own home, had to be overcome initially before becoming a commercial home entrepreneur. It is clear that, from a feminist perspective, this research highlights barriers identified by both the liberal and social feminist schools of thought referred to earlier in this chapter.

Similarly, when asked about the most difficult thing which has had to be overcome in business, answers differed. Business-nature difficulties included continual upgrading of the house on a small profit margin, marketing, getting business in the off-season, and the level of competition. One of the most interesting findings is the fact that 40 per cent of respondents stated that they

Table 3.2 Key difficulties experienced by commercial home entrepreneurs

Difficulty	Experienced (%)
Getting business in the off-season	67
Local competition	47
Marketing	43
Balancing work and home life	40
Staffing problems	33
Time management	33
Covering the costs of the business	33
Keeping accounts	30

have experienced difficulties balancing work and home life (see Table 3.2). One female respondent found that 'living with your family and perhaps ten or 12 guests for six months each year is not ideal', while another noted that 'staying awake long enough for all the work needed to be done' was particularly difficult. Others pointed out that it was difficult to be 'on call 24/7, 7 am until midnight' and 'restricting children in the freedom of their home'.

So how have the entrepreneurs overcome these barriers and dealt with these problems? While problems such as marketing were resolved by spending more, networking and building a good word of mouth, what the women described, in their own words, as 'sheer patience and perseverance', 'determination' and 'family support' were other ways of coping with problems occurring along the way. It is clear that most of these solutions and actions were reactive rather than proactive in nature, and also that the solutions were found mainly within the entrepreneurs themselves or their family support mechanism rather than in formal organisations, business associations or state bodies. No respondents mentioned any regional body, national state agency or business association when asked how they had overcome difficulties.

Networks

It was anticipated that these entrepreneurs may have relied on both formal and informal networks to support their activity and to aid them overcoming their difficulties, as was the case with the homestay sector providing accommodation to language school students (Lynch 2000b). The importance of family members is apparent from Table 3.3, with 90 per cent of respondents relying on family members. This support is reflected in day-to-day assistance with guests and, in many cases, help with running the business comes without any pay. As one respondent noted, family members' support is invaluable as she 'couldn't have managed without them'. This validates findings of

Table 3.3 Percentage of commercial home entrepreneurs who were members of the following networks

Network	Importance (%)
Family members	90
B&B Associations such as Town and Country Homes, Irish Farmhouse and Irish Accommodation Network	77
Other B&B entrepreneurs in the area	73
Failte Ireland	73
Personal networks	47
Other entrepreneurs in the area	37
Other female entrepreneurs	27
County Enterprise Board	17
Local Business Associations	7

several studies (for example, Moore 1990) which showed that women tend to nominate more kin as people with whom they discuss important decisions. The primary support offered by other entrepreneurs is mainly in terms of referring customers.

In terms of formal networks over 90 per cent of respondents were members of one or more professional networks. This result was expected, as commercial homes for the sample were targeted mainly from various professional trade organisations' literature and websites. The positive impact of the Town and Country Homes Association and Failte Ireland was attributed to their selling and marketing support. However, a number of respondents commented on a change in this support. As one respondent said, 'they were more helpful in the past; in recent years they have become less interested in small operators'. The low level of membership of local business associations was also notable.

The perceived impact of state bodies and enterprise boards was mostly indifferent or negative. Rare positive impacts included help with signs, positive effect of the smoking ban, or some training provided by enterprise boards. However, most have negative feelings about public agencies, regarding the lack of commitment by national government to small businesses in rural areas, water rates, or local government's 'allowing planning permissions for housing estates spoiling views and village atmosphere'. Udaras na Gaeltachta was expected to have a positive influence on the sector's development in the Gaeltacht areas, but this was not found to be the case in this survey. The majority expressed dissatisfaction with Udaras na Gaeltachta, making comments such as 'not as much help as one would expect', 'the local office is not promoting Irish speaking homes' and 'offers grants but one needs stamina'.

These feelings explain the lack of active involvement of most of these commercial home owners in formal networks. While they may subscribe to industry groups, they tend to do so simply as a method of marketing. The relationship between the commercial home entrepreneur and the association is distant and, in most cases, simply involves a commercial transaction whereby the commercial home owner pays a subscription to be included in their accommodation listings. This reflects the finding of Mottiar (2007) that lifestyle tourism entrepreneurs in Westport, Ireland did not have a role in formal associations as they believed that they were not large enough or established enough to play a part. It is notable that in Lynch's (2000b) study of networking among people providing accommodation for students of a language school it was found that there were strong links between the hosts and the organisations who they took guests for. The differences between that study and the current one may be explained by the fact that there is less potential for vertical linkages in this case as commercial home owners provide their service directly to the customer and have very few suppliers. Furthermore, the bodies they are associated with tend to be national organisations and so spatial distance makes the operation of strong formal networks extremely difficult.

So, it is clear that these commercial home entrepreneurs rely heavily on personal and social networks. While they are members of some formal networks, this is largely just a commercial relationship whereby they are members of the network in order to advertise their service. Thus these entrepreneurs depend on themselves and their family for entrepreneurial success.

Conclusions

This research set out to increase understanding of commercial home entrepreneurs. It is clear that most are motivated primarily by the desire to supplement household income and to be able to care for children. In the majority of cases they believe that they have fulfilled these key motivations, although the work–life balance still seems to be an issue as they experience difficulties in terms of time and space allocation between family and guests (this issue is discussed further in Chapter 5 of this volume). The lifestyle motivations appear to be very strong among this group, thus supporting the argument that commercial home entrepreneurs are lifestyle entrepreneurs.

From a feminist perspective, these entrepreneurs have not challenged the traditional role of women in society; they have chosen to set up businesses which rely on the gendered female domestic tasks of cooking, cleaning and caring. Their businesses are, as Goffee and Scase (1985) describe, extensions of their domestic work. They have overcome the barriers to female employment and entrepreneurship by choosing to set up a business which will allow them to combine the dual role of parent/homemaker and income earner. In taking this approach, these entrepreneurs have fulfilled their ambitions in terms of the household by contributing to the finances and engaging in child care. However, from a personal point of view more than a quarter of respondents had not attained the higher income that they had been motivated by and had not achieved a better work–life balance. Hence, female home-based work can perpetuate gender inequity by reinforcing women's greater responsibilities for childcare and the management of the family. Individual gain has perhaps been sacrificed, therefore, for the good of the family as a whole. This is an issue that may be interesting to investigate further.

Personal networks and business links can play an important role in terms of overcoming the disadvantages of working alone at home, particularly in a rural isolated location. Such links can also be important in business terms. While these entrepreneurs show use of personal networks, there are few links with local and national government, business associations or county enterprise boards. This highlights an issue that needs to be addressed from a policy perspective.

This chapter has outlined some key issues in terms of female commercial home entrepreneurs to provide a better understanding of what their key motivations are and what barriers or difficulties they experience. It has become clear that these entrepreneurs are motivated primarily by the needs of their home and family, and that they rely on a broad spectrum of family and personal contacts to help them in their businesses. What is also evident is that they appear to function in relative isolation as most are not members of local business associations. Where they do have formal network membership, the purpose is primarily to appear in their accommodation listings. While the majority of entrepreneurs have achieved what they set out to by establishing their businesses, many still grapple with issues of work–life balance and have not attained the higher income they were motivated by. These entrepreneurs are a particular type of entrepreneur who extend the traditional female role in society in an entrepreneurial way. They appear to be what Goffee and Scase (1985) call conventional female entrepreneurs and, as such, they comprise a useful group to analyse for the general female entrepreneurship literature. From the commercial homes literature perspective, the recognition that these individuals are entrepreneurs as much as hosts should underpin all analyses of this sector.

4 Farmstay enterprises

(Re)interpreting public/private domains and 'home' sites and sights

Gayle Jennings and Daniela Stehlik

Introduction

Since the 1970s, impacts of globalisation, climatic crises, environmental pressures and rural farming practices have contributed to substantive changes in agricultural production (Gössling and Mattson 2002; Jennings and Stehlik 2000; Wilson et al. 2001). As a consequence, Australia, like other western industrialised nations, has undergone significant restructuring of its rural industries. This restructuring, especially since the 1980s, has occurred in association with decreases and/or cessation of 'state' support, in particular, subsidisation of agricultural industries. This period of restructuring has been described as a 'post-productive transition' (Ilbery et al. 1998) phase. Farmers who have been able to adapt to this phase, as well as deal with stressors, such as, climatic crises and other shock events, demonstrate 'adaptive capacity' as well as 'resilience' (Australian Bureau of Agricultural Resource Economics, ABARE 2007). The specific capacity of farmers to successfully recoup and maintain their farm-based livelihoods as a result of their responses to crises and stress is described as resilience (Ellis 2000; Walker and Salt 2006). One demonstration of adaptive capacity and resilience has been diversification of farming operations.

One particular innovative diversification response has been the introduction of farm-based tourism experiences into the pluriactivity of farming operations. This response has been undertaken in Australia as well as other western industrialised nations (Evans and Ilbery 1992; Jennings and Stehlik 1999; McGehee et al. 2007; McIntosh and Campbell 2001; Tyrväinen et al. 2001). It should be noted, however, that farm tourism enterprises are not recent phenomena; 'vacation farms' have over 100 years of history (Weaver and Fennell 1997). What is new is the incorporation of farm tourism into farming operations of western industrialised nations as a result of rural restructuring and continued 'shock' events. Key drivers of this innovation have been farm women (Frederick 1993; Garcia-Ramon et al. 1995; Jennings and Stehlik 1999; Knight 1996). Although farm tourism innovations have been diverse, they can be categorised into three types: (1) farmstays – accommodation in a farm setting; (2) farm attractions, which involve demonstration of farming activities; and (3) farm experiences, which are associated with accommodation and involvement in farm activities (Davies and Gilbert 1992). In all three types, tourists buy farm *experiences* rather than farm *products*, although tourists may also consume farm produce as part of their farm experiences.

There is a burgeoning literature on tourism/tourist experiences (Jennings 2006) as well as discussions of the experiential nature of accommodation settings (McIntosh and Siggs 2005). With regard to the theme of this book, the commercial home, this chapter reports on the lived experiences, and in particular, 'the nature or meaning of everyday experiences' (Van Manen 1990: 9), for farmstay providers within the context of farming pluriactivity. Of the three types of farm tourism mentioned above, farmstays and farm experiences fit comfortably into the commercial home interpretive framework described by Lynch and MacWhannell (2000). Moreover, the chapter serves to broaden understandings of home constructs beyond commercial private home settings to consideration of commercial private home enterprises embedded within complementary and competing farming contexts.

Farmstay enterprises: background

The lived experiences of farmstay providers, as a consequence of commercialising farm home spaces and places as well as resultant (re)interpretations of public/private domains and 'home' sites and sights, are the focus of this chapter. The discourses presented are based on a multiple case study conducted at the start of the twenty-first century of farmstay tourism in regional Australia, wherein all the farmstays were operated by women. The sites studied in collaboration with the women undertaking these forms of enterprise were on large properties situated in Central Queensland, Australia. These properties had experienced significant restructuring as a result of drought, falling commodity prices, changing markets and shifts in government policies with regard to support and subsidisation of rural industries. The majority of sites were properties that had been in the same family for many generations. Usually, intergenerational farm connectivity was linked to a husband's family and the women had married *onto* the properties.

Since the study sought to gain a rich and in-depth understanding of lived experiences and consequences of farmstay entrepreneurial activities within the pluriactivity of farming practices, the study used an interpretive social sciences paradigm. It employed a qualitative methodology and generic 'feminist' methodological principles. These informed the methods of participant observation, in-depth interviews, reflexive recordings, diagrams, drawings and photographic essays to generate empirical materials.

The researchers visited each of the farmstay operations included in the study. At the commencement of the study, some twenty operators were identified via tourism brochures, magazines and discussions with tourism associations. A saturation sample was attempted with these operators. There was one refusal from the twenty operators approached, since the business was to be sold in the up-coming fortnight. Data were analysed using constant comparison.

In overview, the study found that, for the receiving farm homes, 'farmstay tourism' impacted on gendered roles and responsibilities, negotiation of public/private domains, and representation of 'farm life'. In relation to this, this chapter discusses the following conceptual dimensions: farmstays as commercial home enterprises; farm women, farmstay work and workloads; farmstays and (re)interpretation of public/private domains; farmstays, farm women and public/private domains; and farmstays and (re)interpretation of 'home' sites and sights.

Farmstays as commercial home enterprises

Within the Australian context, a farmstay is contextualised within agri-tourism, which 'offers a unique country holiday experience that invites visitors to stay on farms and in rural communities [sic] to enjoy agricultural experiences' (Tourism Australia 2007). As one respondent said: ' ... a farmstay is ... a holiday for people to see a different way of life and whatever is happening at the time our guests arrive is what they participate in' (farm woman with five years experience running a farmstay). Although similar to homestays, wherein 'the owners and their guests live under the same roof' (Bed and Breakfast and Farmstay New South Wales and Australian Capital Territory, BBFNSW 2006), some farmstays offer accommodation away from the family home. An additional variation in our study was one farmstay which operated in the off-farm property family home. Regardless of location of the farmstay within, adjacent or at distance to the farmhouse or property, farmstay operation is an additional activity to the normal functioning of the farm.

Farmstays as an entrepreneurial act by women

As already advanced, farmstays are a means of adaptive capacity and resiliency or as Bowler et al. (1996) put it, are a means for 'survival' in order to diversify farm production. Such 'survival' is exemplified by one farm woman in our study, who noted:

> We had to find more income, we had no money for further diversification of farming practices and produce. What we did have was buildings which were unused and I had my skills. I could cook and clean and I like people so I thought I could try a small scale low-key farm tourism operation. We were still a working property although not the size we were before so there were still things for people to see.
>
> (Woman in first year of farmstay operation)

Accordingly, the majority of farm women in our study engaged in farm tourism in order to generate additional sources of income. This was, however, different to an earlier study of farm women in New Zealand (Pearce 1990). This difference demonstrates that farm women are not a 'seamless category of women' (Butler 1990: 4), each has various life experiences and histories which inform their narratives and create 'difference'.

Furthermore, the generation of income situates the farmstays in this study within a commercial home framework (Lynch 2005c). The women in our study also saw value in farmstays because the enterprises connected the providers with other people thereby reducing perceptions of isolation and limited social interaction. Similarly, several studies have also noted social benefits for providers of farm tourism operations (Arahi 1998; Pearce 1990). Subsequently, the farm women in our study could be considered as social entrepreneurs (Lynch 2005c). Another advantage of having farmstay guests, according to some of the women in our study, was that guests were perceived as providing a circuit breaker from economic and climatic stressors:

> I enjoy it. It is relief from our worries here, you talk to other people and get another view on life. Also the city people get to understand our plight. More so it helps to alter the image people have of us as farmers and how we live.
>
> (Farmstay operator, five years of operation, who went from a large-scale operation of 30 guests to a smaller scale of up to ten guests per night)

Women in our study also had other reasons for operating farmstays, such as to educate others: 'I thought it was a way that we could actually show to others what you can do to make the environment more sustainable and more sensitive to environmental needs' (ecotourism farmstay operator of ten years duration). Farmstays were also seen as a means to provide future employment avenues for children and to keep them on the farm. While other commercial home operations are noted to have been predicated on lifestyle choices (Andersson et al. 2002), this was not the case in our study. Consequently, the farm women could not be termed lifestyle entrepreneurs (Buick et al. 2001; Shaw, Williams and Greenwood 1987). However, there were elements of farmstay hosting that provided positive contributions to lifestyle, such as meeting people, as noted previously. Additionally, farmstay tourism had links to identity politics; a majority of farm women indicated that operating a farmstay increased their sense of self-worth and self esteem. Similar rationales for the introduction of farm tourism into the pluriactivity of farms were reported by Clarke (1999) and Ollenburg and Buckley (2007). Lynch (1998) also found a number of complementary motivations in his study of women micro entrepreneurs in host family commercial home enterprises.

Farm women, farmstay work and workloads

One of the impacts associated with the introduction of farmstays into the pluriactivity of farm operations was an increase in women's workloads. Farm women's workloads are associated with three forms: unpaid, paid work and voluntary (Jennings and Stehlik 2000). All three can take place either 'on' or 'off' the farming property. Over the past twenty years literature has focused on both the invisibility and gendered nature of women's contributions to farming activities, particularly, with regard to unpaid contributions (see Alston 1995; Paterson 2002; Sachs 1983; Shortall 1992).

Moreover, as has been recognised in earlier studies, even 'without additional loads, farm women's "domestic" chores usually entail ... far more work than for an urban housewife [sic]' (James 1989: 6). Climatic crises, such as drought experiences, continue to see farm women adding further work roles and responsibilities to their loads, such as, becoming a 'reserve army of [farm] labour' as paid farm staff are laid off (Stehlik et al. 1999). Subsequently, the introduction of farmstay tourism occurs in conjunction with or in opposition to regular farming operations (Jennings and Stehlik 1999), and is therefore not without consequences.

In most cases, farmstay enterprises were added to existing workloads of farm women in both the unpaid and paid work sector. The exception was one farmstay operation which had become the primary farm-based activity and the traditional farming activities had become background staging for the operation. In regard to workloads for farm women, one woman noted:

> I have multiple roles as a farm woman, such as running into town to do traditional farm business, doing the farm accounts, going and helping with anything that needs to be done on the property, being the family carer, managing the household, as well as running the farmstay operation. ... I have to manage the household, other farm responsibilities and operate the farmstay business.
> (Farm woman, married, children no longer at home, farmstay bed and breakfast operation in family home off property in small rural town, operating for over one year)

Farmstay operations also impact on farm women's ability to engage in much needed volunteer work in rural and regional communities and regions: 'The main challenge is ... juggling time between competing interests of working on the property, working in community groups and having tourists coming in. ... ' (farm woman farmstay operator for eight years, near small rural centre). For the farm women who participated in our study, there was a constant negotiation of workloads and movement between household, domestic spaces and places in more public farming spaces and related activities. The majority of the latter public tasks undertaken were not associated with decision-making roles, but rather were 'helping' roles. Additionally, these women indicated that their farmstay enterprises, while situated in the domestic/private domain, clearly placed them into external, public domains. This point was also noted by Lynch (2005a). As a consequence, women became more involved in decision-making and increased their positions of power as well as their social agency. Accordingly, the women's identities shifted from privately situated to being more publicly framed.

This identity shift, as Lynch (2005c) has commented, can generate sites of power conflict, as was evidenced in the lived experiences of farm women involved in our study. In particular, the study found conflict in family relationships as a result of the changing roles of women's work as they moved into more public domains. These conflicts arose from shifts in identity from private to more public identities, the sharing and negotiating of farm home space with guests and overall farming operations. As Aitchison and Reeves (1998: 51) have already commented, 'power, identity, meaning and behaviour are constructed, negotiated and renegotiated according to socio-cultural dynamics,' and this was apparent in this study of farm women operating farmstays in Central Queensland.

As an 'adaptive capability' response of resiliency, however, farmstay tourism has proved to be effective. All the farm women in the study indicated that the money earned went back into the farm rather than establishing a separate income for the women. Although the farmstay tourism enterprises were based on the domestic and non-valued work role of women, the women were definitely value-adding.

Farmstays: (re)interpreting public/private domains

Farmstay tourism offered some of the women of Central Queensland an opportunity to challenge the 'fixed' notion of gender relations exhibited in public/private domains. Here we conceptualise the public/private domains not as a dichotomous 'split' but as space where challenges are possible and resistances likely. In our study, the overall farmstay experience tended to expand out from the farm house onto the farm property, thus challenging 'fixed' notions of public/private spatial domains. In some cases, the tourists resided within the family home; in other cases they were accommodated in other buildings near or at distance to the family home. Subsequently, domestic spaces were extended beyond the garden (the traditional 'border' of gender relations, and one where both wife and husband have a legitimate claim) and into the property, which, until the introduction of farmstays, had been the public, masculine domain of the husband.

However, this expansion is more than just spatial, it is also symbolic. Negotiations as to the relationships within such 'border crossings' (Sibley 1995) are often fraught with what appear to be overt challenges to authority and power. In one case, one farm woman explained that while her attempt to create a farmstay had not met active resistance; she had to run it without help as the farm business was 'more important'. In another case, a woman reported that her husband agreed to the enterprise so long as it did not cost anything because there would be no investment in the undertaking. In a third case, negotiations had meant that no paying guests would be invited into the family house, and that the garden gate became the border between the public/private. This meant additional work as the farmstay enterprise included meals, which had to be run from the family house.

Farmstays: farm women, public/private domains

Whilst the women were moving outside their more traditionally identified 'domestic' spheres of work, they continued to meet resistance from the dominant patriarchal hegemony. Further, women's experiences in farm tourism in Central Queensland were similar to women engaged in tourism work on a global level. Women's work is generally rooted in the domestic sphere. For example, the Scottish highland bed and breakfast industry is primarily associated with women workers because of the 'domestic' nature of bed and breakfast service (Armstrong 1978). Similarly, local guesthouse enterprises in Barbados employ women to fulfil the 'domestic duties' such as housekeeping (Levy and Lerch 1991), and in Sri Lanka, women are associated with the 'domestic' domain of tourism work (Samarasuriya 1982). Samarasuriya (1982) also pointed out that this was found to be the case even for women who had achieved their own 'businesses' such as restaurants and guesthouses. Further, evidence exists in Bali where tourism jobs reify traditional gender roles, with women running losmens (homestays) and craft and souvenir shops (Cukier et al. 1996). Accordingly, women assume work in the domestic sphere. These positions subordinate work in relation to men who occupy positions in the 'public' domain. Relegation of roles associated with the domestic sphere restricts women's access to public spheres of the tourism industry and to positions of power (Armstrong 1978, Chant 1992; Rupena-Osolink 1983/84). Hence, it is appropriate to question 'the extent to which rural tourism can shift the balance of economic power within farm households and help open up rural employment provision for women ... when the involvement ... can be stereotyped as a "natural" extension of their "domestic role"' (Hall 2004b: 169).

More broadly, within farm tourism, reification of gendered roles has been found to occur, with women embedded in the domestic domain and men in public spheres. Access to more public positions are either mediated or, in some cases, denied by men (see also discussions by Brandth and Haugen 2006; Prugl 2004). However, in our study of women venturing into farmstay tourism innovations, whilst farm women drew on their skills developed in the domestic sphere, these skills enabled them to demonstrate social agency and their own resistance to traditional roles. Such agency and resistance further challenged traditional roles and expectations and, as already discussed, moved farm women into more 'public' domains, thereby breaking the silence of their contribution to farming enterprises and the overall nature of women's work – both paid and unpaid work on and off the farm. This finding, while supporting an advance in agency and resistance by both women and men, needs to be qualified. In our study, the women expressed varying opinions regarding empowerment. Their empowerment and involvement in decision-making was mediated because the women were not the direct owners of the property. Our study, then, has some accord with Caballé's (1999) study of farm tourism in Spain, wherein 'gender roles are not modified by farm tourism. Men still have control over all spheres. Woman [sic] only have control over the areas in which they directly contribute their work' (p. 251). Similar comments are purported by Akpinar et al. (2004) with regard to rural women and agro-tourism in Turkey.

Farmstay enterprises: (re)interpretations of 'home' sites and sights

This study found farmstay tourism was an entrepreneurial act by women, which shifted traditional roles and responsibilities and, to some extent, blurred private/public (women/men) spaces. Consequently, when we re-conceptualise space the definition of 'place' as a bounded fixed entity is also challenged, as is its sense of 'authenticity' (Massey 1994: 5). Thus, when conceptualising space and place as it relates to these women's experiences in developing farmstay enterprises, we find, drawing on Massey, that place becomes a 'particular moment', and the space/time dichotomy is itself challenged.

In the course of researching the lived experience of farmstay operators, the study found three emblematic representations of farm life and (re)interpretation of 'home' sites and sights: (1) tourism experience as family life, that is, 'naturalistic' farm life; (2) creation of the 'ideal' environment, that is, 'still life' farm life; (3) mediated experiences, that is, 'impressionistic' farm life. The (re)interpretations were used to manage social impacts of the farm tourism operation on family life and farming operations. Accordingly, differing levels of authenticity, performance and storytelling were engaged in each of the three (re)interpretations of 'home'. Metaphors drawn from the visual arts have been used as conceptual frames for each of the representations, as each of the 'storytellings' has a visual (re)interpretation which represents a 'snapshot' in time.

Farmstay experiences as family life – 'naturalistic' farm life

In this naturalistic representation of 'farm life', the farmstay experience is a complete integration into the lifestyle of the family and incorporates all the spaces the family uses. For example, the house is open to guests to utilise as they wish. There is no private space off limits to the guests. One farmstay operator of five years' experience reflects on this:

> No you can't have private space – I mean there is the children. I ... say to them to 'go out to the verandah to play their games' or 'go out through the office'. But they end up going out through my bedroom. No it doesn't worry me. They've come to share, I think it's the whole idea, they've come to ... experience living in the bush which also includes your house.

These types of experiences were provided by operators who saw host–guest sharing as a mutual exchange – both on a social and business level.

Farmstays as creation of the 'ideal' environment – 'still life' farm life

'Still life' farm life is a (re)interpretation of farm life as an 'ideal' that is carefully managed and staged in both private and public spaces. An 'ideal' life is presented or 'storied' usually as either the 'bush lifestyle' or the 'country lifestyle' of the landed gentry as portrayed in rural lifestyle magazines. To achieve the 'ideal' experience, farm experiences are distanced from the main activity centre or nodes of the farm. Guests rarely enter the 'real' world of the farm setting and farm members unless invited to do so. In the latter case, such engagements are heavily mediated to protect the guest for health and safety reasons. It is also a strategy to keep farmstay guests out of the way of farm operations and to maintain the image of 'ideal' farm experience. In the 'still life' experience, farming demonstrations are primarily orchestrated and performed in the best light and for minimum impact on farm operations. This type of experience is usually provided by operators who see the guests as a means to diversify farm productivity. As the farm woman who operated her farmstay 'off-farm' commented in an interview:

FARM WOMAN: 'I need to be flexible, I just need to know when I've gotta go to the farm that I can go … if you need parts … , you just have to leave. … So our operation is … an evening thing [essentially bed and breakfast], … its not regimented, but yeah, I don't want to be tied to all day tourist care! Even though I enjoy it! And I had the rooms and so we have renovated them for the tourists and they are all self-contained'. [The rooms look like the pictures in the country lifestyle magazines, which are also in the rooms for reading.]

INTERVIEWER: ' … so if someone said to you "I'd like to see your farm", because they saw the photos there, how would you deal with that?'

FARM WOMAN: 'Oh, I'd arrange to go out there, … , there's no problem with that. It would depend if there was a vehicle at the farm that I can take them around in … Otherwise, I'd have to make some arrangement with someone else or send them to some other tourist attractions'.

Mediated experiences – 'impressionistic' farm life

The third reinterpretation of 'farm life' is 'impressionistic. Impressionistic farm life blurs the barriers between naturalistic and still life. The public and private spaces are clearly delineated and articulated to the tourists in order to be able to mediate the border crossings between the public and private divides and between hosts and guests. The reason for this storytelling is to provide some escape for the operators to get away from the guests and also for the guests to get away from the hosts. As one farm operator of four years commented:

> We didn't want people actually staying in the house as part of the operation because I still wanted to work part time, and because we have got such a lovely spot down on the creek so we decided we wanted self-contained accommodation where people could come and take time out, but also if they wanted to participate in the day to day running of the property that was a possibility so we started from there and it has just grown.

The impact of interaction in the impressionistic farm life is mediated to maximise satisfaction for both sides and to minimise negative impacts. Guests are viewed as being valuable for social interaction as well as for monetary benefit, but with some conditions applied to the interactions.

These representations and reinterpretations mirror the traditional discourses of 'the family farm'. Such discourses are inherently patriarchal in nature, wherein women performed domestic roles and their identities as 'farm women' were further extended to incorporate 'farmstay entrepreneurship' into their repertoires.

Conclusions

To reiterate, our study found that for receiving farm homes, 'farmstay tourism' impacted on gendered roles and responsibilities, negotiation of public/private domains, and representation of 'farm life'. Specifically, farmstay tourism as an entrepreneurial act by women resulted in shifts in traditional roles and responsibilities and blurred private/public (women/men) spaces and places. Consequently, it challenged some of the traditional discourses associated with 'the family farm', which serve to subordinate women's positions (see discussions by Brandth and Haugen 1998; Shortall 1992). This was particularly the case in our study wherein the majority of women 'married' on to farms with strong patrilineal generational inheritance practices.

Further, as a means to mediate commercialisation of the farm home and farm life, farmstay experiences represented farm life in three emblematic ways: (1) tourism experience as family life – 'naturalistic' farm life; (2) creation of the 'ideal' environment – 'still life' farm life; (3) mediated experiences – 'impressionistic' farm life. These representations were deliberate responses to manage the introduction and incorporation of commercial home enterprises into farm homes and farm life in order to minimise the negative impacts of farmstay enterprises.

5 Sharing space with visitors

The servicescape of the commercial exurban home

C. Michael Hall

Introduction

Within the developed world, 'exurbanisation', the migration of urban residents to rural environments, has increased greatly since the 1970s. Often characterised as an 'escape to the country' or 'rural dilution' (Smailes 2002) exurban processes are usually associated with a post-productivist countryside in which 'landscapes of production' are transformed into 'landscapes of leisure and consumption' (Butler et al. 1998; Hall and Müller 2004; Williams and Hall 2000, 2002). 'Primary residences there mingle with luxurious second, or holiday, homes and country acreages. These are situated in natural or countryside settings that have usually until recently been worked, but which, through their exurbanization, are increasingly entering the land logic of the metropolis' (Cadieux 2006: 4). Such moves are often motivated by perceptions of an improved quality of life in rural or peri-urban locations, with such ideas seemingly reinforced by lifestyle shows on commercial television, films and novels. In Australia and New Zealand, this has often been witnessed in the processes of 'sea change' or 'tree change' in reference to permanent and temporary (second home) lifestyle migration to high-amenity rural areas (Burnley and Murphy 2004; Walmsley 2003).

Hospitality and tourism are deeply embedded in exurban processes for at least two main reasons (Butler et al. 1998). First, tourism and hospitality have assisted in the promotion of particular images of rurality and rural idylls. Second, for many families and individuals that make the move to rural areas and the peri-urban fringe, hospitality and tourism becomes an important source of income. Tourism and hospitality is therefore simultaneously involved in the consumption and (re)production of idealised exurban spaces by both temporary and more permanent migrants. The development of so called 'lifestyle' businesses by exurbanites has been widely acknowledged in the academic literature. However, there is surprisingly little research on the home spaces of exurban migrants and the ways in which the commercial utilisation of private space may affect perceptions and understandings of the exurban experience and the manner in which notions of home are managed.

This chapter utilises the concept of a servicescape to help examine the way in which the spaces of the commercial home are produced and consumed. Importantly, in the exurban context the spaces of home invariably includes not only the physical structure of houses and buildings and the rooms within but also the surrounding gardens and even countryside, thereby potentially creating new tensions with respect to understandings of public and private space and its construction. In this chapter, these issues are examined with reference to exurban bed and breakfast (B&B) provision in the Canterbury region of the South Island of New Zealand.

The chapter first discusses the servicescape concept and its application to the commercial home. The chapter then discusses some of the contextual research that has previously been undertaken on bed and breakfast and homestay accommodation in New Zealand detailing the results of research undertaken on exurban commercial homes. The chapter then concludes by stressing the often shared visions of rurality of visitors and their hosts in exurban space.

Servicescapes

Servicescapes refer to the physical facility in which a service is delivered and in which the service provider and the customer interact, and to any material or tangible commodities that facilitate the service (Bitner 1992; Lovelock et al. 1998). The servicescape concept builds upon well-established research traditions in design, environmental psychology and marketing, that the design of the physical environment can be an extremely important element in influencing consumption patterns and practices (e.g. Bitner 1990; Booms and Bitner 1982; Donovan and Rossiter 1982; Kotler 1973). The role of servicescapes in the co-creation of experiences has attracted significant interest in hospitality and tourism since the mid-1990s as a result of increased awareness of research and writing in experiential marketing and consumption, perhaps best recognised in the term 'experience economy' (Pine and Gilmore 1998).

However, it is important to recognise that the understanding of servicescapes has gone beyond its initial primary focus on the internal physical environment to recognise the role of external environments and the way place itself is designed and constructed (Sherry 1998a). For example, O'Dell (2005) refers to 'experiencescapes' while Julier (2005) uses the term 'urban designscapes' with reference to the regenerated districts and cultural quarters of new urbanism. Similarly, at a macro-environmental level, Sherry (1998b: 112) refers to 'brandscapes', or the 'material and symbolic environment that consumers build with marketplace products, images, and messages, that they invest with local meaning, and whose totemic significance largely shapes the adaptation consumers make to the modern world'. Brandscapes are utilised by transnational companies such as Starbucks to provide a symbolic retail space that is familiar and comfortable for consumers no matter where they are in the world and which also enables them to physically inhabit and experience brandspace (Thompson and Arsel 2004). Consumers thereby experience what Guliz and Belk (1996) refer to as a 'consumptionscape'.

Servicescapes are extremely significant for experiences because of the way they provide atmospheric cues to consumers. Bitner (1992) proposes that servicescapes consist of three elements; ambient conditions (music, temperature, lighting, noise and odours); spatial layout (functionality, equipment and furnishings) including not only the way the physical environment is arranged, but also 'the size and shape of those items, and the spatial relationships among them' (Bitner 1992: 66); and signs, symbols and artefacts (signage, personal artefacts and style or decor). Wakefield and Blodgett (1996) suggest that signs, symbols and artefacts are the symbols and decoration that can be used to signify and create a particular mood or convey a particular design period, or as a way to let customers know where to go, i.e. location of the bathrooms. All these elements of the physical environment can then be used to create particular images and influence behaviour of those who experience the servicescape (Bitner 1992).

Servicescapes are therefore significant as a stage upon which the theatre of the hospitality experience is set. Indeed, Pine and Gilmore (1998) use a theatre metaphor to define experiences: that services are the stage and the goods are the props. 'An experience occurs when a company intentionally uses services as the stage, and goods as props, to engage individual customers in a way that creates a memorable event' (Pine and Gilmore 1998: 98). They use the example of restaurants such as Planet Hollywood, where the food is used as a prop in an experience referred to as 'eatertainment' (Pine and Gilmore 1998: 99). The extent of their analogy goes on even further to discuss the idea of hiring what they describe as 'theatre troops' (Pine and Gilmore 1998: 99). However, nearly all the servicescape literature, including the growth of interest in the experience economy, is geared towards corporate interests with respect to providing experiences rather than that of the commercial home or the place context of the consumer experience (Clarke and Schmidt 1995). One of the few exceptions to this is Grayson's (1998) research on home-based networked marketing (i.e. Amway, Tupperware) which paid particular attention to the construction of social consensus.

Examination of the use of homespace for commercial accommodation in the exurban environment therefore not only allows for gaining a better understanding of the way in which consumer–producer interactions develop within the context of the internal servicescape but may also shed some light on the role of the external servicescape environment on the co-production of experiences. However, before discussing this further with respect to the study material, some further dimensions of the servicescape literature will be briefly discussed.

As noted above, a primary focus of Grayson's (1998) study of commercial activity in the home was the way in which social interactions are constructed. In the servicescape literature, studies of social exchanges that occur within the servicescape are mainly concerned with the 'nature and quality' of consumer and producer interactions (Bitner 1992: 61). This is either aided or hindered by the servicescape through dimensions such as seating, size and spatial clues. Tombs and McColl-Kennedy (2003) also argue that for some service providers, the social interactions are more important than the servicescape itself: 'for many service organisations … the influence of the physical setting may be minimal compared to the impact that other individuals (customers and service providers) have on the customer's experience' (Tombs and McColl-Kennedy 2003: 448). The implication this has on the servicescape is that its design should allow for interaction between not only customer and customer, but also customer and employee/service provider. In the case of commercial accommodation in private homes a major task is likely to be the management of the interactions between guests as well as guest expectations of the amount of interaction they expect to have, particularly with respect to participation in 'backstage' activities on rural properties.

Physical environments can also extract cognitive responses, meaning that specific elements in the servicescape can trigger a customer's thoughts, attitudes and beliefs about it (Bitner, 1992). Cognitive responses are likely to become more significant in determining behaviour when the experience is new or unfamiliar and the customer is not equipped with a wealth of information. For example, Oh et al. (2007) noted that tourists come to visit the bridges of Madison Country, Iowa to submerge themselves in the romantic fantasy created in a film. 'Tourists flocked to the bridges of Madison County in rural Iowa to immerse, at least temporarily, in the romantic fantasy involving the film's two lovers more than to see the actual details of the bridge' (Oh et al. 2007: 119). Such a situation may be significant for consumers of certain notions of rurality conveyed in the post-productive countryside for which, although not usually conceived of in terms of servicescapes, the design and representation of internal and external physical environments plays a very significant role.

The majority of tourism businesses in peri-urban areas are geared towards daytrippers and short-stay visitors who are seeking easy access to the countryside, with their desire to visit being geared towards certain idealised notions of rurality which are also shared by many of the owners of such businesses (Hall 2005c). Here, visitor and producer motivations for mobility are almost identical with, arguably, tourism serving to produce and reinforce certain idealised images of nature and rurality thereby only further enhancing the amenity values of such locations within exurban processes (Cadieux 2005). Regarding this point, an observation is borne out in Halfacree's (1994) research into exurban migrant decision-making in Lancaster and Mid-Devon, United Kingdom, and Crump's (2003) exploration of exurban migrants' identification of key 'pull' factors in their move to Sonoma County, California, USA. In both cases it was the perceived 'quality' of the rural environment that was the largest factor in explaining the decision to migrate.

The way in which place is produced in the exurban environment therefore becomes a vital part in understanding the way in which the commercial home and the idealised ruralities it embodies is socially constructed and potentially co-produced by hosts, guests and visitors. Nevertheless, the significance of idealised rurality is not without its ironies. As Bruegmann (2005: 84) notes in response to the question: 'But is exurbia sprawl?' exurbanites themselves do not generally 'consider themselves as living in or contributing to sprawl' (90). The irony being, of course, that it is the exurban desire for illusions of rural authenticity that is integral to the dynamics of suburban expansion as well as the ruralities of home-based hospitality. Furthermore, exurban desire is not opposed to urban gentrification. Instead, they may be regarded as 'flipsides of the same coin' (53):

> Back-to-the-land enthusiasts are motivated by desires similar to those involved in the back-to-the-city movement. Both want aesthetic experience of a 'traditional' kind of settlement with all of the conveniences of life usually associated with that kind of landscape. In fact, these are often the same people in different circumstances or at different times of their lives.
>
> (Bruegmann 2005: 90)

It has long been recognised that the connection the emotions of consumers have to the physical environment plays a very important role in consumption. If customers have positive emotions towards the servicescape, it is likely they will stay longer, spend more money and have a positive experience (approach behaviours). If a customer is aroused or excited by an experience, this increases approach behaviours. However, if unpleasant factors are also experienced, arousal may decrease approach behaviours (Bitner 1992). It is important to note that customer feelings about the service environment can be related to the feelings about the organisation or individuals that provide or frame the experience as a whole. Wakefield and Blodgett's (1996) study on the effect sevicescapes have on leisure settings found that those who leave early because they feel dissatisfaction with the physical surroundings are obviously going to spend less money.

Research on the ambient conditions within a servicescape (Bitner 1992) suggests that they have an effect on satisfaction when they are at extremes, for example, too cold or too hot, music too loud or too quiet, lighting too bright or too dull. They are also noticed if the customer experiences them in the environment for a long period of time or if they do not satisfy the customers' expectations. Wakefield and Blodgett (1999) investigated the importance of cleanliness as an ambient condition in leisure settings and found it particularly significant for casino customers. The likely reason for this is that customers are generally spending long periods of time at the casino, thus expectations are increased over that period, as is familiarity with the setting (Wakefield and Blodgett 1999). Another example of the power of ambient conditions in the visitor experience is noted by Oh et al. (2007), where they suggest that tourists may visit Cape Cod, a tourist destination, just for the tranquillity and 'rhythm of the Atlantic Ocean' (Oh et al. 2007: 121). This indicates how a particular aspect of the servicescape can be so powerful that it can be the single reason for a customer entering an experience as well as the significance of 'natural' elements in the physical environment. Although no previous research is available, it is likely that ambient conditions will also be an important consideration in the commercial home.

Use of space is especially important in servicescape considerations (Bitner 1992). A guest can feel too cramped if the area has a lot of furnishings, or other people present. Conversely, too much space can appear unfriendly and daunting (Newman 2007). Spatial layout and functionality for customers is especially significant in those service encounters where customers serve themselves, including self-catering accommodation. Appropriate signs and symbols can therefore inform customers of appropriate actions and behaviours, which may be particularly important in cross-cultural contexts. It is also important when the encounter tasks are not straightforward, as the servicescape must be set out in a way in which the customer can easily see what is expected of them, especially when, as in the situations discussed in this chapter, there is potential for blurring between private, guest and public spaces.

An exploratory study of bed and breakfast servicescapes

Bed and breakfast and other similar accommodation provisions in private homes, such as farmstays and homestays, have become an increasingly important part of the New Zealand hospitality landscape. The exact number of such providers is extremely difficult to determine given that many such services are highly casual and seasonal and rest on owners 'putting a sign by the road' rather than being part of any formal tourism network. From research conducted for a national survey on bed and breakfast providers in 2002–3 (Hall and Rusher 2004, 2005), it is estimated that there are approximately 2,500 bed and breakfast and homestay that are part of formal tourism and accommodation networks, plus as many as four times that amount outside of such networks. This figure only includes accommodation provided when the owners are resident and does not include the rental of holiday homes.

The national survey of 347 bed and breakfast providers undertaken by Hall and Rusher (2004, 2005) indicated that the vast majority of respondents were in the hinterlands of large urban centres and demonstrated the classic profiles of exurbanites in that they had either moved to peri-urban and rural areas for lifestyle reasons or, in some cases, were return migrants, originally from the area but returning after working abroad or elsewhere in New Zealand.

The survey indicated that there were two very significant clusters of business types in relation to dependence on accommodation for income. For the majority of respondents it is a very small portion, with over 47 per cent of respondents earning 20 per cent or less of their total income from accommodation.

At the other extreme almost 24 per cent of respondents depend on the accommodation component for 80 per cent or more of their income. Clearly, such clustering has significant implications for household and income business strategies and reflects the extent to which housing tourists is often only one dimension of income extraction in exurban households. In some households, one person retained a full-time or part-time position that brought in income, while in older households, and usually those for which accommodation was not a major source of income, retirement funds or other investments were important. Most respondents to the survey were relatively casual in their business approach with only 15 per cent of respondents registering their business with the Companies Office, although 67 per cent were registered for Goods and Services Tax (GST). Accommodation was also highly seasonal with less than a third of businesses claiming to be open year-round. Nevertheless, the survey did indicate that despite emphasis given to lifestyle and quality of life with respect to the development of the business, making a profit was still regarded as extremely important, even for those bed and breakfasts that were not the mainstay of household income (Hall and Rusher 2005). Social reasons for developing the bed and breakfast in terms of social contact with visitors were also extremely significant. Such insights are important as they reflect the notion of entrepreneurship strategies that is geared towards long-term maximisation of household quality of life attributes rather than immediate profit maximisation (Morrison 2006; see also Mottiar and Laurincikova, this volume).

The social dimensions – and tensions – of hosting a bed and breakfast or homestay accommodation have been recognised in previous New Zealand research (Oppermann 1998; Tucker 2003b; Tucker and Keen 2005; Warren 1998). However, such developments have at times not come without perceived negative or unexpected consequences. Although not solely concerned with rural homestay businesses, Warren's (1998) survey of rural businesses echoes a number of concerns found in the New Zealand and international literature regarding the development of rural bed and breakfasts and the relationship between business and lifestyle issues. While 70 per cent of her respondents enjoyed greater social contact with visitors and 49 per cent saw tourism as an opportunity to meet people from other cultures, 35 per cent also experienced a loss of personal time and 20 per cent a lack of personal space. Interestingly, the social dimension of B&Bs has also been identified in surveys of accommodation users. In examining the motivations which surround choice of lodging in New Zealand, Johnston-Walker (1998) observed that bed and breakfast guests place far more emphasis on social interaction than do hotel guests and, significantly for understanding the role of servicescape in the commercial home, aesthetics, setting and friendly service were also regarded as extremely important by visitors.

The national survey of bed and breakfasts and associated literature provided the basis for the conduct of a series of semi-structured interviews with respondents. In addition, several interviews were conducted with bed and breakfast households that were not part of the initial survey but had been suggested by other respondents. A total of 18 interviews were conducted in the Canterbury region of the South Island of New Zealand. All interviewees were located within a three-hour drive of the city of Christchurch, the major international gateway of the South Island and all were located in the peri-urban area. In addition, opportunity was taken to walk around properties including gardens and, in several cases, to also meet and talk with guests. The original focus of the interviews was on the issue of the implications of sharing space with visitors. However, following the conduct of several inter-views this interest expanded into a broader concern with issues surrounding the servicescape and place and place-making. The results are discussed in relation to the three dimensions of servicescapes recognised in Bitner's (1992) seminal work: ambient conditions, spatial layout, and signs, symbols and artefacts.

Ambient conditions

A common theme in discussion with respondents was a concern with pro-viding the right 'atmosphere'. This was expressed not only in terms of ensuring that rooms were 'warm enough' or 'smelt fresh' but that also that guests felt comfortable in terms of the design atmosphere of 'being in the country'. Most respondents placed cut flowers or herbs in guest bedrooms and other guest spaces, while scented waters were also widely used. A sig-nificant dimension as well was ensuring that the 'noises' experienced by visitors, especially at evening and night time, fitted in with notions of rur-ality. One respondent stated that they kept chickens, 'as much for the noises they make as we do for the eggs', while several commented on the impor-tance of the quiet of the countryside and the opportunity to hear birdsong because 'that's why we moved here'.

The identification of particular types of noise in the external physical environment rather than the internal as being important for both visitors and their hosts became an interesting discussion point in considering notions of home, as home was regarded not just as the built structure of the house but also the surrounding countryside (for related discussion, see Tucker's chapter, this volume). Indeed, it was clearly realised that in many cases the garden was a very clear extension of home, in terms of not only being a designed space but also being used to represent homeliness and rurality to visitors. This became especially apparent when walking around gardens with respondents and the importance that was stressed on sharing the smells and sights of the garden with visitors. In fact, the garden was often regarded as a space that could be more easily shared with visitors than many parts of the house, not so much because it was less personal to the owners, but more so because it seems to provide a ready-made common ground with visitors.

With some guests I sometimes feel like I lose a bit of privacy inside the house, I occasionally feel like I have to run back to my room. However, the garden is wonderful, we never have such feelings there. As we are only open in the warmer months we also take every opportunity to eat out there with guests rather than inside, and it can keep guests busy for hours as well.

The importance of the sights and sounds of the garden were intrinsic to all respondents, while in several instances the vegetable garden or orchards (which in some cases were also another source of income) also became a significant part of the commercial home experience.

Spatial layout

The layout of a property has important implications for the capacity to distinguish between areas that are private to households and those that are accessible to guests. Key differences emerged between those who had the opportunity to design the house for guests and those who used existing properties and refurbished them. According to one respondent, 'We never would have had guests here if we didn't have the idea of what we wanted from the start. Designing it from scratch meant that we could clearly indicate which areas guests could use and which were private while still all being under the one roof.' This can be contrasted with that of another interviewee who stated: 'Although guests have their own ensuite and bedroom, you still end up bumping into each other in the hallway or the kitchen ... I wish we had a different house. The problem is you can't escape very easily.' Indeed, several key rooms were identified as being points where privacy could be most easily lost: bathrooms, kitchens and hallways. Bathrooms were considered particularly private places, with several interviewees noting that even though both guests and the household had their own private bathrooms the shared bathroom often caused personal difficulties with respect to concepts of privacy and hygiene, though guests usually would be told not to use such facilities.

Given that cooking and meals are often a feature of bed and breakfasts it was surprising that so many respondents mentioned the kitchen as a space in which it was felt that privacy was intruded upon. According to one respondent, 'It's my space, it's nice that people offer to help or would like to watch but I sometimes wish they would have a glass of wine and wait for the meal and talk then'. However, it was noticeable that there was a difference in attitude between those who had guests year-round and those for whom hosting was quite seasonal, with the former being far more concerned about guests being in the kitchen.

Signs, symbols and artefacts

A feature of over half of the respondents was the provision of country decor which nearly all regarded as conveying an ambience of either retro or contemporary country furnishings, especially through use of such design icons as Cornishware, woven baskets, stressed pine furniture and Laura Ashley. The provision of country style and decor was regarded as very important and was seen as something 'shared' between host and guest. As one person commented with respect to selection of decor: 'We expect it, they expect it, it's actually something we share and like. In some ways it's almost a common design thing between us ... Perhaps we all read the same magazines like *Country Style* or *House and Garden* [laughter].' One respondent even noted, 'of course [design] style is important, after all its what we came out here to enjoy ... as do our guests'. As noted above design style extended from the house into the external environment with garden also being regarded as important in conveying design sensibilities. Often described by respondents as 'an extension of what's inside' the garden conveyed rural atmosphere with several people noting that the garden was actually even more important than the external appearance of the house. This was especially so when, as noted by more than one respondent, 'It's amazing what you can hide underneath Virginia Creeper' (another interviewee also mentioned ivy!).

As noted above, the garden was usually regarded as a friendly common or shared space between host and guest. Perhaps just as significantly it was also described by several respondents as a place in which 'stories' could be told and shared. According to one interviewee, 'So many of our visitors are interested in gardens and in the plants, it always becomes a place where we can share stories of the difficulties we may have had in getting something to grow or of our garden triumphs'. Interestingly, the role of certain objects becoming the basis for storytelling was also noted inside the house, although here the positioning of pictures, furniture or other objects was usually done quite consciously as a way of potentially allowing conversations to start. For example, one interviewee stated: 'We have found it really important to have an "ice-breaker", something in the room that allows us to start an easy conversation with guests. We rarely have a guest who is not interested in some aspect of the house, family or local history ... we just have to make sure we have something that allows visitors and us ourselves, I guess [starts laughing], to have a point of connection.'

Conclusions

This chapter has focused on the commercial exurban home to illustrate the role that servicescapes play in helping to create the experiences of hosts and guests. In some cases elements of the servicescape are being deliberately used to create conversations and generate successful social interaction. In the case of the bed and breakfasts visited as part of this research particular attention was usually given to using the servicescape, including its social dimensions, to generate clues for visitors about what to expect and how to behave in a commercial home environment. Such activities are important because, as in

Grayson's (1998) study of network marketing, 'today's social world does not generally consider the home to be an appropriate servicescape. Business is not usually welcome in the household' (Grayson 1998: 458). This situation still applies in the case of bed and breakfasts where both guests and hosts are seeking far higher degrees of social interaction than would be normal for commercial accommodation as each encounter has to negotiate the relative access of guests to various spaces within the home. Moreover, given that emphasis is given to the 'homelike' nature of the experience, this is usually done via social and physical clues rather than a set of instructions. As one interviewee commented, 'We always tell people that they have the run of the house and that they can go wherever they like, but we all know that's not really true!'

An additional important element in the interviews conducted for this research is the extent to which elements of the servicescape are co-created, or at least jointly constructed over time, because of the common perspectives of host and guest. The garden, in particular, but also to a significant extent the interior decor, is regarded as displaying shared design values and interests between visitors and households. As suggested above, this may well be strongly related to the shared understandings of exurban ruralities. Both host and guest are attracted by particular representations of what a country garden or a cottage garden should look like, as well as a number of elements of what should contribute to the decor. Much of the servicescape of the bed and breakfasts included in this study should therefore not be regarded as a backstage experience but rather as a shared stage that promotes a mutually sought after social interaction that conveys the appropriate atmospherics of 'home', as well as providing a transformative space from the public to the private.

Figure 5.1 seeks to place the commercial home within changing conceptions of private space in Western society. Building on the insights of Lawrence (1990) and Grayson (1998), it suggests that the exurban commercial home represents a further development of pre-industrial and industrial conceptions of public and private space. However, the commercial home is not a return to a Romantic pre-industrial state, even though that impression may sometimes be conveyed by idealised accounts of rurality (Butler et al. 1998). Instead, the exurban commercial home provides a temporary private space for the mobile traveller (along with the car) with the garden and decor providing a collective connective servicescape for host and guest. Significantly, servicescape elements such as artefacts are often deliberately utilised to ease the collective space-ambiguity experienced within the commercial home so as to provide easier transition between spaces and signify the private space of the household.

Of course this idealised account does not mean that such clear boundaries are always achieved and that private space is not invaded. However, the loss of private space appears to be related as much to the mode of operation (year round versus seasonal) and the level of household financial dependence

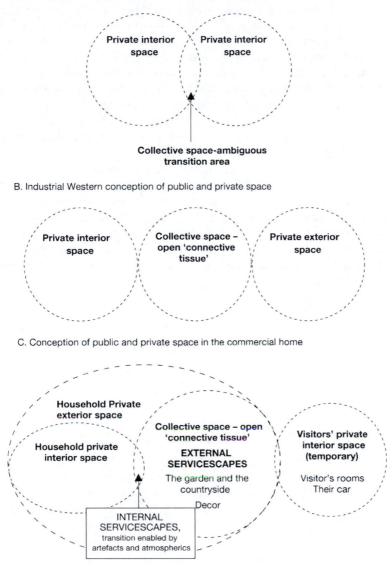

Figure 5.1 Changing conceptions of public and private space.

on income from accommodation as it does from the presence of guests per se. The development and management of the bed and breakfast servicescape, even if households may not think in such terms, has become a key strategy to manage potential loss of privacy and the sharing of personal and family space. All respondents stated that they wished that they had better information about the potential for loss of personal space and its implications before embarking on the business venture, while several noted that ultimately they believed that it would be a determining factor as to the longer term operation of a commercial home venture. Nevertheless, the social and economic benefits of managing the bed and breakfast and the lifestyle benefits that were gained were still regarded as outweighing the loss of private space.

Although limited to an exploratory study, the interviews with bed and breakfast operators highlight the need for a greater appreciation of servicescapes and the physical environment in the experiences of both the producers and consumers of hospitality experiences. Servicescapes are critical to the visitor experience but many of their elements are co-created as part of the cultural circuit of capital between host and guest and, in the case of the present study, their shared understandings and perspectives of exurban ruralities. In tourism and hospitality studies the primary focus of research on servicescapes has been very much geared towards corporate commercial usage of the concept. In contrast, the present study suggests that understandings of servicescape and the wider role of place and the physical environment needs to be given attention if we are to better understand not only social interaction and control but also the tourism and hospitality experiences of host and guest.

6 Exploring the importance of setting to the rural tourism experience for rural commercial home entrepreneurs and their guests

Barbara A. Carmichael and Kelley A. McClinchey

Introduction

This chapter explores the importance of the physical and human dimensions of the rural setting for the quality of tourism experiences for both hosts and guests. It is suggested that 'place' in which tourism experience occurs may be conceptualised on a number of scales and involves different geographical elements (Carmichael 2005). A conceptual framework is presented that shows that the physical and human environments can be experienced at both the regional level and at the accommodation site level (i.e. at different spatial scales). Perceptions of the rural landscape and the physical and built environment in the region influence the rural tourism experience for both hosts and guests. Similarly, at the accommodation site, the physical environment is important and includes heritage, quaintness, architecture, gardens, interiors and aesthetics. Furthermore human elements are deemed important within the setting and environment. With reference to setting, Lynch (2005b: 535) acknowledges that 'impressions of the homestay building, its nomenclature and the locality' are all important, as well as the fact that the setting seems to have a behavioural effect sometimes leading to social conformity, use of social rules and role play and perhaps dissonance. Furthermore, social interactions with other visitors and with local residents affect visitor and host perceptions of the quality of the tourism product, both within the region and at the accommodation itself.

In this chapter, a conceptual scheme is presented and placed within the context of a literature review of the concepts of rural landscapes, rural lifestyles and home settings. Second, the conceptual framework is tested out using a case study in South-western Ontario of bed and breakfast operators and their guests.

Contextualising rural tourism experiences in terms of setting

Figure 6.1 shows a conceptual framework of the rural tourism experience at different geographical scales for different geographical elements. It combines regional setting and activity/accommodation site scales (spatial dimensions) with physical elements (natural and built environment) and human elements (social interaction environment). This figure is based on a conceptual framework that is modified from a similar framework that was first applied by one of the authors to the wine tourism experience in a wine region and at winery attractions (Carmichael 2005). Figure 6.1 shows four cells. In cell 1, perceptions of the rural landscape and the physical and built environment in the region influence the overall tourism experience. In cell 2, at the accommodation or activity site, the setting is important and includes accessibility, buildings, and the aesthetics while cells 3 and 4 show the influences of human elements. Social interactions with other visitors and with local residents and hosts affect tourists' perceptions of the rural tourism product, both within the region in terms of rural lifestyles (cell 3) and at the accommodation or activity site itself in terms of home hospitality (cell 4).

This chapter will focus on the 'commercial home' experience from the perceptions and perspectives of both hosts and guests. According to Lynch (2005b), the commercial home is a distinctive hybrid between a home and a hotel since a 'homestay' is involved that influences guest behaviour. As noted in Chapter 1 of this volume, Lynch and MacWhannell (2000) distinguish between 'traditional commercial homes', 'virtual reality commercial homes' and 'backdrop commercial homes'. In this case study, most rural accommodation properties are of the 'traditional commercial home type', where the home

Geographical Elements

	Physical and Built Environment	Human and Social Environment
Regional Setting	1. Rural Landscape • cultivated fields • small towns • infrastructure • farms	3. Rural Lifestyles • rural idyll • rural livlihoods
Accommodation Site	2. Home Property • buildings and gardens • servicescape • ambience • accessibility	4. Visitor Interactions • home hospitality • service quality • interations with hosts • interations with other guests

(Geographical Scale)

Figure 6.1 Dimensions of the rural setting for commercial home entrepreneurs and their guests.
Source: Author's conceptualization.

concept is strongly present. They range from bed and breakfasts to farmstays to village inns with no more than twelve bedrooms. Some offer self-catering facilities as an off-shoot from the main property. Two of the village inns could be considered as 'virtual reality commercial homes' as they were not privately owned but instead were operated by private corporations with visitors receiving assistance from managers on duty.

For visitors staying in 'homestay' accommodations, such as in bed and breakfasts where tourism entrepreneurs live, work and also call home, experiences at the accommodation site may have a strong impact on visitor satisfaction. Perceptions of the 'servicescape' (see also Hall's chapter, this volume) in which they are staying (in terms of attractive surroundings) and the service quality (in terms of the welcome they receive) are based on the unique experiences that may be achieved by being received into someone's home as a paying guest.

This context of commercial home tourism may also be rewarding for the hosts, not just from revenues earned but also because of the enjoyment of the interaction with their guests. In terms of setting, the home (often large and sometimes heritage) may be refurbished and remain affordable from revenues earned. Hosts enjoy living in rural settings and interacting with the local community. They are able to maintain a rural lifestyle and quality of life. Thus there are 'trade-off' benefits from sharing a family home with paying guests.

The regional experience

The regional rural landscape experience (cell 1)

It is likely that the rural tourism experience is not limited to a particular site or attraction and that several elements of the wider experience will impact on the on-site experience. Therefore, the rural landscape is an integral part of the tourism experience. Tourists view tourist sites and landscapes with much greater sensitivity to the visual elements of the landscape than is normally found in everyday life. They take photographs, buy postcards and make purchases that enable their 'gaze' to be reproduced and recaptured (Urry 1990). Furthermore, it is a rural landscape that reflects a way of life on which it is difficult to place a value. Farm-based tourism includes accommodation facilities on working farms and farm-based activities/attractions (Sharpley and Vass 2006). However, tourists may enjoy rural landscapes without having to stay on a farm or participate in farm-based activities. Indeed, previous research suggests that it is the 'role of the farm and the farmer to supply the background that provides farm tourism with its unique features' (Fleisher and Tchetchik 2005: 493) and that farm activities are not essential for visitor enjoyment (Walford 2001, cited in Fleisher and Tchetchik 2005). Consequently, many rural bed and breakfast establishments take advantage of a setting in proximity to farm landscapes, and bed and breakfasts on farms do not necessarily have to provide farm-based activities.

Rural lifestyles (cell 3)

The cultural meaning of a rural lifestyle contributes to tourist images and expectations as well as to the enjoyment of local residents. 'Rural' refers to people, places, lifestyles, artefacts, values, and social relationships (Willits et al. 1990). Valentine (1997) describes the imagining of rural as a peaceful, tranquil, close-knit community. This is a common romantic vision of rural life, or the 'rural idyll', based on nostalgia and sense of belonging and where people can escape from the city (Valentine 1997). As Bunce (1994: 2) points out: 'The affection for the countryside may reflect fundamental human values and psychological needs which can be traced to a basic human desire for harmony with land and nature, for a sense of community and place for simplicity of lifestyle.' While this rural idyll may be a myth there is no doubt that this type of image contributes to the attractiveness of rural regions both for touring and sightseeing and for the enjoyment of rural living.

Accommodation site experiences

Home property and physical attributes (cell 2)

In the tourism marketing literature, the concept of place is often described merely in terms of distribution channels. However, discussions of the tourism product also identify the importance of the physical environment, atmosphere and ambience. A 'servicescape' refers to the built environment, that is the manmade physical surroundings rather than the natural or social environment (Bitner 1992; Hall, this volume). Reimer and Kuehn (2005) extend the definition of servicescape to include employees' dress, brochure appeal, architecture, interior design, noise, cleanliness, temperature, music, colour and lighting. Atmosphere is appreciated through the senses and thus has visual, aural, olfactory and tactile dimensions (Kotler et al. 2003). Sensory images within the home provide insights into the personality of the hosts, especially if the guests are able to view hosts' memorabilia and artefacts scattered around the dwelling.

Wakefield and Blodgett (1996) suggest that the effect of servicescape on customer behavioural intentions is well documented and that customer satisfaction, particularly from a hedonistic perspective, is influenced by the nature and quality of the physical setting. In the tourism context, servicescape affects mood and customer quality perceptions in restaurants (Namasivayam and Matilla 2007). Furthermore, it affects level of excitement, sense of crowding and satisfaction in leisure settings (Wakefield and Blodgett 1994).

Depending on the division of private and public space within a hospitality setting, guests may gain access to 'back-regions' within the home (Goffman 1959), and be invited to join hosts in what they may perceive to be more private spaces. Hosts and guests in this type of accommodation both tend to expect a 'homey atmosphere' and a 'home away from home' (Lynch 2005a). Cleanliness and tidiness of home and garden ('trade dress' in marketing terms) are also likely to affect the quality of guest expectations, experience and satisfaction in this type of 'servicescape'. Kotler et al. (2003: 54) identify the importance of 'trade dress' to hospitality companies and the need to protect the distinctive nature of their total visual image and overall appearance, as well as to manage effectively their physical surroundings. However, as Lynch (2005a) suggests, home is a complex construct with temporal, social, cultural, personal and emotional dimensions that merit further investigation. These dimensions are influenced by the physical and human settings in which experiences are perceived and behaviours take place. Previous research on home meanings suggests there are three relevant aspects: personal, social and physical (Sixsmith 1986). The conceptual framework presented in this chapter focuses on the social and physical settings in which the outcome is the personal perceptions of the meaning of home to the individual, who, in this case, is either a host or a guest in the home setting.

Visitor interactions (cell 4)

A small-scale setting within a commercial home ensures a high degree of interaction between host and guest (Stringer 1981). However, this interaction is concentrated into formal time periods: arrival, breakfast, departure. The dining-room setting is also one in which social interaction occurs with other guests through seating arrangements, sometimes at one large table. One of the authors of this chapter recalls a breakfast situation at a bed and breakfast in Ireland where the guests were given out song sheets and were encouraged to sing the verses of 'Danny Boy' together. Flags representing the nationalities of the guests seated at the table were prominently displayed. In such situations encounters with other guests tend to be quite formal and polite but are variable. Sometimes there are shared experiences which are exchanged quite genuinely but at other times there seems to be a false camaraderie (author's observations).

Case study of rural accommodation entrepreneurs and their guests

Study area

The Waterloo and Wellington counties in South-western Ontario, Canada, chosen for the study, have a rich cultural heritage, based on settlement by Mennonites, Scottish, English and German settlers and their distinctive rural cultural landscapes. The close proximity of the urban market in Toronto enables rural tourism to be a profitable venture for entrepreneurs. Filling a much needed demand, rural residents offer accommodations in the form of bed and breakfasts, country inns and farm vacations.

Research methodology

Data were collected using personal interviews with hosts, content analysis of brochures, a visitor questionnaire survey and field observation at the accommodation sites. A list of farm vacations and country bed and breakfast establishments revealed a target population of 71 rural accommodations within the Waterloo–Wellington area. The interview procedure resulted in the completion of personal interviews with 40 rural operators. Interviews were conducted at the rural accommodation properties and took approximately 45 minutes to complete. Rural accommodation brochures were collected from 34 of the 40 respondents. Brochures were transcribed manually for key descriptive words and phrases which were coded and grouped according to relevant themes. Visitor questionnaires were distributed at the completion of the rural host interview in 20 of the 40 rural accommodations. This was a partially selected sample based on geographic location, type and size of rural accommodation. There were 280 visitor questionnaires distributed and 106 were returned (response rate of 37.9 per cent).

Findings

Rural accommodation characteristics

The types of tourism accommodations participating in the study were farm vacations (5 per cent), village bed and breakfasts or country bed and breakfasts (83 per cent), and inns (12 per cent) (Table 6.1). Village bed and breakfasts (23 per cent) differ from country bed and breakfasts (60 per cent) in their locations since village bed and breakfasts are located within the main parts of villages. On the other hand, village inns tend to have more rooms and offer more amenities. Farm vacations differ from bed and breakfasts in that they are on working farms and may have farm-related activities available for guests. Only two of the eight working farms offered farm-related activities as well as accommodation.

Most of the rural accommodations were open all year round (83 per cent). Seasonal establishments were open from approximately April to December. The majority of rural entrepreneurs mentioned that their accommodation was a part-time business (65 per cent). Most rural accommodations were privately owned and operated by both the male and female of the household (55 per cent), although females most frequently interacted with guests (58 per cent). Two of the village inns were not privately owned but were operated by private corporations. It is notable that the primary hosts with whom the interviews were conducted were predominantly female. Eighty per cent of operators were in business for ten years or less and only 5 per cent were operating their accommodation for more than 15 years. Furthermore, many were newcomers, having lived in the study area for ten years or less.

Table 6.1 Rural accommodation characteristics (n = 40)

Characteristic	Percent
Accommodation type:	
Farm vacation	5
Country bed and breakfast	60
Village bed and breakfast	23
Village inn	12
Seasonality:	
Yes	17
No	83
Number of rooms:	
Smaller country or village B&Bs	1–3 rooms
Larger country or village B&Bs	4–7 rooms
Village inns	8–12 rooms
Full or part-time business:	
Full-time	35
Part-time	65
Gender of host interviewed:	
Male	2
Female	38
Both	55
Corporate	5
(one female and one male)	
Gender of host who mainly deals with guests:	
Male	7
Female	58
Both	30
Private Corporation	5
Number of years in operation:	
0 to 5	48
6 to 10	33
11 to 15	15
16 to 20	3
21 or more	2
Number of years host been a resident:	
0 to 10	50
11 to 20	20
21 to 30	13
31 to 40	10
41 or more	7

Testing the conceptual framework

RURAL SETTING AND LANDSCAPE (CELL 1)

The importance of rural setting is shown from the hosts' perspective revealed in an open-ended question that asked hosts what most attracts guests to their accommodation. More responses than any other related to the rural setting

Table 6.2 Hosts' and visitors' ranking of visitor motivations for staying in rural accommodations

Motivation	Hosts' Ranking	Visitors' Ranking
Escape into Country	1	3
Relaxing Environment	2	1
Tourist Attractions	3	3
Natural Environment	4	6
Friendly Hospitality	5	5
Rural Landscape	6	2
Host/Guest Interaction	7	7
New Experience	8	8
Learn about Rural Lifestyles	9	11
Inexpensive Vacation	10	9
Active Vacation	11	12
Visit with Family and Friends	12	10

and landscape as being what most attracts guests to their accommodation (13 out of 39 respondents). They used the descriptive words 'rural setting' and 'landscape', as well as 'surroundings, environment and countryside'. One host stated that, 'it is the rural area rather than the accommodation that most attracts guests to stay'.

Both hosts and guests were asked to rank from one (most important) to twelve (least important) a series of pre-selected visitor motivations for staying in rural accommodations. A Mann Whitney U test was used to test for statistically significant differences between rural entrepreneurs' rankings and visitors' rankings. A significant difference only existed at the 0.05 level for inexpensive vacation (p = 0.022), thus hosts had a good idea of what motivates visitors. Both lists ranked aspects of rural setting and the rural landscape as important motivations. Hosts commented, 'there seems to be a need to escape large city life'; 'the sheer number of visitors to our area is a strong statement of how people enjoy the escape from their busy lives in the city as well as finding a unique community to spend a little of their vacation time'; and 'there is something worth preserving here, something worth keeping'.

In an open-ended question, hosts were asked to list aspects of the rural landscape they like best. The natural environment such as rivers, trees, rolling hills and changing seasons was listed most frequently (62.5 per cent) and second was a farm-related environment, including farms, fields and well-kept cultivated land (27.5 per cent). Sense of community, neighbours, towns and home (15 per cent) were mentioned just as often as uncluttered, open spaces (15 per cent).

HOME SERVICESCAPE AND AMBIENCE (CELL 2)

For rural accommodations, the home is a very important aspect of the tourism product. It features strongly in the advertising material and is an integral part of the tourism experience. Interview data and content analysis of accommodation brochures revealed how the home is perceived by hosts and also how its image is portrayed. A content analysis of the words and phrases of rural accommodation brochures (Table 6.3) showed descriptions of a century home, old heritage home and antiques in the home being stated more often than other descriptions about environment, landscape or nearby attractions.

Other brochure descriptors involved type of experience that guests would have while staying at the accommodation, such as relaxation (35 per cent), country hospitality (26 per cent), quiet, peaceful and tranquil. Some described rural landscape such as the farming area and Mennonite country. Others outlined the importance that setting plays on the bed and breakfast as perceived by the rural accommodation hosts. One rural host quoted in the brochure described the morning experience at the bed and breakfast as well as experience at the end of a busy day: 'Wake up to the aroma of fresh-ground, brewed coffee, muffins/breads and heartier fare, which you may enjoy in our dining room, kitchen or outside covered porch. A large yard and deck, 2 sitting areas with piano, fieldstone fireplace, cathedral ceiling and television invite you to relax before and after a busy day of sightseeing, shopping, live theatre or golfing, all 30 minutes or less away.' Other rural operators focused on describing the home and rural landscape: 'A century stone house set amidst 97 acres of picturesque rolling hills and woodlands'; 'Welcome to our "turn of the century" Victorian home while you enjoy the peace of a small village ... ' and ' ... is an enchanting Victorian house nestled among trees

Table 6.3 Rural descriptions from content analysis of accommodation brochures

Phrase and Description	Frequency	Percent
Century home, old home, century farm	17	50
Relaxation – described as part of a phrase such as 'relax by the fire place', 'relax on the porch'	12	35
Farming area, country, fields	11	32
Country hospitality – described also as warm welcome, friendly	9	26
Quiet– used in descriptions of area surrounding accommodation (i.e. 'quiet countryside')	7	21
Activities described nearby:	10	29
Attractions (theatre, Stratford, Drayton)	22	65
Shopping	8	24
Antiques	11	32
Cultural-heritage attractions – Fergus Highland Games, Elmira Maple Syrup Festival, Wellesley Apple Butter and Cheese Festival, Museums	20	59
Mennonite Country	10	29
Peaceful	2	6
Tranquility	2	6

and flowers in a park-like setting'. More specifically, 'An 1860 Gothic Revival style Inn restored with all the modern comforts and amenities ... Antique period furnishings complement the pre-Confederation elegance of this historically designated property'. Brochures also described the type of interaction expected when guests arrived: 'Relax and enjoy your stay in our comfortable, quiet home' and 'retreat to nature in the heart of Mennonite farming country. We offer full country breakfasts with a view of our trout pond, stream and apple orchard. Relax beside the fireplace.' Other rural operators stated: 'Leave behind all your working day worries and let us pamper you'; 'We offer you old-fashioned country hospitality in an historic home filled with antiques and original art'; 'This is your home away from home'.

Personal interview data also shows insights into the home construct. Rural operators were asked to state in their own words their motivations for starting their businesses. Their responses revealed the importance of the home as a social space, a place of shelter and an opportunity space for enjoyment and achievement. Their responses included: to meet people (n = 12), provide income (n = 9), fill an empty house (n = 6), provide accommodation (n = 5), preserve heritage of home (n = 4), take on a retirement project (n = 4) and experience something new (n = 3).

In response to the open-ended question 'What most attracts guests to their accommodation?', 11 out of 39 hosts perceived that their old home, century

Table 6.4 Field observations of rural accommodation homes

Description	0 (not prominent)	1	2	3	4 (very prominent)	Mean	Standard deviation
Manicured flower gardens	2	2	11	10	9	2.65	1.13
Century/older home	2	2	5	5	14	2.44	1.64
Naturalised lawns and landscape	10	3	2	7	12	2.24	1.71
Park-like lawns and landscape	4	6	13	6	5	2.06	1.20
Antiques/old furnishings	8	5	6	8	7	2.02	1.49
Theme rooms/ decorated	5	9	8	7	5	1.97	1.31
Country crafts/ patterns/decor	6	7	9	6	6	1.97	1.36
Stone architecture	14	3	5	5	7	1.64	1.63
Ginger bread trim/ fancy detailing	10	11	2	9	2	1.47	1.33
Rustic/natural exterior	17	9	4	1	3	0.941	1.25
Modern home	23	2	3	2	4	0.882	1.45
Working farm	16	7	2	1	8	1.68	1.75

Notes: frequency is shown n = 34.

home or style of the home was very important. A question on the visitor questionnaire asked which criteria made their stay enjoyable and they were to select all that applied. Guests selected clean, comfortable accommodation as the criteria which made their stay most enjoyable (85.5 per cent). Other factors were friendly hospitality (80.2 per cent), quiet relaxing atmosphere (78.3 per cent), good meals (72.6 per cent), rural landscape (50 per cent), nearby rural attractions (41.5 per cent) and other (6.65 per cent).

Host interviews took place at the rural accommodations and, as part of the data collection, field observations were documented. A list of criteria referred to the exterior of the home including heritage, architecture, construction, as well as the rest of the property (Table 6.4).

The wide variety in the responses showed that rural hosts' homes were quite unique. There were very few modern homes, quite a number of older heritage homes as well as homes with antiques or older furniture and homes with country crafts. Many of the homes had manicured flower gardens and some had park-like lawns and property which highlights the point that bed and breakfast operators take pride in their homes and property and understand the importance of a neat, tidy and well-kept exterior. Rural hosts who also operated a working farm (8 locations) also had beautiful manicured flower gardens and well-kept lawns.

RURAL LIFESTYLES (CELL 3)

Rural operators were asked what aspects of rural life they liked best. In this open-ended question, hosts responded most often with descriptions about living closer to nature, the outdoors and wildlife (n = 10). Other descriptions of rural life appreciated by hosts were neighbours and friendly community (n = 9), quiet (n = 9), privacy (n = 7), slower pace (n = 7) peaceful (n = 3), gardening (n = 30), producing own natural food (n = 3), farm life, rural setting (n = 2), proximity to communities (n = 2) and raising a family (n = 2).

When hosts were asked what most attracts guests to their accommodation, several hosts stated that it is the people and the friendly hospitality. Rural operators commented: 'It is the way that they [the guests] are pampered'; 'people come back because of what we offer'; 'it is a family oriented atmosphere'; and 'we sit and chat with our guests'. Some hosts mentioned that they gave guests privacy when they were eating breakfast and only joined them at the table when they were invited, which was often the case. This type of social space thus appears to be fluid and to be negotiated separately depending on the needs of the guests. Several hosts referred to food and the cooking as important aspects that visitors are attracted to. One host mentioned that some visitors even take pictures of the breakfast table with all the food displayed. This is a 'marker' of the visit and may be considered as a ritual space. One host, in referring to how comfortable they make their guests feel, stated that they consider themselves 'an ambassador' for the area.

Rural operators were also asked to state their personal benefits from operating a rural accommodation establishment. Rural hosts could list as many benefits as applied and 80 per cent of hosts stated that 'meeting people' was their main benefit from operating the business. For 42.5 per cent of the hosts, another benefit was to generate income. One host stated that a 'farming lifestyle can be economically challenging, therefore this business offers them an additional income as well as the tax benefits for keeping the house in an appropriate condition for the bed and breakfast'. Other benefits that contributed to their rural lifestyle were 'learning from others' (22.5 per cent), 'the satisfaction from making people happy' (10 per cent), 'making friendships' (10 per cent) and 'providing diversity in their life' (5 per cent). Another rural host stated that having guests from different parts of the country and even the world is like 'travelling without travelling'. It is apparent that host–guest interaction is important for hosts in that it contributes in several different ways to their rural lifestyle. Furthermore, such lifestyle benefits outweighed the profit motivation for the majority of the entrepreneurs in these commercial home operations.

VISITOR INTERACTIONS (CELL 4)

The interaction with visitors in the commercial home is unique. Guests share a part of the home that is intended as host–guest space but is traditionally considered a private place. Therefore, hosts and guests are able to participate in an intimate business relationship that may even extend into a closer friendship-like connection. The majority of the visitors are couples, staying one to two nights and about 40 per cent are repeat visitors. Some maintain a relationship with their hosts and return on a regular basis.

As mentioned earlier, hosts benefit from and are motivated by the desire to meet other people. One host commented, 'Where else can you stay at home and meet people at the same time?' They reported gaining from the stories in the morning from their guests, meeting interesting people from all over the world, learning about other places and providing their children with an atmosphere they are lacking. Rural hosts also perceive that a close visitor–host interaction enables them to exchange ideas and learn from others, but also enables them to teach guests about rural life. This interaction between hosts and guests enables the hosts to provide a 'brokering role' by giving guests insider knowledge and recommendation for the regional attractions and way of life. One host stated that rural accommodation 'provides an appreciation for the country and allows people to appreciate agriculture more; they see where their food comes from and gain a greater respect for the rural area'.

Conclusions

This chapter aimed to deconstruct the quality of the visitor and host experiences in the commercial home setting. A four-fold matrix was applied to identify the geographical scales (regional and accommodation unit) and geographical elements (physical and human environments) that describe the home setting. This conceptual model was broadly applied to the commercial home context. However, it became apparent that there were overlapping meanings, especially in the data that described the concept of home. Physical meanings, social meanings and individual benefits were difficult to disaggregate from each other. All wove together to contribute to the hospitality experienced by both hosts and guests. This finding of the multi-faceted meaning of place is not unlike the findings of other researchers, for example, Gustafson (2001). He found three themes to classify meanings of place (self, others and environment) but found that the meanings of place expressed by his respondents were 'often situated in the relationship between self/others and/or environment rather than just unambiguously belonging to just one of these categories.' (p. 9). Similarly Sixsmith (1986: 289) had suggested three 'experiential modes' to classify the meanings attributed to home: personal, social and physical. Sixsmith (1986) was investigating meaning for one's own private home, which is perhaps less complex than the variety of emotions generated by sharing one's space with guests. Equally complex are the perceptions and meanings of that home for the guests sharing the space, since they are engaging in a monetary transaction as well as reflecting on the meaning of their own homes.

This study reveals that the profit motive is not the major motive for many of the rural accommodation operators. This fits with other research on small business enterprises in tourism (Ateljevic and Doorne 2000; Morrison et al. 1999) as well as with farm tourism (Ollenburg and Buckley 2007). Meeting people is perceived as an important lifestyle benefit from the operation of commercial home enterprises, and often lifestyle aspirations are more important than profits. Benefits from living in a pleasant rural environment, owning an interesting property and meeting different types of people, as well as the flexibility of operating only part of the year are reasons for being willing to open up one's home and allowing some of the privacy of home to be shared by others. As discussed by Manzo (2003), home is a complex concept with multiple meanings. It is more than just the dwelling place as 'it connotes a more active and mobile relationship of individuals to the physical, social and psychological spaces around them' (Saegert 1985: 287). Hence, it is difficult to disaggregate these multiple settings at the centre of the production and the consumption of the tourism experience.

This research reinforces the importance of understanding the complex relationships between service quality and the setting of the tourism experience (Williams and Buswell 2003). Furthermore, the management of the 'environmental encounter' and its linkage with the 'service encounter' would clearly assist in creating repeat business and long term relationships. The servicescapes in the varied accommodation facilities in this study were comfortable and attractive in design both inside and outside of the commercial home. Many offered a quiet but friendly retreat. While direct relationships between servicescape with repeat business behaviour was not directly explored in this research, all operators did have attractive servicescapes as well as many return visitors.

This chapter has thus shown the importance and meaning of the rural landscape, rural lifestyles accommodation attractiveness and servicescapes for commercial home settings. Whilst few of the accommodations in this area are located on working farms, and only two offer farm based activities, it is the rural farm setting and backdrop that has the strongest appeal for visitors to this culturally varied landscape.

Part II
The commercial home lens

7 The discourse of home hosting

Examining the personal experiences of commercial home hosts

Alison J. McIntosh and Candice Harris

Introduction

This chapter adopts the commercial home as an investigative lens to examine wider debates surrounding personal experiences within the context of tourism. In particular, it considers the personal narratives of hosts to understand the nature of their personal relationship with their commercial home, and, specifically, the impact of hosting on their personal, private and family life. In contrast, previous studies have predominantly examined the role of the accommodation host as business manager, service provider or tourist guide. Instead, we seek to provide insight into the hosting experience, grounded in the personal narratives which hosts themselves describe and define in their own words. We seek to address the questions: How do hosts describe their relationship with their commercial home? What do they see as their responsibilities during hosting? What impact does hosting have on their daily life and life events? What impact does it hold for other life stakeholders? How do hosts manage these impacts?

The commercial home hosting experience

Hosting within the personal or family home is unique. The nature and construction of the commercial home experience provided for guests is to a large extent determined by the homeowner and occupants; their personality, motivations, expectations, experience, interpersonal skills, own tidiness and style, management strategies, tolerance and attempts to make the accommodation experience 'homely'. Greater than is the case for other forms of commercial accommodation, the commercial home also has significant spatial and emotional importance to its owners. The home is ultimately a place of security, interpersonal relationships and meaning. Thus, when the home has a commercial domain, the impact of hosting within the home on a host's personal and family life, and private space, can be immense. There is less separation between work activities and home life (Harris and McIntosh 2007), and less privacy in areas of the home from visiting strangers. This has consequences for the nature of the host–guest relationship (Tucker and Keen 2005), and the performance and life-cycle of the business.

Previous research has identified the significance of the home setting in the construction of the 'hospitality' experience from the guest's perspective (Lynch 2000c; Lynch and MacWhannell 2000), and from the perspective of host-guest dynamics (Pearce 1990; Stringer 1981). Previous studies have also reported on the key characteristics of the commercial home enterprise, including demographic profile of hosts, entrepreneurial type, geographic, employment and economic factors, characteristics of the home business and guest profile (see Lynch 2005a), as well as issues relating to the construction of the product or performance of the home hosting experience. There is a lack of research examining the personal experiences of hosts and how hosting impacts their life. More commonly, the host perspective is considered in relation to gender roles, lifestyle motivations, or the influence of host personality and interests on the construction of the commercial home product.

Fundamental to an evaluation of the personal perspectives of tourism experience are the subjective meanings, subjective experiences and situations of individuals. Predominantly, previous studies have analysed the personal experiences of tourism from the perspectives of travellers rather than hosts, particularly through tourist narratives (Noy 2004). Consequently, prior experiential analyses reinforce the distinctiveness of tourism from everyday life experiences. More recent discourse, however, has included examination of the interaction between work/volunteering and tourism (Wearing 2001), age-related or family life-cycles (Collins and Tisdell 2002; Gibson and Yiannakis 2002), and of the position of tourism within wider human mobility (Hall 2005b); thereby effecting a broader analysis of tourism within a wider social context over the life span and experiences of individuals. However, with the exception of life-stage or life-cycle analysis, most of the historical focus in tourism studies has been on the effect of tourism on an individual's life, as opposed to including also a flip-side view of the effect of an individual's life on tourism.

A notable exception includes the study by White and White (2004) of older long-term travellers to the Australian Outback. The authors describe how personal life events and changes precipitated the desire for a period of extended travel. Such events included, for example, changed family circumstances such as in the death of a partner or as an 'empty nester', the end of a marriage, the end of good health or of a phase in working life, of retirement from working life, a disconnection from social/community bonds and networks, or dissatisfaction with the repetitive routines of everyday life. Another example is Tucker's (2005) study which compares how the particular life-stages of a young group and an elderly group affected each party's performances of a sightseeing tour of New Zealand.

In the context of commercial homes, it is the subjective experiences of hosts, and the influence of their life events, which shape their experiences and ultimately impact on the nature of tourism or hospitality business and the host–guest encounter. In the pursuit of a richer understanding of the personal experiences of commercial home hosts, we therefore support the increased recognition afforded to qualitative research in order to achieve a more in-depth, subjective, reflexive and emic insight into the nature of the experiences of tourists (and hosts) in the tourism setting; especially that which is grounded in the narratives and lived experiences that respondents themselves describe (Noy 2004). Tourism also involves many contextual influences, as people are not always in control of the planning and experience of their vacation and, as such, there is a need for the relativism that qualitative research brings (Decrop and Snelders 2005). In respect of commercial home hosting, it is this latter perspective which formed the context for the present study.

The study

An in-depth qualitative study conducted in April 2006 revealed the personal experiences of twelve commercial home hosts in the Waikato and Auckland regions of the north island of New Zealand. Nine sites were visited in total; husband and wife couples were interviewed at three sites. At the other six sites, four women and two men were interviewed individually. Located in both a rural and urban region of New Zealand, the commercial home hosts interviewed were predominantly aged over 40 years, and the large majority were 'retired' (as they described themselves). For most participants, their previous working lives had been spent as teachers/educators. The others had been based in other people orientated careers around caring (nursing) and sales professions. All but two of the hosts we interviewed hosted guests in the family home (rather than in self-contained accommodation); as such, all occupants were reported to play a role in hosting. Only three hosts interviewed had children living in their home which is not surprising given the age of the majority of interviewees.

All the respondents were owners of their commercial home; most had been in business for less than five years, did not own any other business (other than two who were farmers and one who had a home-based framing business) and did not employ any additional staff to work in the commercial home. It was also reported that none of the hosts relied solely on the commercial income they earn from hosting, describing it as generating 'pocket money', 'a way of staying in the family home' and offering a 'tax benefit'. As such, the hosts appeared to be in a comfortable financial position in their retirement. Furthermore, they were hosting in properties which had appreciated in value due to the significant growth in the New Zealand property market in recent years. Most commonly, the commercial homes had at least three bedrooms in total, with two being available for guests. If requested, an evening meal was almost always available to guests in addition to bed and breakfast. Guests were predominantly international tourists visiting New Zealand, staying mainly one or two nights in total. The type of commercial home included in this study fits the 'traditional commercial home' type identified by Lynch and MacWhannell (2000).

The in-depth interviews were conversational in style to evoke the personal narratives of respondents. Within the interview, hosts were asked mainly open-ended questions relating to the establishment of their venture; their experiences of operating the commercial home; their relationship with their commercial home, for example the extent to which the commercial home is a home and the extent to which it is a business, private/public zones within the home, personal behaviour around guests and strategies for managing work–life balance; and the nature of the host's partner/children's relationship with the commercial home. The interviews were tape-recorded to facilitate ease of conversation and to record the narrative of respondents accurately. Each interview lasted at least an hour, with three interviews taking closer to two hours. Additional time was then spent with respondents conducting a guided tour of the home and taking photos to facilitate discussion of their relationship with particular aspects of their commercial home.

Data was analysed using content analysis to establish key common themes emerging from the interviews. Particular attention was given to applying Critical Discourse Analysis (CDA) in the analysis of transcripts. CDA concentrates on the processes by which power is reproduced or reinforced and roles are established through language. It can be used to access and structure perspective and meaning in the accounts of participants (Llewellyn and Northcott 2005). The main aim of CDA is to explore the links between language use and social practice (Phillips and Jorgensen 2004). Furthermore, CDA considers the context of language use to be crucial (Wodak and Meyer 2001). A full 'critical' account of discourse requires theorisation and description of both the social processes and structures surrounding the production of a text, and of the social structures and processes within which individuals or groups as social historical subjects, create meanings in their interactions with texts (Fairclough and Kress 1993). The model of CDA proposed by Fairclough and Kress provides an analytical framework consisting of three dimensions: First, text (the linguistic features of the text); second, discursive practice (processes relating to the production and consumption of the text); third, social practice (the wider social practice to which the communicative event belongs) (Phillips and Jorgensen 2004).

The personal narratives of commercial home hosts

In reporting their personal experiences of commercial home hosting, the hosts interviewed expressed common narratives. These experiences are presented below and relate to: 1) the host's life-stage as a reason for establishing the commercial home; 2) their relationship with their commercial home as a 'home' first and foremost, rather than a 'home-based' business; and 3) common strategies hosts have adopted for minimising the impact of hosting on their personal and family life.

Life-stage influences as a reason for home hosting

As mentioned above, all of the participants interviewed were aged over 40 years, and the large majority were over the age of 60 and 'retired'. The motivation for starting the commercial home enterprise for many of them was synonymous with a life-stage change, choosing such a venture to provide them with a new role after their official career had ended and also new direction when the children had left home, or after a marriage break-up. This motivation has similarly been noted in previous studies (see Pearce 1990; Stringer 1981). The commercial home was described as keeping them busy, giving them a sense of purpose and enabling them to remain in the large family home:

> Basically, when my wife and I split up and all the kids had grown up and left home, I thought what am I going to do? Was I going to move out which is what I would have had to have done or can I actually do this and run it as a business?
>
> I think one of the reasons why I took it up was that when my marriage broke up, I'm historically quite an introverted person so I thought if I'm living by myself I'm liable to get to that kind of state. And also I was brought up in an environment with lots of people around.
>
> It's a good use of an empty house. This home was brought to hold the family. We had five kids between us at the time.

Most of the respondents whose main career had come to an end reported that they had been in a 'people' orientated career:

> I was a teacher all my life and the last 12 years before I retired I was an academic.
>
> I was a nurse. He was an insurance agent for 20 odd years which was a little bit different – and in the army too for about 13 or 14 years.

Another, unexpected, finding was how candid many of the participants were in admitting that hosting provided them with wider social contact. Commonly, participants spoke of having fairly small networks of friends and/or family and yet wanting to be in an environment that would provide them with frequent personal contact:

> I think in a way you'd be pretty miserable if you didn't want to share it with other people, we've been farming all our lives, and we haven't got a wide circle of friends.
>
> We don't have a huge gaggle of friends. We're not hugely social people. We've got a lot of friends but I'm ashamed to say not very many locally and we don't have a huge family, so maybe we're looking at it as a surrogate family! But we like people.

Hosts and guests are found to have much in common with each other, with the commercial home acting as a vehicle for the meeting of 'kindred spirits' in quite a serendipitous way. Sharing a love of travel was a common theme influencing the participant's motivation for hosting, along with sharing other interests in common at their life-stage, given the large majority were over the age of 60 years:

> I retired in 1988. ... Because I've always had a lot of friends from overseas, I really enjoy having overseas people and I decided to go for it.
>
> I actually really enjoy the guests. ... professional people from a range of walks and they can really have good conversation. They often have travelled a lot and we have too.

Overall, running the commercial home always kept the hosts busy, providing them with a purposeful role to perform.

> I think without it I'd be all shrivelled up in a little house by myself all shrivelled up and doing nothing. But now I've got a few little chores to do and I can type up something on the computer and solve some of the problems for the bed and breakfast society.
>
> Well I'm retired so it gives me something to do. A very important thing with my life is that it's given me a discipline like we've had four children and once they leave home it's very easy I think to slip into a slovenly way and not taking too much care over things. But for me to get up and have breakfast ready, and it's not everyday so it's not a problem and for me it gives me a reason for getting up and having a purpose for the day.

The commercial home as a 'home' more than a business

Overall, it is clear that the large majority of hosts we interviewed position their premises as a 'home' first and foremost; both in terms of their own thinking but also further reinforced by the guests' ability to relax and treat it as if they were at home.

> It's more of a home thing instead of doing it as a business thing ... because they're round the table and they take us as we are, one comes in and stands inside and says I'm starving. I think they feel part of the family. It's what a lot of them have said, they feel a part of the family and that's what we like.
>
> Well, we're a home, we're a home more than a business. I mean to be perfectly honest we're not making much money out of it. It is our home, if people want to come and stay here, they come, we treat them as we would treat friends or relatives.

As the premises were viewed as a home first and foremost, hosts reported that there was a need for both hosts and guests to be accepting of this:

> I put myself in their position. A lot of it for us is genuine. We have to be genuine here because it isn't our total business. People have to accept that there will be gumboots at the back door and smelly overalls because that's reality.
>
> If we're a bit untidy and people come in, I say this is our family room, take us as you find us. People are just usually happy to take us as we are.

While hosts were adamant that they did not act in a formal manner as they were technically 'in their own home', they did stress that it is important to make some degree of effort. A common theme within the issue of suitable attire for hosting was that you needed to be clean and tidy, which for many of them means changing out of the gardening clothes prior to interacting with guests.

> No, well I might put a clean pair of trousers ... I think that it's a bit of give and take, we accept them as they are as long as they accept us as we are. Within the bounds of good manners, but its no good trying to pretend you're somebody you're not because you soon get found out.

Sometimes, hosts reported that the formalities of hosting turned into 'irritations' to running their commercial home. In particular, hosts described situations where they had to put themselves out for guests:

> Going to have a shower over in the garage. It's not ideally set up. When we came here there was no garage, we built the garage and we also added in a shower and a toilet. When we have guests, they have the use of the bathroom, we use the outside. And having to go outside on a freezing cold night to have a shower – that takes the edge off it a bit.
>
> Once you make a commitment to a guest, that absolutely has to take priority. I suffer from migraines and I have had occasions when I've literally had to rush out of the room and go and vomit, not that the guests have known, but you just manage.

On the whole, hosts reported their experiences of hosting as positive, with mutual respect between host and guest:

> We find that they respect our privacy as well. They want to have their space and they respect our privacy, so rarely do we have any problems.

Because the commercial home is first and foremost a 'home', this requires all family members to be part of the experience, by making guests feel welcome and respecting the needs of guests:

It has a good effect on our daughter too, she meets a lot of different people. It gives her an insight into how big the world actually is.

Yes, my husband definitely. [My son] at fifteen has often got home-work. He's great, and says hi, but he'll perhaps go in there and watch TV and that's fine too. But my husband enjoys it, and the guests enjoy him. They're coming here because it's a farm-stay so they've often got a lot of questions and they're fascinated by what we do and why we do it.

Some participants were quite happy to mix time with friends and family with their guests, demonstrating that hosting does not need to be a separate 'work' area of their life. Instead they are happy to facilitate such groups mixing and often find that they also have complementary interests:

Yeah, and another thing that happens is that quite often I'll invite a lot of my friends around. Normally if I'm cooking a dinner I'll invite quite a few friends with similar interests or different interests and they all enjoy coming down and meeting them, and we have some good chin-wags around the table.

Strategies for keeping the commercial home a 'home'

Despite the strong finding that they have a home first and the business is very much secondary, the longer hosts had had the commercial home, the more knowledge they had amassed enabling them to achieve greater pro-ductivity by working smarter not harder. In the early days of hosting, several participants spoke about being 'on edge', 'uptight' or 'nervous', which led them to invest huge amounts of time and energy and even 'over-hosting' guests.

I think when we started it was difficult to know, to what degree people wanted to communicate.

I know when I first started, it was big! The whole thing seemed huge and you want to get it right and the cooking, the timing.

As they gained more experience, the activity of preparing the home for guests, providing hospitality, engaging with guests and cleaning up once they depart all seemed less daunting. Along with a more relaxed and confident attitude, the participants had also established routines and systems that enable them to look after the commercial side of the home efficiently, thus having more time to enjoy hosting as well as other activities in their lives.

Yeah, and that's why you've just got to learn to relax and they've just basically got to take you as they find you. You've got to be yourself, so just relax and enjoy it.

You have to hone up on your organisational skills and you have to be very compatible and you can't think of you as an individual having certain tasks to perform and leave the others to your partner. You've got to be prepared to step in and do whatever's necessary.

While the benefits and sense of enjoyment the participants received from hosting far outweigh the downsides of minor irritations, it was also found that the participants had set limits on their capacity to host. These limits were set often in quite an active way, for example by blocking out nights as not available, excusing themselves from guest interaction when they had to go out for the night due to another obligation, or giving priority to family and friends coming to stay. As such, hosts reported that they had never been affected by having to host during times of major life events or crises.

More passive strategies were also used to set capacity limits, for example not answering the phone, not offering a dinner, or not actively marketing the home. Whether the strategies were active or passive, they were undertaken by the hosts in order to preserve enthusiasm and energy for the commercial home, and to balance other obligations they have in their lives:

> Well we could have had more you know, but it depends on how often. Like last week, we had six out of seven nights, and then you can go for a long time without anybody. But we cope. In being a bed and breakfast, we've got the opportunity, well opportunity's not quite the right word, but you can say no if you don't want them.
>
> If you're going to enjoy it, you've got to be reasonably flexible. I know I work at the church shop from time to time and you never know when you're going to have visitors so you can say yes I'll do that tomorrow, and hello we've got visitors that night and then you've got to excuse yourself. Most people are understanding about it.

Capacity limits were also set in consideration of, and in consultation with, wider life stakeholders such as friends and family. Although many of the participants said that their family supports their hosting endeavours, this was balanced with the demands from wider family to be able to 'come home' for celebrations such as birthdays and Christmas to have the home for just family, without guests.

> I had one yesterday which I had to turn away because they wanted to turn up on the 24th and 25th of December ... My daughters are most unimpressed so I've taken a solemn vow that I will not have people at Christmas no matter how nice. I've got to respect my family.
>
> [The family] don't mind, they're all away and doing their own thing so they're quite happy with it. It means there's always some beds here when they come to stay.

A discourse of home hosting: 'We have never really had a problem'

A particular issue, for which Fairclough and Kress's (1993) CDA framework can be used to analyse, is the typical narrative offered by hosts when asked about any problems or issues encountered, namely that they had never experienced real problems with guests. Only minor instances and irritations were offered during the interviews when asked about problems they had experienced with guests and/or with running the commercial home:

> We've never had any problems. The only thing I have lost is a facecloth that matches. In the last newsletter, somebody was saying every time they put navy blue towels out they go walk-about. But we haven't got any navy blue towels.
>
> We've only ever had one problem with a guest and that wasn't a problem. She was just a little bit insensitive.
>
> We've just had really nice people.

Clearly, at the 'text' level, there is an emphasis on 'nice guests' who cause, if any, only minor problems or irritations. Hosts stressed the minimal nature of problems, which enabled them to respond to the question we asked them yet keep the 'good experience' intact in terms of hosts providing good hospitality and guests enjoying their stay. As Stringer (1981) noted, the home hosting service can yield a 'highly focused, almost obsessive, quality ... the need to provide "homely accommodation"' (p. 363). The provision of 'homeliness' might be a 'special skill' to lift host's 'occupation above a mundane and purely monetary level' (ibid.: 364).

Analysis of the discursive practice focuses on how the text is produced and how it is consumed. In this study, several production conditions could have had a bearing on the 'positive reporting' by host participants when asked about problems they had experienced. For example, ethical approval was gained for this study from the University Ethics Committee; therefore, to meet ethics and informed consent requirements when out in the field, participants were given an information sheet, consent form and full details of how the information would be used, and our roles as researchers. They were told about how information would be used to support this current chapter and about the book it would be published in. While all this is necessary and sound research practice, we are aware that it also makes the act of gaining narratives from participants very 'formal', and thus may lead to possible 'positivity bias' (Pearce 1990). We are also very aware that our roles as 'academic researchers' also can construct us in the participant's eyes as high-level analysers of their home enterprises, and thereby the nature of their operations, their lives. Whilst previous researchers may not have disclosed their role and the purpose of their investigation, unless specifically asked (for example, Pearce 1990), this can not always uncover the expressed experiences and attitudes of hosts to certain topics. In the case of the study presented here, it is felt that the University Ethics requirements did have an influence on the 'public' experience we were given when interviewing. We question whether the hosts were comfortable sharing the blurred boundaries of their public/private life with guests on a micro-level, but that the idea of sharing it on a macro-level by disclosing their stories on tape to be analysed by researchers and disseminated through research publications led to a potentially 'sanitised' script of hosting being reported.

Social practice analysis examines the social world to which the communicative event belongs. As a key output from this study is this book chapter, for which we also took photos of their operation, we question whether this further encouraged 'positive reporting' when asked about problems experienced, as hosts were concerned that their operation could be identified through the photos (for which they gave their consent). The social practice of hosting for money in exchange for warm hospitality and a secure place of lodging may also be underpinning the lack of problems as reported by the hosts interviewed. After all, a 'gracious host' should not moan about guests, particularly in a potentially public manner, such as through research for an international book which is a potential form of publicity for their business.

An interesting and unexpected finding in this study is that the majority of hosts had retired from people-oriented careers. As such, they probably would have learned appropriate 'people skills' to deal with difficult situations. Furthermore, as the majority of hosts were former teachers, we expect that their tolerance levels for less than desirable behaviour would be fairly high. The majority of hosts were also aged over 50 years and, potentially therefore, are in a generational cohort where 'polite people do not complain'.

The almost unanimous discourse of the hosts experiencing no or only minimal problems and impacts on their lives lead us to question – were we being hosted? What we mean by this is that we question if we were being hosted in a similar manner to how they would host their guests, that is by hosts presenting themselves as easy going, hospitable, polite, fun, 'real New Zealanders' and respectful of previous guests. The culmination of these characteristics presented hosting as a form of utopia for those wanting to debunk the stereotype of retirement. This may be the case for many; however, we also consider that maybe the actual reality of our time in the field was that we were interviewing, while they were hosting. Certainly we were spoilt by meeting friendly people, enjoying generous morning and afternoon teas, and we were given free access to view and photograph aspects of their homes.

Conclusions

Through the investigative lens of the commercial home, personal experiences of hosts were examined through their narratives of hosting to understand the nature of their personal relationship with their commercial home, and, specifically, the impact of hosting on their personal and family life. It appears that many of the commercial home hosts interviewed are self-marginalised, choosing to make a significant life-stage change and enter a new 'role' after their 'official' career has ended. They share similar motivations; they are 'people-orientated' individuals looking for wider social contact and the opportunity to share in hearing the travel stories of guests. The commercial home thus often becomes a vehicle for the meeting of 'kindred spirits'.

The 'home' is a significant dimension in the commercial home product and one that seemingly necessitates negotiation and strategies on the part of the host so that impacts are minimised (Pearce 1990; Stringer 1981). Through the relatively homogeneous narratives the hosts shared, we propose that a 'hosting discourse' is evident. Particular features of this discourse are the importance of a typical New Zealand home-life or 'homely' experience, that problems with guests are rarely experienced, and the personal life-stage and motivations for hosting. Alternatively, because the commercial home is seemingly a vehicle for the meeting of 'kindred spirits', perhaps 'like' people are attracted to this particular form of hospitality and thus, there remain few, if any, impacts on an individual host's life, other than what they can control or expect in terms of familial norms when inviting guests into one's home. In this sense, is commercial home hosting merely a question of 'learning the rules'? Indeed, Pearce (1990) noted the importance of host and guest not only sharing the same attitudes and values, but also the same meta-cognitive beliefs (what they expect from the interaction). The dominant narrative of hosting that was found seems to allude to an ethnocentricity of the commercial home, as a formal institution, whereby hosts and guests operate according to the formal and informal rules, and engage in con-versation dialogue whether one agrees or not. While the hosts identified that their home was definitely 'a home' more than a 'business', the wider narra-tives that emerged implied a certain level of 'formality' shaping both host and guest behaviour. The fact that life events or specific interactions with guests appeared to only minimally impact on hosting in their commercial home, as reported in this study, perhaps confirms the need for a flexible schedule and people-oriented personality and skills as prerequisites for balancing home and work harmoniously within the commercial home.

As is often the case in research, we are thus left at the end of this study with several questions and avenues for further research. To advance research on personal experiences in tourism, particularly in contexts such as the commercial home, wider questions must be posed in future research: How can certain ontologies, epistemologies and methodologies be used to under-pin research designed and approached to capture personal experiences, per-haps encouraging a less formal setting and framework for the enablement and capture of personal narratives within the wider life course of the indivi-dual? How are pluralities in the tourism experience, such as through the influence of gender and cultural diversity, to be captured in future research? How does this influence the negotiation between host and guest? To put the subject at the forefront of the exercise, we also need to engage in reflexive practice to consider our own position, standpoint and world views. These shape how we approach research, what our objectives are and how we interact with participants. What is our responsibility to our researched when we are perhaps told about diverse experiences? How can we privilege the importance of their experiences in our writing and publishing forms? What can we learn from the value of their personal experiences for advancing theory? As a final reflection: perhaps if we are to address these research questions, we first need to remove the descriptive labels of 'tourism' or 'tourist', 'host' or 'hospitality', and talk about the life-course and experiences of the people involved, in order to look at the complex phenomenon of tourism and hospitality as an investigative lens into its wider context?

8 Time to trade?

Perspectives of temporality in the commercial home enterprise

Philip J. Goulding

Introduction

The phenomenon of a temporally or 'seasonally' defined tourism economy is a significant feature of tourism in many parts of the world, particularly in the cool temperate latitudes such as the fringes of northwest Europe (Baum and Hagen 1999; Getz and Nilsson 2004; Lundtorp et al. 2001). In such places, market imbalances are typically characterised by demand concentration into a short temporal peak, offset by months of surplus capacity in the face of depressed levels of business. The seasonality experienced by service providers is thus part of the landscape of tourism related economic life, often epitomised by the temporal closure of tourism supporting amenities and small businesses. This is especially so in the commercial home accommodation sector which consists of essentially home-based enterprises.

In Scotland, much of the tourist accommodation stock comprises bed and breakfasts, guesthouses, small family-run hotels and self-catering properties in essentially domestic environments. Indeed, so pervasive is the small-scale family-run micro-enterprise in Scottish tourism that it has been described as the 'cornerstone' of the country's accommodation sector (Morrison 1998b:135). Within this context, then, it is highly significant that one in six of Scotland's bed and breakfast and guesthouse establishments close for business at some point during the year, rising to over 40 per cent in January (TNS Travel and Tourism 2005).

It would be wide of the mark to suggest that all manifestations of the temporality of service provision are necessarily derived from market conditions. Indeed, this issue frames the following exploration of temporality in the commercial home enterprise. The aims of the chapter are twofold: The first is to examine notions of 'temporality' and 'seasonality' in the home-based accommodation operation, identifying different manifestations of temporality; the second is to explore aspects of the dynamic between motivations and behaviours associated with seasonal trading in the accommodation sector. Particular attention is given to 'lifestyle proprietorship' which purportedly affords temporal flexibility in a commercial home environment and a basis for flexible, independently constructed trading patterns.

The chapter draws on findings from a large-scale survey of temporal trading behaviours among home-based accommodation operators in Scotland (N = 592), conducted by the author between autumn 2004 and spring 2005. The implications of the findings are discussed in terms of opportunities for further investigation and their relevance to the emerging conceptual understanding of the commercial home enterprise.

Notions of temporality

Seasonality

Temporal analysis of tourism has traditionally centred on the notion of 'seasonality'. This term has emerged as shorthand to encapsulate temporal imbalances in the functioning of the visitor and service supplier market. Grant et al. (1997) refer to the peaks and troughs of visitor numbers during a calendar year. In economic terminology, 'seasonal variation' is understood to represent the 'rhythmic annual pattern' (Hirschey et al. 1993: 375) of a particular measurement indicator such as output, sales, consumption or profitability.

For commercial accommodation operators this perspective of 'seasonality' is epitomised by room and bed occupancy patterns across the year and concomitant impacts on revenue yield, marginal costs and profitability. However, seasonality is increasingly accepted as not merely a numeric phenomenon, but rather as a condition that has social, cultural and environmental as well as economic ramifications for individual service providers and destinations alike (Commons and Page 2001). Indeed, 'seasonality' in tourism is imbued with widely differing perceptual approaches and meanings. Hartmann (1986) argues that differences in the language of seasonal terminologies reflect the more fundamental meanings and distinctions of natural 'seasons' which in turn are part of the cultural identity of the user. He asserts that 'latitudinal and regional experiences of seasonal change' (p. 28) are significant to our understanding, identifying an ethnocentric dimension to the phenomenon. Allcock (1995) also argues that there is a cultural perspective to understanding seasonality in tourism. Seasons are, he notes, '*socially significant* periods of time' (ibid.: 93) rather than natural events. As such, seasons represent a cycle or set of human activity, such as annual cycles of agricultural labour, production or indeed leisure activity. In the case of many of Scotland's small home-based accommodation units, 'the season' is a sociological construction and cultural descriptor for a defined period of operational activity, often from Easter until the end of September or October.

The perceived level of season at any particular time may be destination- or business-specific, reflecting its particular market mix and degree of peaking or relative emptiness. 'Peak', 'high', 'shoulder' and 'low' are thus terms more reflective of destination conditions than the dynamics of origin markets. The start of the 'high season' in one locality may not be interpreted similarly by bed and breakfast or guesthouse operators in the next or indeed the same locality, irrespective of indicators such as occupancy and utilisation levels. Therefore, seasonal comparison becomes clouded by terminological inconsistency and perception, spatially, operationally and culturally. It is against this backdrop to which the seasonal patterns of small, home-based accommodation businesses are often described and misunderstood. Within this debate, there is the further dimension of short-term periodic temporal variation that also prevails in the *modus operandi* of commercial home trading behaviour.

Periodic variation

Periodic patterns of tourism activity are characterised as week-by-week variations, fluctuations according to the day of the week or between weekdays and weekends and even in levels of activity within an operational day (Bar On 1975; Holloway 1998). 'Periodicity' or short-term variation therefore contributes to an understanding of temporal cycles in tourism.

While these may be seen as distinct from longer-term patterns of seasonality, periodic fluctuations may themselves influence the supply-behaviour of accommodation businesses. For example, it is acknowledged that many small tourism businesses in seasonal operating environments experience periods of intense work patterns during peak seasons which impact on their trading patterns and behaviours at other times (Getz et al. 2004; Morrison and Teixeira 2004). Rest, relaxation, mental and physical 'downtime' during the operational day or occasional recovery days of business closure epitomize this temporal relationship in the commercial home setting (Goulding 2006). Indeed the prevalence of periodic downtime within the mode of operation serves to heighten the distinctiveness between commercial home and other operational norms.

Temporal downtime may therefore represent a more meaningful descriptor than seasonality or periodicity in operational and economic terms, and has recently been acknowledged accordingly at the European Union level (Richards 2006). Figure 8.1 illustrates a conceptual framework of temporality exhibited within the trading/operational patterns of small accommodation businesses in Scotland and thus represents a supply-side perspective. The principal temporal dimensions of seasonality and periodicity reflect both fixity and flexibility in temporal behaviours and are thus dynamic. Moreover, such supply-side temporality is typically conditioned by a mix of factors pertaining to the destination, business and proprietor demographic.

In summary, the literature has treated temporal variation mainly in terms of seasonal fluctuation from a demand-driven perspective, in which the vagaries of the market are the gateposts dictating the opening and closing patterns of tourism businesses and the levels of service provided at certain times of the year. However, this paints a significantly over-simplified canvas of the

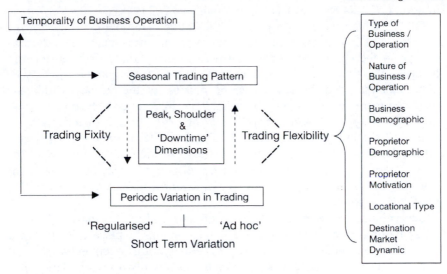

Figure 8.1 Conceptual framework of supply-side temporality.
Source: Goulding 2006.

temporal trading realities of many commercial home enterprises, for whom the dynamic of the market represents but one element of their temporal trading decision. Indeed, the range of non-market related influences on businesses' trading patterns are wide and diffuse, embracing climatic, economic, destination and intrinsic personal factors (Goulding 2006). Moreover, the rise of lifestyle businesses and the changing demographic of commercial home enterprise proprietorship requires a re-evaluation of the temporal role of business operation.

Before exploring these issues further, it is pertinent to reflect on the commercial home enterprise construct as it relates to seasonal trading accommodation entities within Scotland's tourism economy.

The commercial home enterprise (CHE) in Scotland's temporal tourism economy

Adopting the broad characterisation as a home or home construct that generates income (Lynch 2005c), it becomes apparent how pervasive the CHE is as a temporal entity within Scotland's tourism economy. However, it is first important to recognise that the CHE concept encapsulates more than just an economic exchange between paying guest and proprietor. It encapsulates the added dimensions of host–guest interaction within a private home setting where public space is shared and where the importance of the host(s) is emphasised through symbols of emotional attachment to the home. 'Home' is thus represented as a powerful cultural, emotional and temporal construct in addition to its physical facets (Di Domenico 2003; Lynch 2004).

Other distinguishing facets previously identified are the importance of the lifestyle entrepreneur as a motivational type, of owner-manager values as central to the construct, of personal networks, of family involvement and lifecycle, the significance of gender (with a noted predominance of CHE 'entrepreneuse') and the sense of embeddedness of the business within the local community and economy (Lynch 2005c: 549). Of course, some of these may equally apply to businesses out with the CHE concept such as the non-home-centred independent visitor attraction or the manager-operated corporate franchise. However, it is the holistic application of these facets, of the centrality and meanings of home and the distinctive types of accommodation service setting that provide the basis of operational temporality within the CHE construct.

Such a construct is potentially compelling in informing the role of temporal trading behaviours, insofar as home connotes a place of retreat and privacy. Within the Scottish context, CHEs are variously represented by bed and breakfasts, guesthouses, small hotels, host-family accommodation (for example, hosting summer-exchange students) (Lynch 1998) and some forms of self-catering establishments such as cottages and apartments. It is observed that collectively these types of accommodation are small in terms of letting capacity (mostly fewer than 12 letting bedrooms, as recorded by Lynch 2005c) although there is by no means consistency in this dimension of analysis among related literatures (for example, Morrison et al. 1996; Slattery 2002). Scale of operation equates with temporal flexibility, whereby spontaneous, short-term closure becomes more accessible and logistically less problematic to the home based micro-entrepreneur (Goulding 2006).

Temporality is further embedded in the CHE construct through the facets of private home ownership and the inevitably close interactions between resident host and guest. On the one hand, the business may necessitate an intense periodic involvement where the proprietor is required to or feels the need to be on call twenty four hours a day whenever guests are resident. On the other hand, such immediacy and intensity of contact engender the need for compensatory withdrawal, whereby private space is recaptured through temporal closure, either at the margins of 'the season' or interstitially, for example, by not taking bookings during defined periods. One in five home-based operators in Scotland admits to such behaviours (Goulding 2006). Moreover the temporal flexibility of smallness allows for opportunism in seizing business during otherwise closed periods, a practice conducted by 40 per cent of Scotland's seasonally closed accommodation businesses (Goulding 2006).

The remotely operated (non-resident proprietor) business, typically a holiday- or second-home let out commercially by the owner as a self-catering unit, poses a temporal variant. Here, the notion of temporality is definable mainly in terms of the 'letting season' without the short-term periodic elements of respite typically experienced by the resident guesthouse or bed and breakfast proprietor. Moreover, host–guest contact in such circumstances is often by proxy, in which the non-resident domestic housekeeper or key holder provides the principal point of 'in situ' contact.

In practice, businesses that fit the CHE concept occupy a significant place in Scotland's tourist accommodation provision (Di Domenico 2003; Morrison 1998b; VisitScotland 2002). Published operating information suggests that many of them display tendencies towards seasonally fixed trading periods in Scotland, compared with larger establishments such as country house hotels, branded hotels and motels. Thus, for the CHE, temporality is expressed both in terms of temporariness and extended downtime, the latter of which may involve several months of closure.

The degree of pervasiveness of temporal operation can be seen from returns to the Scottish Accommodation Occupancy Survey. Although a snapshot in time, Table 8.1 shows, according to four key accommodation sectors, the extent of 'closed' returns from proprietors in the 2004 national survey. Closure rates are based on the respective monthly return rate rather than as a proportion of the month of maximum sample size.

An unknown element is the degree to which such monthly fluctuation is due to the non-submission of occupancy data due to temporary ad hoc or seasonal closure on the one hand or permanent business closure on the other.

Despite these limitations, the national survey for the year in question reflects a commercial accommodation provision largely composed of small,

Table 8.1 Accommodation units notified as 'closed' in the Scottish Accommodation Occupancy Survey, 2004

Months	Hotel		Guesthouses and Bed and Breakfasts		Self Catering	
	No. closed	% of sample	No. closed	% of sample	No. closed	% of sample
January	42	13.1	134	41.5	299	26.3
February	40	12.0	130	40.0	312	27.8
March	22	7.2	92	29.1	202	17.0
April	2	0.7	18	5.8	48	3.6
May	1	0.3	6	1.9	30	2.3
June	1	0.3	2	0.6	30	2.3
July	0	0	2	0.6	29	2.2
August	0	0	2	0.6	68	5.0
September	0	0	6	2.0	45	3.5
October	2	0.7	25	8.8	39	3.3
November	19	7.0	100	34.1	219	19.8
December	26	9.6	117	39.9	208	19.6
Average	*13*	*4.4*	*53*	*17.4*	*127*	*10.4*

Source: TNS Travel and Tourism, 2005.

independent businesses that display significant, though varied, degrees of
seasonal trading across the sectors. This is most extreme among guesthouse
and bed and breakfast operations in which for four months of the year, more
than one third of the stock is closed for business. Moreover, this level of
closure remains comparable with the 1999 SAOS survey response data
(System Three 2000) and thus represents a systemic condition.

While the hard data suggests a clear propensity for temporalism among a
minority of Scotland's CHE population, what remains more elusive is the
role of causal influences as explanatory factors. Oft-cited in the small hospitality business literatures is the role of 'lifestyle proprietorship' in seasonal
destinations (Andrew et al. 2001; Getz et al. 2004; Shaw and Williams 2002).
This is explored next.

Temporality and lifestyle in the commercial home enterprise

Surprisingly few links have been established empirically between lifestyle
enterprise and the temporality of the business operation in home-based
commercial accommodation. Indeed, empirical and theoretical relationships
between seasonal trading and lifestyle proprietorship remain undeveloped,
even though in recent years there have been attempts to bridge the conceptual gap, most notably through the gaze of the family business. Getz and
Carlsen's (2000) Western Australia study of rural accommodation based
family businesses and studies in Canmore (Canada) and Bornholm (Getz
and Petersen 2004) provide examples among the few such studies where
seasonality and the use of downtime by proprietors are explored.

As a starting point, 'free' or 'discretionary' time manifested either as
short-term periodic flexibility or as temporal blocks may represent a facet of
lifestyle if based on choice. Andrew et al. (2001) propose that temporal
trading may indeed represent a lifestyle accessory to the (hospitality) operator. They also suggest that a consequence of this is reduced propensity to
invest in marketing, training and quality upgrading. Implicit in such logic,
however, is that the use of non-trading or downtime periods for activities
such as business planning, staff development, repairs or investment in the
property would seem to be inimical to lifestyle proprietorship. Di Domenico
(2003: 29) suggests that for dual income households in which the tourism
related business ' ... can be integrated into the family lifestyle', the off-
season period may afford leisure opportunities for the operator. Her view
echoes that highlighted in Getz and Carlsen's (2000) Australian family business study, in which seasonality is seen to offer families ' ... a lull during
which pursuit of family and lifestyle goals can dominate' (p. 555). Moreover,
seasonality fits with 'family first' values and priorities among their study
group.

Getz et al. (2004) highlight the tensions between lifestyle businesses and
seasonality from a different perspective. They observe that in some locations
the temporal increases in workload caused by seasonal demand fluctuations

may actually serve to conceal from proprietors the lifestyle benefits that initially motivated the business start-up. In other words, extremely busy high seasons can counter or devalue the lifestyle benefits sought (such as relaxation, time to catch up on non-business chores and socialising) offered by low-season respite. The antithesis of this view is provided by Andrew et al. (2001) who propose that for significant parts of the year, accommodation operators are free to enjoy their chosen lifestyle. Thus the debate on whether or not seasonal trading confers lifestyle benefits is bound up with issues around the physical and mental health and well-being arising from the work patterns and associated work–life balance.

A related manifestation of this tension is found in the problem of business inheritance. The temporal nature of the operation, resulting from seasonal demand patterns, may cause negative perceptions by heirs or next of kin to the prospect of taking over the commercial home based family business. This is recorded by Getz and Nilsson (2004) in their study of seasonal tourism operators in Bornholm, and encapsulated in an interview accordingly: 'Our children are not interested in this business because of the long working hours in high season' (Getz et al. 2004: 110). Interestingly, it is the negative aspect of long high season working hours rather than the potential respite benefits during periods of closure that feature as barriers to business inheritance in Getz and Nilsson's (2004) Bornholm study.

An 'emotional attachment associated with the physical space' of the commercial family home (Morrison and Teixeira 2004: 247) can be a central motivating factor within the various accommodation sectors. Goulding et al. (2004) observe that seasonal trading may represent a key stratagem for achieving such an attachment. In this sense, the temporal downtime allows proprietors to have control over the balance of priority between, on the one hand, showcasing their domestic environment to visitors for a certain period during the year and on the other, the intrinsic benefits achievable through closure of the business for parts of the financial year. Commercial home enterprise proprietors such as those running bed and breakfast, guesthouse and on-site self catering businesses are afforded significant flexibility in this respect.

More generally, the characterisation of the lifestyle entrepreneur as one of a number of entrepreneurial guises identifies seasonality as a contextually motivational and aspirational factor for entering or starting a seasonal business. Brown (1987), as reported in Getz et al. (2004: 14), concludes that taking a long seasonal break from work is a motivator for some family business owners, albeit a growth-impeding factor. The notion of seasonal trading preference is thus an underpinning factor, though seldom overtly articulated as such. As Getz et al. (2004: 14) note, for some operators the 'off-season' ' … comes as a relief, enabling rest, vacations and time for necessary work around the house and business'. For more commercially oriented businesses, incorporating non-operating periods into the trading calendar may serve different preferences, such as business planning and maintenance (Grant et al. 1997: A5), or counter-cyclical earning activities (Flognfeldt 2001; Getz and Nilsson 2004).

The point is also made that for some small home-based family businesses, seasonality is seen as a fact of life rather than as a threat (Lundtorp et al. 2001), as has been demonstrated in Getz and Nilsson's (2004) Bornholm study. Among their survey respondents, 57.5 percent (n = 46) claimed to trade seasonally, i.e. through closure of the business for part of the year, either by choice ('lifestyle or health considerations') or because of the non-viability of staying open during off-peak times (p. 28). Most seasonal traders exhibit what the authors term 'coping' response strategies to Bornholm's extreme seasonality, in which temporal closure is an adaptation to seasonality.

However, most revealing from Getz and Nilsson's work is that while there is an element of lifestyle-oriented or 'family first' motivations underpinning the seasonal trading behaviours of commercial home based enterprises, the majority of business owners prefer a longer, more profitable tourism season. Thus their study reveals that 'lifestyle-orientation' and seasonal trading are seen to coincide de facto within this case study area. At the same time there appears to be an aspirational divergence among some of the lifestyle-oriented business proprietors. On the one hand, some operators profess to prefer a longer season, but on the other hand they abstain from engaging in 'combating' response behaviours.

Irrespective of whether small commercial home enterprises do or do not seek to grow, lifestyle entrepreneurship and lifestyle orientation form a realistic paradigm in accounting for temporal trading behaviours, as illustrated in Figure 8.2.

The lifestyle-orientation category is most likely to engender preference for seasonal closure or flexible temporal trading (e.g. periodic closure). Ultimately however, various conditioning factors will influence the nature of the business response to seasonality and whether, in the case of closure, such behaviour is a preferred or compelled course of action. The status of the business and the proprietor within the business household, the household demographic, well-being and personal lifecycle factors represent some of these. They in turn influence the role of temporal trading in commercial home enterprises.

Roles of temporal trading in Scottish commercial home enterprises

The operational behaviours and aspirations of CHEs cannot always be explained from a purely economic rationale (Andrew et al. 2001; Holmengen and Bredvold 2003; Morrison 2002; Williams et al. 1989). This applies when their motivational spectrum encompasses factors such as physical and psychological comfort, personal health, socialisation and even environmental awareness, alongside revenue generation.

Among the 'lifestyle-affirming' CHE proprietor population in Scotland there is a wide diversity of circumstance, including among them farming

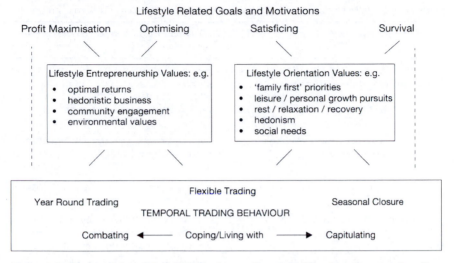

Figure 8.2 Conceptual model of CHE business orientation, lifestyle and seasonal trading.

households, near-to-retirement proprietors, long established and more recently started businesses (Goulding 2006). These are also spread across the various accommodation types and household contexts. For some, operational temporality more closely represents a purposive role within a particular work–life or demographic balance, such as fitting in with farming or other business commitments or with the requirements or contingencies of health and well-being, than simply being a lifestyle preference per se.

A number of distinct roles attributed to seasonal trading emerged from a previous study among CHE operators in the Scottish Borders (Goulding et al. 2004). A summary of these is shown in Table 8.2. There are clear inter-linkages between some of the identified roles emerging from the individual narratives. For example, attributes of stability and control (No. 2) afforded to proprietors by temporal or flexible trading may be prerequisites to enable them or their partners to undertake other remunerated work. In this author's subsequent large-scale Scottish survey, the incidence of dual- or multiple occupations in seasonal tourism households is around a third, with farming and land management occupations predominant (Goulding 2006). Apart from the propensity to operate other tourism and hospitality-related services around the commercial home enterprise, a diverse range of professional services is also operated by proprietors or other members of the household. Construction- and property-related businesses and retail- and education-related occupations are also in evidence as complementary occupations in Scotland's seasonal and periodic CHE households (Goulding 2006).

A range of attributes are revealed pertaining to mental health and personal welfare, both of the proprietor and his/her family, and also relating to employees. Articulation of the need to escape or rest at the end of the season

Table 8.2 Purposive roles of seasonal trading by commercial home enterprise proprietors

Role of Seasonal Trading	Examples of Statements by Exploratory Study Interviewees
1 as an inherent motivation for entering the tourism/hospitality trades	'we decided to give it up [former trade] and bought the [holiday-home park] which became a family home for all of us. We only operate seven months a year.'
2 provides a framework for living – e.g. stability, predictability, control	'we are private, therefore to a certain extent we have been able to do what we like…'
3 complements other business interests	'the season I now have is what I choose to fit in with my life'
4 complements time-related lifestyle goals	'normally our holidays are taking groups …away on trips abroad…so we're not actually on our holidays…'
5 enhances emotional attachment to physical space, the home, material possessions, hobby	'out of season the house becomes ours again' 'you don't want the place swarming with tourists [all year round]…it detracts from the beauty of living…'
6 balances proprietor's environmental concerns/values	'…nor do we think it's environmentally sound…if you're cycling on that you're damaging that'…[referring to off-road cycling in the winter months]
7 fulfils social roles/allows family commitments	'at Christmas and the New Year you have the family here, grandchildren here, that's important'
8 'downtime' allows physical and mental rest and recovery	'the staff can't wait for the end of the season so they can have a rest' 'at the end of six months you've got to have a holiday…you're becoming stale, you get short tempered'

Source: Goulding et al. 2004.

echo other previous empirical studies of seasonality and destination communities, such as Jordan's (1980) work in Vermont and more recently Flognfeldt's (2001) study of seasonal workers and proprietors in Jotunheimen, Norway. In the latter study, the author notes the incidence of seasonal employees and employers taking long holidays during low seasons.

Two further connections between temporal trading and the home environment are observed. First, there is the aspect of emotional attachment to the physical space as home, central to the CHE concept (Lynch 2005c, 1998). Several proprietors offer the opinion that temporal trading allows a sense of peace and ownership to be restored at the end of 'the season', a much reiterated sentiment, through the expressed importance of free time, privacy and self-occupancy of the property (Table 8.2, Statement 5).

Second, a small minority of interviewees articulate the benefits of seasonal tourism to the state of the physical environment. Such views add support to the debate on the role of post-seasonal recovery to communities as described by Butler (2001), Baum and Hagen (1999) and Flognfeldt (1988). Moreover they provide an interesting perspective on Morrison's (2002) assertion that accommodation owner-managers can be committed to sustaining the local environment and community for a range of moral and lifestyle, as well as commercial motivations or, in Lynch's (2005c: 549) terminology, 'embedding' in the local community.

A further factor underscores the purposive roles for seasonal trading. In the Scotland wide study, a general preference for seasonal trading emerged as a strong motivational force. Indeed, 70 per cent of the proprietor population are inclined to operate the business accordingly rather than year round. Among bed and breakfast operators the proportion is even higher (Goulding 2006). Such proprietors span both the demographic spectrum and the divide between growth- and non-growth orientations. This suggests that such seasonal trading preference transcends the traditional paradigms of lifestyle, family-life-cycle and economic versus non-economic goals.

Conclusions

An overarching aim of this chapter has been to highlight the range and complexity of inter-relationships between the commercial home enterprise and notions of temporality. A specifically supply-side lens has been adopted to investigative operational flexibility and seasonal downtime among CHE businesses. In peripheral, rural Scotland as elsewhere among the rural cool temperate regions of north-west Europe and North America, the seasonal tourism economy is often far more complex than explained purely from the demand dynamic of the market place. Moreover, while conditions of extreme seasonality as characterised by Getz and Nilsson (2004) are generalisable to parts of Scotland and other peripheral North Atlantic destinations, as yet little empirical evidence captures the complexity of operational temporality and its underlying behaviours and motivations.

Against this backdrop, a large-scale study in Scotland revealed that commercial home enterprises spanning a range of accommodation types engage in seasonal trading and often also in periodic trading flexibility through ad hoc or planned short-term closure. While the range of factors influencing such behaviours is wide, there is little doubt that, for some, lifestyle business objectives and orientation underlie temporal downtime. However, lifestyle entrepreneurialism and orientation remain nebulous, under-theorised concepts. Indeed, the CHE concept provides a more unifying and explanatory lens than either 'lifestyle business' or 'family business' in shedding insights on temporality from a provider perspective.

As observed by Lynch (2005c; 1998), Di Domenico (2003) and Morrison (2002) among others, commercial home hosting evokes a distinct blurring of motivational and behavioural boundaries between entrepreneurialism, life-style and hobbyist business operation. Among the non-market and non-profit oriented factors, personal life-cycle, physical and mental health and well-being as well as work–life balance factors are influential to proprietors' temporal behaviours. Operational temporality is thus seen to be often pur-posive and encompasses numerous potential roles for the proprietorial family or sole operator. Moreover, a substantial minority of Scotland's temporally operating CHE proprietors are in households of dual or multiple occupa-tions, especially those in farming localities, where the dictates of competing income generating activities may override the need or ability to open the CHE to paying guests at certain times. Such domestic and economic role balancing supports the strength of preference for seasonal trading and temporal flexibility among many CHE operators in Scotland.

In the traditional guise of bed and breakfast, guesthouse or small hotel, the commercial home construct is thus instrumental to the temporality of operation. The home environment provides a natural retreat from the demands of long periods of intense hosting activity and empowers the host to shut down, temporarily or for more prolonged periods, both in opera-tional and psychological terms. During periods of inactivity from touristic hosting, the commercial home becomes temporally and temporarily non-commercial and reverts to its other social functions and economic domains.

Empirical studies of temporality among CHE operations have barely scratched the surface of the complex relationships between operational behaviours and motivational dynamics and the place-role of the physical home construct. There are clear public policy implications in learning more about such inter-relationships. From a local economic development perspec-tive, the economic impacts in places exhibiting clusters of lifestyle-oriented businesses or long-term seasonal closure of accommodation and amenities have received relatively little attention. Moreover, the debates on the positive social, community and environmental impacts of temporal tourism activity have yet to encroach on the role of the commercial home enterprise in fos-tering such impacts. It is hoped that some of the issues raised in the preceding pages may stir further enquiry in those directions.

9 Behaving appropriately

Managing expectations of hosts and guests in small hotels in the UK

Anne Benmore

Introduction

The main theme of this chapter is that the home construct, as a distinguishing characteristic of the commercial home (Lynch 2005c: 535), significantly influences the behaviour of owners and paying guests in these establishments. Here, the commercial home is conceptualised as ' ... the private home as a site of commercial hospitality provision' or 'hotel-home' hybrid (Di Domenico and Lynch 2007a: 118). It is further contended that commercial home owners, as hosts within the hospitality relationship (Guerrier and Adib 2000: 266), effectively manage their own and guests' behaviour within their homes, through flexible and autonomous use of emotional labour (Harris 2002; Hochschild 1983). They do this by adroitly operating within and across the three domains of hospitality; social, private and commercial (Lashley 2000a). The dual lenses of emotional labour and hospitality thus provide a powerful cross-disciplinary framework through which the complexities of host and guest behaviours in commercial homes can be better understood.

The chapter draws on twenty commercial homes selected from a wider study of over twenty-five small and large hotels in a major UK resort. This sample of twenty conforms to the definition of the 'commercial home', as 'types of accommodation where visitors or guests pay to stay in private homes, where interaction takes place with a host and/or family usually living upon the premises and with whom public space is, to a degree, shared' (Lynch 2005c: 534). As small hotels, this sample are categorised as 'traditional commercial homes' (Lynch and MacWhannell 2000) and have eleven bedrooms or less (Lynch 2005c). In all cases, hosts live on the premises (with partner and family if applicable); the hotel thus comprising both private home and commercial business. The hotels are run by the owner(s), with any staffing being on a casual basis, for example to help with cleaning and preparing the bedrooms. Space is used flexibly according to the owner's personal needs and financial circumstances; for example, the number of bedrooms that are let or retained for personal use, and the extent to which guests share the lounge. Guests mostly include a mix of business travellers and holidaymakers whose stay is generally between one and fourteen nights. However, some guests are longer-term, for example students and contract workers.

The larger study from which this sample is taken focused on how hosts and guests experience emotional labour. Qualitative data was acquired through semi-structured interviews with hosts, and through open questionnaires and telephone interviews with a self-selected sample of guests from the same hotels. Owners of the hotels made the questionnaires available to guests, who then returned them direct to me.

To support the main contention of this chapter, two particular features of the commercial home – private home status and host–guest interactions within the home – exemplify how perceptions of the 'home' (Lynch 2005c: 535) influence how hosts and guests experience commercial home hospitality. Hence the remainder of the chapter is structured around these two key themes. First, it is argued that host and guest behaviours are shaped by each party's perceptions of the commercial home as a 'home', in the context of the guests paying to stay in that private home. Second, it is proposed that perceptions of the 'home' element influence how guests feel they can and should interact with the host, who, though providing commercial hospitality, lives in the commercial premises. Within these two key areas, host and guest behaviours will be examined in depth, across the three domains of hospitality (Lashley 2000a). Data from the research study will illustrate how hosts and guests negotiate behaviours that each considers appropriate to the context of guests paying for commercial hospitality in the host's private home and interacting with a host who lives on the business premises.

Conceptual framework

Concepts of the commercial home, hospitality work and emotional labour support this chapter.

The commercial home

Drawing on the definition of the commercial home (Lynch 2005c: 534) cited above, the importance of the 'home' in this context is emphasised by Lynch who suggests that 'home is " … a powerful physical, cultural, emotional, and temporal construct"' (Lynch 2005c: 535). He further argues that it can constitute a haven to 'truly be oneself and affirm one's identity' (Lynch 2005a: 41). Not surprisingly, then, commercial home owners' perceptions of the 'home' shape how they choose to share that home with paying guests. Such feelings toward using the home to provide commercial hospitality may also be reflected in the host's specific motives for running a commercial home. Aside from the profit motive, these can range from, for example, lifestyle and family related goals (Getz and Carlsen 2000) to 'having the company' and 'meeting different people' (Tucker and Lynch 2004: 22).

Perceptions of a commercial home as a *home*, by both hosts and guests, also influence how they interact. These interactions – between host and guest – are another key feature of the commercial home and reflect the centrality of the host–guest relationship to the hospitality product (Hoque 2000; Tucker 2003a; Tucker 2003b; Tucker and Lynch 2004). However, this relationship can be ambiguous as to its 'commercial/family orientation' (Lynch 1999: 120). The host's role is influential here; for example, as hospitable 'friend' or commercial provider (Darke and Gurney 2000).

Hospitality work

Hospitality work is integral to running a commercial home, where the function of hospitality is to 'establish a relationship or to promote an already established relationship' (Tucker and Lynch 2004: 22). However, 'to be effective, hospitality requires the guest to feel that the host is being hospitable through feelings of generosity, a desire to please, and a genuine regard for the guest as an individual' (Lashley 2000a: 15). The complexities these descriptions imply can be better understood using a conceptualisation of hospitality as three independent but overlapping domains, 'social', 'private' and 'commercial', through which hospitality activities can be analysed (Lashley 2000a: 5). This model is used in this chapter to provide a framework through which the two features of the commercial home – guests paying for commercial hospitality in the private home and guests interacting with the host who lives on the premises – are examined.

The social domain can reflect a host's value system, by establishing and reinforcing a desired social order through the host's relationships with guests. Negotiating the different social expectations this demands requires interactive skills common to the commercial domain (Clark 1995; Go et al. 1996). This helps the host to manage hospitality provision, which involves 'a series of complex negotiations between guests and service providers about what is and what is not acceptable behaviour' (Guerrier and Adib 2000: 266). However, the established social order may be challenged if host–guest expectations are misaligned, for example 'if guests choose to step over the boundaries' (Brotherton and Wood 2000: 139). Tucker and Lynch's (2004) idea of host–guest matching through psychographics can be useful here. However, a further challenge to commercial home hosts is the traditions of hospitality toward strangers, to meet their needs and protect them (Beardsworth and Keil 1997; O'Gorman 2007; Selwyn 2000). Hospitality's twin sister 'hostility' is never far away, so 'managing' strangers to share your home can be problematic.

Moving to the private domain, Lashley (2000a: 10) argues that commercial enterprises can learn from understanding the 'nurturing and altruistic motives of those who cook, serve beverages, make beds and create a safe environment', since these 'shape to some extent expectations of the non-domestic provision of hospitality activities'. Private domain hospitality is characterised by hospitableness, involving 'a genuine desire to please guests and make them happy' (Lashley 2000a: 11). Here, the host has 'an appropriate motive' (Telfer 1996: 86); not trying to win favour from, seduce or profit from the guest. A private host may want guests to be an 'admiring audience to an accomplished home-making performance' or may wish to 'preclude any outsiders visiting because they create extra work and destroy a hard-won sense of the home as haven' (Darke and Gurney 2000: 80). A host's motives may also be influenced by their view of the housework necessary to provide hospitality. However, this is inherently contradictory; it can be tedious and repetitive, but the homemaker can also work autonomously. Additionally, 'performance' standards are self-imposed but evaluated by both self and others, which can be problematic for the 'house proud' (commercial) homeowner (Oakley 1974: 106).

Commercial domain hospitality is distinguished by its 'market driven relationship which allows a customer a freedom of action that individuals would not dream of demanding in a domestic setting' (Lashley 2000a: 12). It generally involves demeaning (house) work (Oakley 1974) and 'dirty work', where staff must deal with guests' 'intimate bodily functions' (Guerrier and Adib 2000: 261). The work is also commonly gendered (Guerrier and Adib 2000). Commercial host–guest relationships are typically non-reciprocal. The host's motive is ulterior (to secure a profit) and the money exchange absolves the guest from any feeling of mutual obligation and loyalty (Lashley 2000a) This emphasis impacts on how guests perceive hospitableness; 'on receiving genuine hospitality, the individual feels genuinely wanted and welcome. This is not the same as being welcomed as a valued customer' (Lashley 2000a: 13).

Emotional labour

The use of emotional labour to provide commercial hospitality is well documented (Guerrier and Adib 2003; Ritzer 2007). The conceptualisation of emotional labour used here draws on Hochschild (1979, 1983) and Harris (2002), beginning with Hochschild's (1983: 7) description of emotional labour as 'the management of feeling to create a publicly observable facial and bodily display'. Emotional *labour* can be distinguished from emotion *work* (Fineman 2003: 20; Hochschild 1979: 561), where the latter refers to emotional effort expended in the private sphere to manage social situations, whilst the former refers to appropriation of private emotion management for the pursuit of profit. Hence emotion *work* becomes emotional *labour* when emotion management is transmuted from the private to the public domain, for commercial gain (Hochschild 1983).

Hochschild (1983: 118–119) argues that emotional labour requires transmutation of three elements: emotion work, feeling rules and social exchange. The first two become public acts with little or no discretion, with social exchange allowing ' ... much less room for individual navigation of the emotional waters'. Feeling rules convey what the emotional labourer thinks he or she ought to feel, and express, in particular situations, such as hospitality exchange. The labourer identifies these rules by focusing on 'the pinch between "what I *do* feel" and "what I *should* feel"' (Hochschild 1983: 6). In terms of emotional display, Fineman (2003: 21) argues that 'Surface acting is simulating emotions not actually felt. Deep acting involves suppressing what you privately feel, to come in line with what the employer wants you to feel'. Here, display rules define emotions that should be expressed or hidden (Mann 1997: 6). Ashforth and Humphrey (1993: 94) add a third option of 'no acting', when an individual's emotional display aligns with their inner feeling, requiring no need to act. Commercial homeowners, being self-employed, arguably impose such rules on themselves.

Harris (2002) develops earlier ideas (for example, Morris and Feldman 1996) to offer a three-dimensional model of emotional labour; its origins, extent and content, and consequences. He also distinguishes between 'private' and 'public' emotional labour, the former taking place 'back stage' and the latter referring to 'front stage exchanges'. Although Harris' study referred to barristers and solicitors, a parallel can be drawn with front-of-house and back-of-house operations in the commercial home (Goffman 1959). Harris also suggests that consequences of emotional labour can be both negative and positive, in contrast to Hochschild's (1983) primary concern with emotional dissonance.

The ensuing discussion examines two key features of the commercial home; that guests are paying for commercial hospitality in a private home and that they interact with a host who lives on the premises. The discussion is intended to show how these aspects of the commercial home shape host and guest behaviours. The behaviours that are explored are interrogated and explained through the concepts of hospitality (Lashley 2000a) and emotional labour (Harris 2002; Hochschild 1983).

Managing paying guests in the commercial home

Social domain

Commercial home hosts in this study commonly selected guests to suit the hospitality provided. Matching guests to the business and protecting the home in this way demanded regular use of emotional labour. Hosts would create feeling rules for themselves as reminders of the social boundaries they wished to maintain. These rules were manifested through emotional displays that facilitated appropriate guest selection. Hence the host communicated the particular home identity he had created for the business, such as a 'hostel' style environment or contemporary 'urban chic' hotel. To match this image, hosts commonly employed well-honed routines to assess the suitability of potential guests on the phone or at the door. They negotiated polite refusals to those who would not 'fit' the particular culture of their hotel. One host, for example, reported 'attuning his antennae' to judge the suitability of potential guests. All manner of emotions were involved here, from suppressing disquiet to being welcoming and friendly. However, what is interesting is that since the 'rules' of emotional labour emanated from the host himself, he appeared to have far more autonomy than his counterparts in larger corporations, in defining the nature and employment of emotional labour. Consequences arising from its use could thus be less stressful than for employees in larger organisations (Hochschild 1983; Williams 2003).

Nevertheless, assessing potential guests still caused concern, since within the context of selecting guests to share one's commercial home, a host is mindful of the ever-present challenge of dealing with 'strangers' (Selwyn 2000). Hospitality traditions suggest strangers should be welcomed into one's home for protection and comfort (O'Gorman 2007), but for commercial home hosts, the 'stranger' may not necessarily be someone 'in need' but could be anybody wishing to 'buy' the hospitality on offer. As such, they are 'unknown' and can hence pose a threat to the host and other guests (Selwyn 2000). The hosts in this study responded differently to this challenge, with their use of emotional labour being equally diverse. Some went to extra-ordinary lengths to assess the 'stranger danger'. One host for example, donned steel-capped shoes and an array of personal armoury and alarms before tackling night-time disturbances, saying he felt lucky not to have been physically harmed. Many others learned through early experience to 'remove the problem' by nurturing 'repeat business' to largely negate any need to 'deal with strangers'.

Most hosts refused to take people who appeared drunk, involved with drugs, or appear homeless. They wanted to avoid the emotional labour that they anticipated would be associated with the unpredictable and messy behaviour such people might exhibit. However, for others, assessing (and often refusing) strangers posed a dilemma; the host's natural hospitableness wanted to say 'yes' but common sense said 'no' (see also Telfer 2000). For these hosts, managing their emotions proved difficult; they struggled with what they really felt and what they thought they ought to feel in refusing strangers access to their commercial home. Some felt 'guilty' or 'mean' for refusing people just because they looked suspicious or 'shabby', since this jarred with the traditions of providing hospitality to strangers. So here, using emotional labour to protect the home and business appeared to conflict with the cultural origins of hospitality traditions (O'Gorman 2007: Selwyn 2000). However, hosts justified their decisions by saying 'you just don't know who you're letting into your home', reinforcing the unknown dimension of the stranger.

Private domain

In the private domain, emotional labour was evident in how hosts engaged in the 'housework' necessary to provide hospitality to paying guests. Hosts generally appeared to agree that housework was a double-edged sword; they enjoyed autonomy over the work but were aware that their performance was under constant scrutiny. Both hosts and guests assessed the standard of housework, with a host's own evaluation set against his self-imposed standards. Maintaining these standards commonly involved the host expending emotional labour. Their own feeling rules constantly reminded them when the work had to be done and if it was done well enough. Their views toward both their home and hospitality provision shaped their attitudes toward the work involved. A common sentiment was 'It's hard work but it's our home and we take pride in that', resonant of hosts who welcomed guests as audiences to admire 'an accomplished home-making performance'.

However, others did not relish the extra work that guests could generate, to 'destroy a hard-won sense of the home as haven' (Darke and Gurney 2000: 80). For example, one commented, 'When they leave the floor strewn with crisp packets and cans it makes me really mad – it's a lovely room'. The emotional toll on this host is not unlike the emotional consequences of feeling house-proud 'in one's own circle' (Oakley 1974: 106). Yet others took a philosophical view toward the work as a necessary evil. As one put it: 'I hate the work but it has to be done.' For these hosts, investment in emotional labour was heavy, and the 'acting' required for the desired performance was considerable. As some commented: 'It never ends, it never ends' and 'It's the same old, same old – every day'. However, for others no acting was required. One host, for example, felt doing housework meant literally 'being himself'. He enthused 'I know it sounds sad, but I *love* cleaning, I just *love* cleaning' and 'When I've finished all the rooms I look back and feel really proud'.

Commercial domain

Not surprisingly, the intrinsic characteristic of the commercial home as a profit making venture evoked transactional perspectives from some paying guests. The 'I've paid for it so I'll have it' mentality was manifested by a minority of guests in this study. A typical example was parents ordering full cooked breakfasts for small children, just because they had paid for it. Hosts drew on emotional labour to find ways to 'manage' these situations to avoid waste, which they found annoying, and in a way that avoided conflict with the guest. One host, for example, by-passed the parents and spoke directly to the children; a strategy that gave few parents latitude to intervene without embarrassment to themselves. However, some guest behaviours tested even the most relaxed and accommodating host. One hotelier endured an incident where she found great difficulty controlling her anger and indignation and not revealing 'inappropriate' emotion (Mann 2004: 206). A guest openly allowed her daughter to 'make a new pattern' on the duvets, with permanent felt–tip pen. The parent seemed to treat the matter as a joke and had no qualms that this was acceptable to 'amuse' her daughter. The hotelier was struggling in her first year of trading and 'could have cried' that brand new sets of bed linen were 'ruined'. The guest was clearly oblivious to the feelings of hurt and violation she had caused. Such guest behaviour is consistent with the idea that commercial hospitality guests are free to do as they please within a purely transactional (as opposed to reciprocal) relationship (Lashley 2000a: 13).

Managing host–guest interactions in the commercial home

Social domain

Selecting guests to share one's commercial home is only the first stage in hosts' management of the social framework they have established (Lashley 2000a). The next challenge is to manage their relationship with the guests throughout their stay. Thus hosts have to find ways to ensure that guests behave appropriately by adhering to the prevailing social order, because 'norms' of social orderliness established by a host can be easily upset (Lynch 2005a: 45). Guests might 'choose to step over the boundaries' (Brotherton and Wood 2000: 139), thus challenging prevailing feeling rules (Hochschild 1983) that guide how hosts and guests normally behave toward one another. In this study, hosts' motives for managing social order in this way appeared to be twofold; wishing to protect the home, and to ensure that guests did not behave in ways that could harm the business by upsetting other guests. For example, most hosts would not allow guests to come down to breakfast in their pyjamas, or to swear openly in front of fellow guests. A few did, however, 'turn a blind eye' if the hotel was not busy, even allowing a guest with curlers in her hair!

For some hosts, managing relationships with guests meant no more than 'creating a climate of respect'; whilst others felt it necessary to implement all manner of 'house rules' to constantly reinforce the standard of behaviour expected. Whichever approach was used, hosts employed emotional labour to constantly reinforce the social standards they desired. Through feeling rules and emotional display rules (Hochschild 1979, 1983) a host reminded himself how he should feel in order to express emotions that would elicit an appropriate emotional response and behaviour in the guest. For example, if a host felt it was reasonable for party groups to 'have a good time', he might convey the impression that they could 'let their hair down', but within limits. In return, guests tended to repay that trust by 'having a good time' whilst respecting the host and other guests. Conversely, a party of guests greeted with 'a reading of the riot act' might feel disgruntled and so behave as they pleased, disrespecting others by slamming doors and shouting at three o'clock in the morning.

However, when guests did step over the boundaries of 'reasonable' behaviour, for example by being rude or abusive, a host could feel violated and hurt. Faced with such emotions hosts struggled to maintain their demeanour of appropriate emotional display (Hochschild 1983). A frequent consequence of such incidents was that the host subsequently reviewed his selection strategy. As one put it: 'You have to refine, refine, refine.' However, terminating the relationship was an option very much within the host's control, in contrast to corporate counterparts (Seymour and Sandiford 2005: 560). In one case, gay hosts took immediate action to remove guests exhibiting homophobic behaviour, refusing to tolerate such personal abuse. As one said, 'We don't have to put up with such people'.

Private domain

It was also evident in this study that commercial home hosts commonly drew on private domain hospitality by endeavouring to be hospitable toward guests. For a significant number this appeared to concur with how they would behave toward *any* guest in their home, so paying guests were treated very much as friends and family. As one put it, 'When you're all ready and waiting for them to arrive, it's like having the family over', with many others commenting that they had made a lot of friends through hosting. Most hosts also implied that their 'naturalness' was 'being themselves', whether front-, or back-of-house (Douglas 1991; Guerrier 1999: 43). These 'natural' behaviours suggested that hosts' perceptions of the 'performance' required and the effort needed to execute that performance were closely aligned, thus requiring no need to act (Ashforth and Humphrey 1993: 94). However, even these hosts acknowledged that it could be hard to maintain their performance at certain times, for example toward the end of the season. A typical sentiment was, 'I'm really myself doing this, but it does get hard when you're tired'. Additionally, a few readily admitted to 'putting on an act', but felt the act was 'genuine'. For these hosts, 'being hospitable' did not come naturally, but they suggested that what was important was not that they needed to act, but that the guest felt the 'performance' was genuine. This view was corroborated by guests who reported that, although they mostly felt hosts were genuinely hospitable, they did not mind if the 'performance' was to some extent an 'act', provided it *felt* genuine; that the host was 'trying to be helpful'.

What appeared inconclusive in the study, for both hosts and guests, was what each felt should be the appropriate balance of 'friendliness' and 'commerciality' in the host–guest relationship. The dilemma for both parties was whether the relationship should be primarily a hospitable exchange or commercial transaction. This lack of clarity could affect the appropriateness of emotional display (Hochschild 1979, 1983). For example, a host might be *too* hospitable, compromising his professionalism by expressing 'natural' emotion (Harris 2002). Guests' expectations compounded this conundrum; many reported that they wanted hosts to be friendly, courteous and helpful, and to make time 'to talk to me' but not to be 'too intrusive'. Hence they seemed to want interaction whilst retaining their privacy. The 'commercial' and 'home' notions of the commercial home concept thus appeared to generate some ambiguity in how the host–guest relationship was interpreted by both parties. Similar ambiguity has been reported in other studies concerned with smaller commercial homes, for example, Lashley et al. (2007) and Lynch (1999).

This ambiguity could give rise to tensions if host–guest expectations were mismatched (Lashley 2000a: 11). In these circumstances, feeling rules employed by the host to maintain the relationship did not necessarily elicit the expected response from the guest. This could trigger negative feelings in hosts, affecting how they reacted to the guest, and thus putting the host–guest relationship in jeopardy. In one example in this study, a host who seemed friendly, accommodating and professional experienced an incident that tested her ability to maintain her composure and contain her indignation. A couple from a strict religious group booked to stay for a few days and asked if there might be 'some room' in the fridge for 'a little food'. The hotelier was happy to do what she could to oblige. However, she felt the boundaries of the host–guest relationship were severely breached when a refrigerated lorry appeared with enough pallets of plated meals to feed a whole family for several days. The couple had assumed she had room to store this food, that they could use the microwave to reheat the meals when required, and that it was 'OK' to invite the rest of the family to eat with them. The host felt these guests had abused the 'home' element of her hotel and had taken liberties that strained the prevailing social order (Lashley 2000a), pushing her need for emotional labour to unreasonable limits. This example also illustrates the tensions that can arise in home-hotel hybrids when cultural traditions are misunderstood or in conflict (Selwyn 2000).

Commercial domain

As well as the influence of private hospitality, not surprisingly, this study also revealed that hosts' commercial motives had a significant effect on the host–guest relationship. These motives were shaped by hosts' reasons for running the business and their personal circumstances. One host, for example, bought a hotel to avoid living on benefits and so had to take whatever guests she could to make a living, whilst another had left a successful career to run a hotel as much as a lifestyle choice as a need or desire to make money (Getz and Carlsen 2000). What is interesting is that whatever the business motive, hosts exerted considerable control over relationships with guests. They did this in different ways, adapting their use of emotional labour to suit both their circumstances and clientele. In the latter case, for example, the hotelier could 'pick and choose' whom to take, and indeed whether or not to take any guests at all if he felt like some time off. However, in the first example, the host had to take anyone, from students and asylum seekers to stag and hen parties. This (necessary) business strategy inevitably brought with it all manner of unsavoury characters and unwelcome behaviours. To cope with this the host deliberately cultivated an 'act' to manage guest behaviours by whatever means necessary, to protect her home and livelihood. She admitted that this was 'definitely not me', but that the act was essential to maintain her business. Her interactions with guests could be aggressive and involve bad language to communicate her expectations and elicit desired responses;

keeping out 'undesirables' and avoiding damage to her property. 'Get out of my f***ing hotel' was not unknown for this hotelier. She was uncomfortable with this use of emotional labour, but felt it necessary to survive.

It was also evident in this study that hosts had to employ emotional labour to manage the 'dirty' work that is characteristic of commercial hospitality (Guerrier and Adib 2000: 261). However, 'dirty work' as such was not perceived as a major problem or a reason to dislike the work. Rather, it was the circumstances in which it arose that tended to cause disquiet, where guests transgressed social boundaries that the host understood to prevail. For example, relatives of elderly guests sometimes booked them in without telling the hotelier that the guest was incontinent. In one case the host felt physically sick from the stench that greeted her every day she had to clean the room for an entire fortnight. Dealing with this situation demanded heavy investment in emotional labour. The host's feelings of exploitation were clearly evident; recounting this story, she could barely disguise her disgust and alluded to feeling nauseous just reliving the events. Hence hosts' attitudes toward the 'dirty' side of the work seemed to be much more about feeling 'violated' within the host–guest relationship than about a view of the work itself. Typically, such transgressions resulted in 'house rules' being tightened in future. For example, a number of hosts reported that once they had experienced stag party guests wetting beds and breaking furniture, they refused to take such groups again unless they signed a 'bond' agreeing to pay for any damage.

However, the sense of abuse felt by hosts confronted by such situations appeared heightened if the 'dirty work' that was expected also seemed to be gendered. One female host for example, was 'outraged' when a male guest presented her with a bag of personal washing, saying 'Can you run these through for me love?' Prevailing feeling rules were challenged; this was not how she expected a guest to behave. She used emotional labour autonomously and 'put him firmly in his place', leaving him in no doubt as to how she felt about his (unreasonable) request. The guest may have considered this emotional display inappropriate but the host was not prepared to tolerate such treatment, even though the guest was paying. However, sometimes the guest appeared to wrest control from the host; as one host commented when greeted by a room left filthy by a 'nice family', 'What do they think I am?' Hence guest behaviours could sometimes leave hosts feeling indignant at the violation of themselves and their home, evoking emotions of anger and hurt. Overall, however, commercial hosts in this study appeared to retain considerable control over their home and business, using emotional labour in whatever way they deemed appropriate.

Conclusions

This discussion illustrates how commercial home hosts in this study adeptly operated within and across the social, private and commercial domains of hospitality (Lashley 2000a), to manage their own and guests' expectations of appropriate behaviour in their home. They achieved this by tailoring their use of emotional labour to suit their particular circumstances and clientele. Employing emotional labour in this flexible and autonomous manner to protect the home and business distinguishes its use in the commercial home from its ubiquitous employment in the corporate hospitality sector (Hochschild 1983; Ritzer 2007). These behaviours by commercial home hosts were in turn shaped by their own and guests' perceptions of the 'home' element of the home-hotel hybrid (Di Domenico and Lynch 2007). This is to be expected given the integral nature of 'the home' to the commercial home concept (Lynch 2005a). Controlling access to the business was commonplace; assessing 'strangers' and keeping out 'undesirables' who might violate the home, whilst at the same time welcoming guests judged to be respectful admirers of what is being provided. Hosts' freedom to select paying guests to share their home in this way, and their management of relationships with those guests, distinguishes the commercial home from the traditional hotel paradigm.

10 The cave-homes of Göreme

Performing tourism hospitality in gendered space

Hazel Tucker

Introduction

> Kelebek Pension has a wonderful location, right in the heart of Göreme's historic old village, with spectacular views looking out towards Uchisar and Cavusin. Until 1993 Kelebek was my family home, and like most homes in Göreme, it was made of a mixture of cave rooms and stone-arched rooms which had been added later. Today the pension has 16 rooms, some of them in the fairy chimneys, some in caves and some of them in the traditional arched rooms where my family used to live ... We hope you will enjoy trying out the cave lifestyle with us ...
>
> (Kelebek Hotel)

Commercial homes can arguably represent 'the quintessential *place* of modernity' as they can be associated with authenticity and 'the reinvention of a kind of local identity' (Lynch et al. 2007: 124). Indeed, as tourism has developed in the region surrounding Göreme in central Turkey since the 1980s, local entrepreneurs have developed the use of their cave-homes, in their representation of local place and identity, as tourist accommodation establishments and as tourist attractions. There are two clearly differentiated types of commercial home production in Göreme. The main use of the cave-houses as 'commercial homes' is as cave-*pansiyon*s ('*pansiyon*' is the Turkish word for the term 'pension' more commonly used throughout southern Europe), or guesthouses and, in these, tourists are mainly hosted by local men as it is these men who own and operate the tourist accommodation establishments. The other type of commercial home in Göreme is more in line with Lynch and MacWhannell's (2000) idea of 'backdrop' homes, referring to the use of houses as visitor attractions. Importantly, it is the women of the village who, whilst being largely separated from the mainstream business of hosting tourists in *pansiyon*s, have embarked on the more informal entrepreneurial activity of showing their private cave-house to tourists in the hope of selling them handicraft items.

Based on my ethnographic fieldwork and long-term involvement in Göreme village, this chapter discusses tourist interest in the cave-houses and focuses in particular on how villager men and women, differentially, have responded to this interest by performing a 'cave-dweller' identity within their home-space. By discussing the two types of 'commercial (cave) home' in Göreme, the chapter is intended to highlight the gender influences on the way in which home-identity is performed for tourists in the 'commercial home' context. The chapter thus contributes to theory concerning the gendered nature both of tourism hospitality and of hospitality spaces.

Gendered space, home and commercial hospitality

The interrelationship between gender, home and tourism hospitality has been considered with regard to a variety of settings (for example, Bouquet 1982; Garcia-Ramon et al. 1995; Ireland 1993; Long and Wall 1995), establishing the point that performances of hospitality within the commercial home are indeed highly gendered (Darke and Gurney 2000). However, much of the research linking gender and tourism production has focused on gender roles and the sexual division of labour, emphasising the prescriptive nature of gender norms to explain how these norms have either prevented women from participating equally with men in the tourism workplace (e.g. Harvey et al. 1995; Levy and Lerch 1991; Long and Kindon 1997; Scott 1997; Wilkinson and Prativi 1995) or, alternatively, have allowed women to earn extra income by engaging in 'domestic' work in small and micro tourism hospitality enterprises (Bouquet 1982; Garcia-Ramon et al. 1995; Gibson 2001; Long and Wall 1995). What these latter studies drew attention to is that it is traditional gender roles, and particularly the division of labour by gender, which in large part have enabled women to participate in small-scale, and especially rural, commercial home entrepreneurial activity, precisely because such work does not compromise women's other (re)productive duties within the household (Long and Kindon 1997; Stringer 1991).

Few studies, to date, have considered the part that gendered *spatial* separation has to play in commercial home production activities nor have they focused on the part that gendered relations within home-space play in the commercial home (Tucker 2007). Whilst Saunders (1990) has argued that men and women view the home in essentially the same way, this being as a haven for relaxation and loving relationships, Darke (1994), in contrast, has argued that gender differentiation is inevitable since 'home' is so integrally bound up with identity and the 'self'. Further to this, Darke (1994) argues that women feel a strong sense of ambivalence towards the meaning of home because, while home represents for women the burden of work, their work in the home and consequently the home itself can be a strong source of identity, pride and satisfaction.

Furthermore, the question of whether the notion of 'home' is more closely associated with the house in which ones lives or the wider place or country to which one belongs might itself be gender-related. As Immerfall (1998) notes, home is inevitably bound to place because 'home' is the moment in time and space in which the creation of individual identity, social relations and collective meanings are created. If one were to also draw upon Simmel's (1983) understanding of home as the focal point of particular kinds of relations, then home has a necessary spatial dimension according to the 'spatial extension' of those particular forms of relations gathered around each person (Nowicka 2007). For example, if 'domestic'/'private' space and 'public' space are constructed as differential focal points of interaction for men and women, then the home meanings associated with the domestic/private house versus those associated with the wider (more public) place in which the house is located will also differ between men and women.

As the chapter will go on to make clear, in Göreme society the *domestic* space of the house is clearly women's place for the majority of the day whilst the place for men during the day time is the *public* space of the village such as the village centre, businesses and the tea-house. It therefore follows that women's identity and associations of 'home' are closely aligned with the domestic space of her house, whereas men's identity and associations of 'home' are more attached to the wider (public) place of Göreme village. As the chapter will go on to discuss, this point has particular implications for the ways in which men and women in Göreme differentially perform 'home' in the commercial home context.

The issue of the gendered demarcation between a 'public' and a 'private'/ 'domestic' sphere has long gained considerable attention in feminist anthropology (e.g. Ardener 1981; Buitelaar 1998; Rosaldo and Lamphere 1974) and cultural geography (Blunt and Rose 1994; Massey 1994; Mills 2005). For example, it is common knowledge that social organisation in Muslim countries such as Turkey is primarily based on a sexual division of space (Buitelaar 1998). Indeed, there is in Göreme society, in accordance with Islamic codes and practice (Delaney 1991), strict segregation of the sexes with a well-defined distribution of economic and social activity according to gender (Tucker 2003a). Göreme village is divided into residential quarters (*mahalle*) which surround the village centre (*çarşa*) and, as mentioned above, the centre of the village is primarily considered public and thus male space. These days, also, the village centre is the main tourism business area of the village and, since it is inappropriate for women to spend any time in that area, they are largely excluded from the tourism business domain in the village. It is therefore in the ideological social and spatial gender separation in Göreme that tourism work and tourism hospitality are highly gendered.

When looking at the interrelationship between the home, gender and commercial hospitality, therefore, it is crucial to include consideration of how the gendered *spatial* divisions between the public and domestic spheres interact with the spatial processes of tourism and hospitality. This chapter does this by discussing the ways in which Göreme men and women, differentially, have come to use their cave-homes as tourism hospitality establishments. Firstly, the chapter introduces tourist interest in the cave-homes through a description of the Göreme area and tourism development there. This is followed by a discussion of the development and use of the cave-houses as tourist accommodation establishments, or *pansiyon*s, and the men's hosting performances within those tourist accommodation spaces. The next section goes on to focus on the Göreme women's performances of a 'cave-dweller' identity through their informal entrepreneurial activity in their (private) cave-homes.

Tourist interest in 'cave-houses'

The area of Göreme and the wider region known as Cappadocia consists of soft volcanic rock which has gradually eroded to form valleys filled with natural columns and cones, which are locally termed 'fairy chimneys'. For centuries, the sides of the valleys and the fairy chimneys have been carved and hollowed to form dwellings, stables and places of worship that still pattern the villages in the area today. Tourism has derived from and perpetuated an aesthetic valuing of the rock cones and caves of Cappadocia, serving to promote their preservation along with the cave-dwelling lifestyle of the 'troglodytes' who inhabit them (Tucker 2003a). Embedded in the volcanic landscape, also, are Byzantine monastic remains, including numerous thousand year old churches carved out of the rock. This Christian heritage was the focus of the Göreme area's designation in 1985 as a UNESCO World Heritage Site. The cave-churches together with the contemporary cave-dwelling way of life in the villages also led to the creation of the Göreme National Park at that time.

In the wider Cappadocia region tourism developed fairly rapidly during the latter part of the 1980s, with some towns seeing the construction of large-scale hotels to accommodate the increasing 'mass cultural tourism' in the area. However, Göreme village, with its population of approximately 2,000 permanent inhabitants, is situated in the heart of the Göreme National Park and developed a reputation as a 'backpacker' place, with small accommodation and other tourism-related businesses that cater mostly to the independent traveller market. Tucker (2003a) has previously discussed these tourists' apparent Romantic search for a simple and pre-modern world in the Cappadocia villages. This Romantic search is met most conclusively in the notion of people still living in caves, and the mostly independent tourists staying in Göreme spend much of their time wandering through the back streets to gaze at the 'troglodyte' village life, as well as walking in the valleys which surround Göreme village exploring and clambering in and out of the caves and churches they find there.

Repeatedly seeing the visiting tourists' fascination with the caves, the people of Göreme came to appreciate the value of the caves and the opportunity to sell tourists the chance to become cave-dwellers themselves. In the early days of tourism development, they started offering accommodation in rooms of their cave-houses and the cave-houses were thus slowly turned into '*pansiyon*'. In 1984 there were three cave-house *pansiyon*s in the village. Throughout the late 1980s and early 1990s, increasing numbers of Göreme villagers became aware of the aesthetic and economic value of their cave-houses and associated 'cave-life' and decided to refit their family home to be suitable for tourist accommodation. In addition, many of the older, crumbling cave-houses that were previously abandoned were reclaimed by the families who originally lived in them to be restored and turned into *pansiyons*. By the mid-1990s, there were approximately fifty cave-house *pansiyons* in the village (Tucker 2003a). Just as Di Domenico and Lynch (2007a: 121) have pointed out that the internal dwelling spaces of the (commercial) home reflect and embody the external space surrounding the home, the cave-*pansiyons* of Göreme embody the very vernacular housing style of Göreme and the wider Cappadocia region.

Approximately fifty cave-house accommodation establishments exist through to today, with many having become increasingly up-market. A survey of the *pansiyons* conducted in 2005 showed that approximately 20 were still at the cheaper end and were clearly aimed at the lower-budget backpacker traveller, with dormitory rooms and backpacker cave-bars. Another 20 were in the mid-range aimed at the slightly higher budget and perhaps more mature, independent traveller. The remaining 8 or so had been renovated to become what could be termed 'boutique' hotel-*pansiyons*, with such additions as en-suite spa (cave) bathrooms, terrace restaurants and swimming pools. Many of these establishments now have their own websites, a certain selection of them have also long been advertised in the variety of independent travellers guidebooks, and all *pansiyons* have a promotional display panel in the bus station in the centre of the village. Advertisements highlight their 'traditional' cave rooms and their breakfast-terraces overlooking views of the village and the fairy chimneys, as the promotional extract at the start of this chapter together with the following one show:

> Cave Hotel Saksagan is an old house built into fairy chimneys, which has been restored in 1998. The hotel offers you the warmness of your own home in Göreme, with rooms that present you history, nature and culture together. Saksagan Hotel provides a super view overlooking Göreme. Rooms are located within fairy-chimneys and carved into rocks. All rooms are clean and spacious, and decorated in the Ottoman Style ... Breakfast is served on the terrace, with its magical view, or in the garden accompanied by birds in song ...
>
> (Cave Hotel Saksagan)

The *pansiyon* accommodation in Göreme fits perfectly with the expectations of the independent traveller market for various reasons. First, the *pansiyons* are small-scale tourism businesses and so allow the tourists to indulge in the idea that they are not participating in 'mass' tourist activity. They also allow the tourists to meet with other like-minded travellers to swap tales of their travels and to experience an important sense of community in their travelling. Most importantly, though, since most of the *pansiyons* are set in converted cave-houses, Göreme's *pansiyon*s are suitably 'other' and consistent with the place, allowing tourists to engage in the fantasy that they are also, for a time, cave people. In line with Di Domenico and Lynch's (2007a) discussion of Scottish place-identity being reflected in bed and breakfast establishments in Scotland, Göreme's cave-*pansiyon*s clearly reflect the place-identity inherent in the tourist gaze on Göreme and the wider Cappadocia region.

The first of the cave-*pansiyon*s established in Göreme were developed by local families deciding to rent out rooms in their family home to tourists. These establishments became 'family *pansiyon*' accommodation, with wives and daughters involved in the daily running of the business. However, because of the gendered spatial separation in Göreme society, as tourism grew and the *pansiyon*s became more developed, the family unit tended to be moved into another house. This was in order that the original cave-home could be turned completely over to tourist accommodation and, importantly, to ensure that the women of the household were appropriately separated from the 'public' tourism arena. In other words, the cave-houses that were turned into *pansiyon*s were no longer considered 'domestic' space and therefore were inappropriate spaces for women to be present. Women were thus largely excluded from participating in the hosting of tourists in what were previously their cave-homes, whilst men became the key tourism hospitality providers. In the above-mentioned survey of *pansiyon* accommodation in 2005, of the 50 or so establishments only five were advertised as 'family-*pansiyon*s' with mention of the hosting family.

Men's hosting performances in cave-*pansiyon*s

Since women have generally been excluded from *pansiyon*s, the owner-operators have tended to employ one or more 'boys' (often a younger relative of the owner-operator) to conduct the house-keeping and kitchen work (but see Tucker 2007 for a discussion of women beginning to be employed in the larger, more established of the *pansiyon*s in recent years). This process has allowed the men running these commercial homes to decode their old cave-houses as domestic (and thus feminine) space and to recode them as public and masculine space. For the villagers in general, consequently, *pansiyon*s have become 'male space', where men can play as well as work.

To compound this, the usual construction of village houses is such that rooms are set around a courtyard which is separated from the road by a high wall. This wall is intended to clearly separate domestic from public space and to maintain the privacy of the women inside. *Pansiyon*s which are formed out of the original cave-houses are therefore also walled and separated from everyday village life. The common area of the *pansiyon*s where tourists eat breakfast, drink beer and commune with other tourists is usually situated in the courtyard area, with tourists also having access to upper-level roof terraces in order that they can enjoy the view of the village life below and the valleys beyond. *Pansiyon*s are thus set up so that tourists can see out but people outside of the *pansiyon* cannot see in, and so activities that take place within the *pansiyon* are, in many respects, 'private' to the *pansiyon*.

So whilst these businesses are places of work for the Göreme men, they are also spatially separated from other aspects of village life. The *pansiyon*s therefore act as *liminal* zones which provide new contexts in which the men are relatively free from the village way of life and village rules. This idea was expressed in an interview with a village entrepreneur when asked how he felt when in his *pansiyon*:

> It's like a free zone – I can't walk in shorts on the street but I can here. So I must be careful to change when I go back into Göreme. I can't walk with a girlfriend through Göreme holding hands, so I'm happier here – I feel more free ...

The men who host tourists in the *pansiyon*s thus experience some sort of suspension of normal life, free to an extent from the usual rules and able to join in with the play of tourism. This sense of being apart from the village life whilst in the *pansiyon*s is compounded by the point that, during the summer tourist season at least, the men work very long hours and often sleep in their businesses. During the summer, they may rarely go 'home' to their family, even if that home is only some metres away from their business. While there are some negative aspects in their experience of being 'outside' of the village while hosting tourists in *pansiyon* accommodation, the men invariably enjoy being able to join in the play of tourism. For many local men, and depending on their age, *pansiyon*s represent a free zone where they can drink beer, meet (and sometimes sleep with) tourist girls, and generally hide from the watchful eye of their elders.

Among the non-'family-*pansiyon*s', beyond the fact that they are obviously in an original cave-house, it is variable as to the extent to which they are explicitly performed as the hosts' original cave-*home*. It is noteworthy to mention here that as tourism developed into the late 1990s and 2000s, many of the original *pansiyon* owner-operators went into retirement and rented their *pansiyon* out to younger male entrepreneurs from the village, often a nephew or other relative. The guests' experience may thus become even further removed from the idea that the *pansiyon* is the host's old cave-'home'. However, even these younger hosts are still hosting guests in their 'home-village' and it is the close, unmediated contact between hosts and guests that, more than anything else, provides tourists with experiences of local identity and a sense of being 'hosted' in the villagers' home. Furthermore, because men's place and focal point of interaction is within the public spaces of the village, men are far more likely than women to identify the wider village, beyond the domestic house and neighbourhood, as 'home'. Their performances of 'home' in the *pansiyon*s are therefore based on the wider place of Göreme rather than just the (cave-) house.

These performances inevitably include the play of being 'troglodytes' in a cave-land fantasy (Tucker 2001, 2002). Together with the tourists, the Göreme men play and experiment with their own identities, engaging in an ironic play on touristic representations concerning their cavey identity. Indeed, one Göreme man named his *pansiyon* 'Flintstones *Pansiyon*', after the cartoon comedy anachronistically depicting cave-dwelling people living out a modern lifestyle in a pre-historic cave-land environment. Many other businesses follow the same theme, with names such as 'Troglodyte *Pansiyon*', 'Rock Valley *Pansiyon*', and the 'Flintstones Cave Bar'. Again, these performances relate to Di Domenico and Lynch's (2007a) discussion of how hospitality performances in commercial homes often entail performances of the external place in the inside 'stage' of the commercial home. For many tourists, Göreme has become a fantasy-land of caves and troglodytes, where tourists can stay in a cave room and be hosted by a local troglodyte who chats to them about how he was born and brought up in a cave.

Rather than these performances portraying a 'traditional' identity of the Göreme men in a feminized 'Other' sense (see Morgan and Pritchard 1998; van Eeden 2007), however, since the performances of the troglodyte identity are carried out through the idiom of fun and irony, the men are simultaneously playing to and *resisting* the 'pre-modern' cave-man representations of themselves in tourist discourse and official rhetoric (Tucker 2002, 2003a). This process is largely helped by the point that, through their hospitality in the commercial cave-homes, the men are firmly established as 'hosts' to the tourist guests visiting *their* village. The power of the hospitable host is an established element of the social dimensions of hospitality (Heal 1990; Robinson and Lynch 2006; Sant Cassia 1999; Tucker 2003b), and as Tucker (2003a: 128) has previously remarked, '*pansiyon*s are spaces where tourists' behaviours and attitudes can be controlled by villagers'. As well as the obligation to behave in certain appropriate ways in the village and to follow up on hosts' recommendations concerning which restaurants, carpet shop and tour agency in the village to patronise, the close, unmediated contact between host and guests in the *pansiyon*s also enables the hosts to work their meetings with tourists free from the underpinnings of inequality encoded in the tourist gaze.

Women's cave-home-based entrepreneurship

As outlined above, there exists in Göreme a spatial and social duality with the women's domain centred in and around the household and tourism business and the central area of the village almost entirely the domain of men (Tucker 2003a, 2007). Despite urban women in Turkey enjoying increasing levels of equality and participation in the workforce (Kandiyoti 2002; Sönmez 2001), Göreme and the wider Cappadocia region remains a pocket of social ultra-conservatism more widely associated with the Islamic Middle East. As tourism has developed there, tourism work has been considered a man's activity, with women generally only being able to access the tourism economy indirectly through the earnings of their husband or other male family members.

Being separated from the tourism domain, the village women have largely continued to engage in garden-agriculture and other 'household' and reproductive duties. The women themselves and the cave-houses they inhabit have thus come to represent the 'traditional' in Göreme, and some women have capitalised on this point through engaging in informal entrepreneurial activity by inviting tourists in to view their cave-house and then attempting to sell them handicrafts they had made. These entrepreneurial activities began during the late 1980s and early 1990s with a few women who live on the outskirts of the village having arrangements with tour guides to bring their bus groups of international tourists to visit their house (Tucker 2003a). The guide always showed the group around the cave-house with the help of the woman as prop and then the tourists were shown a selection of handicrafts in the hope that they would buy some. Now this practice has spread so that many women living throughout the village have started inviting passing tourists in to visit their cave-house.

As mentioned above, the entrepreneurial activities of these women fit with Lynch and MacWhannell's (2000) concept of the 'backdrop' commercial home, whereby the house becomes a visitor attraction. In Göreme, the attraction is visiting a 'real' cave-house. Tourists' acceptance of such invitations is likely to stem from a desire to experience a perceived 'authentically social' (Selwyn 1996). Moreover, the fact that these encounters are generally experienced as serendipitous for the tourists adds to the perception that they are 'authentic' encounters (Tucker 2003a). The visits generally involve the tourists being shown various rooms in the house and, of particular interest, are usually the kitchen and food storage caves in which 'traditional' food preparation practices can be seen. The tourists are also usually invited to sit for a while to drink Turkish coffee or eat some fruit, and then the 'hostess' brings out some handicrafts, usually knitted or embroidered items, which tourists feel obliged to buy. Whilst, by the end of the encounter, tourists usually feel that they have succeeded in getting 'backstage' into a villager's home, tourists often come away with a sense of ambivalence about their encounter, feeling both satisfied at having seen a 'real' village cave-home but also discomfort and the sense that they were duped into buying something (Tucker 2009).

The village women inviting tourists into their homes also feel a sense of ambivalence towards their entrepreneurial activities. First, there is much gossip around the village about this activity and how the women's waiting on their doorstep for tourists to pass was akin to begging. As one elderly woman told me, 'It's more than shameful. I could never do that. If you are going to work, go and work like a person.' There is also likely to be ambivalence relating to the meanings of 'home' for these women. If home for women is the site of work and of the mundane and the prosaic, then performing home as an 'attraction' is likely to be fragile and difficult. Related to this, in Göreme there is ambivalence surrounding the meanings of 'tradition' that the women, in association with their cave-houses, represent for tourists. The women are largely aware that they should be and are performing the 'traditional' Other to tourists. However, they simultaneously desire to escape the traditional identity placed upon them by the tourist gaze and are actually far more proud of the automatic washing machine or microwave they may have than the earthenware pots storing home-made bulgar wheat in their cave-kitchen. Drawing upon Aitchison (2000), van Eeden (2007: 193) has pointed out the gendered dimensions of Orientalist discourse, arguing that Orientalism has constructed women as Other and the feminised object of the male colonial (and tourist) gaze. The Göreme women's ambivalence in their commercial home performances shows a desire to resist that objectifying gaze.

This resistance is, to some degree, achieved through their commercial home activities, with their performances of their cave-homes, like the men's performances, inevitably involving a negotiation between representing a 'traditional' identity for tourists and yet at the same time emerging from that identity. The way in which this simultaneous process occurs is quite different for the women and the men, however. In the women's case, it is simply because the encounters involve the women interacting with tourists that they are empowered as 'host' to these outsiders. Their home is *their* space and the tourism production they are participating in is of their making and choosing. The women engaging in this type of entrepreneurial activity acknowledge that they would not be able to work in tourism other than doing this sort of activity because they would not obtain permission from their husband to work in the 'public' sphere. Having their cave-house as an attraction and selling handicrafts from home therefore provides them with an opportunity that they would otherwise not have to engage with the tourism economy and to earn some money of their own. Since tourism activity has entered what is otherwise considered domestic space, these spaces are reconfigured through commercial home hospitality and thus the gender identities they produce are also being reconfigured.

Conclusions

This chapter has discussed the provision of tourism hospitality in the gendered space of the cave-houses of Göreme in central Turkey, showing the different ways in which the cave-houses have been performed by men and women in their 'commercial home' performances. The chapter has also shown how, when discussing the relation of gender to the commercial home, as well as considerations relating to gender roles and the division of labour, it is important to consider the gendered meanings associated with 'domestic'/ 'private' space and, in converse, 'public' space. In Göreme society, because of strict gender segregation whereby women have no *place* in public space, the 'public' spaces of tourism business are male domain. Thus, as the cave-houses of Göreme became turned into tourist accommodation establishments, the space of the cave-*pansiyon*s became 'public', and therefore male space, and men became the main 'hosts' in these commercial homes.

Related to these spatial dimensions, the importance of considering the ways in which the meaning of home in itself is spatially gendered has also been highlighted. That is, the meaning of home can differ between men and women concerning the extent to which the locus of home-meaning is the *house* or the wider *place*. In Göreme, because women's place is always in the realms of domestic space, the 'house' is the focus of home. In contrast, men's place, during the day time at least, is away from the house and its associated domesticity and so the locus of significant interaction and identity formation for men is the wider public space of the village. It follows that the men's performances of 'home' within the commercial cave-homes of Göreme, rather than being performances of the domestic cave-house per se, are performances of the cave identity of the wider village. Well aware of the importance that tourists place upon the unique cave qualities of Göreme, the tourism entrepreneurs explicitly perform these qualities *together with* the tourists in the commercial home spaces of their cave-*pansiyon*s. By performing this cave-identity through the idioms both of hospitality and irony, moreover, the men manage simultaneously to play to and resist the 'pre-modern' cave-man representation of themselves encoded in the tourist gaze.

In contrast, the home-performances of the Göreme women in their commercial home enterprises come far closer to the feminized 'pre-modern' Other represented as the object of the tourist gaze. Furthermore, in contrast to the men, the women are less able to resist the objectifying tourist gaze through their hospitality performances. This is because home-performances for the women combine with home-meanings that relate the home to the prosaic, the mundane and to the burden of domestic work. Performing their cave-homes as tourist 'attractions' is for women, therefore, shrouded in ambivalence.

However, these commercial home entrepreneurial activities are also shifting the boundaries between 'public' and 'domestic' meanings associated with both the 'house' and 'home'. The provision of commercial home hospitality in what is otherwise considered the domestic space of the house works, to an extent, to reconfigure this space as public space, thus affording women the opportunity to reconfigure their subject position within that space. For the men, what was previously the domestic space of the cave-house becomes public/tourism space, but also private/liminal space separated from the rest of the village. In these liminal spaces, the men are able to playfully perform their cave-home of Göreme village *for* tourists and also *together with* tourists. Hence, this discussion has shown not only that the provision of commercial home hospitality in the cave-houses of Göreme village is overtly gendered, but also how the gendered space of 'home' can be reconstructed and re-inhabited precisely through that provision of commercial home hospitality to tourists.

11 Rural dimensions of the commercial home

Elisabeth Kastenholz and Marion Sparrer

Introduction

In this chapter light will be shed on the 'commercial home' concept in the rural context in three European regions. If we understand a 'commercial home' as a type of accommodation where visitors pay to stay in private homes and where interaction takes place with a host and/or family usually living upon the premises (Lynch 2005c), this type of establishment is frequently encountered in the rural setting.

The rural 'commercial home' may be a working farm, where the home concept has to be confronted with two different types of economic activities simultaneously reflecting different lifestyles: tourism and agriculture. Rural tourism establishments must additionally be understood in the context of a wider local economic and social structure of a community, i.e. as potential development tools. This feature and the associated public expectations also impact on the type of 'commercial homes' and corresponding tourist experiences that characterise this tourism form and naturally go beyond the home-based accommodation experience. Rural tourism and the associated products, services and experiences differ from country to country, from region to region and from establishment to establishment.

The aim of this chapter is to analyse the rural tourism commercial home construct in three different countries/regions, namely in Portugal, Spain (Galicia/A Coruña) and Northern Germany (Frisia/Wittmund), attempting a comparison that will help clarify different concepts of the 'commercial home' and how it contributes to a more complex rural tourism product by providing quite distinct experiences to both visitors and hosts. The three countries/regions were selected for this study because of the different levels and directions of development of rural tourism present. The data about Galicia and Frisia result from Sparrer's PhD research (2005) whilst the data on Portugal integrates results from several studies (Kastenholz 2002; Ribeiro 2003; Silva 2006; Silvano 2005). Sparrer's (2005) qualitative research project was undertaken in 2002 and 2003, and included in-depth interviews conducted with the owners of rural accommodations in Wittmund and A Coruña, as well as a survey of guests (mainly domestic tourists) during the summer of 2002, aiming at eliciting opinions, perceptions and motivations of demand and supply. Kastenholz's (2002) study was a survey financed by the Regional Coordination Commission of North Portugal (CCRN), with the objective of analysing the tourist market in rural areas in the region. Through a carefully chosen cluster-sampling procedure, conducted at diverse attraction sites and tourist facilities at different points in time (88 per cent of the tourists were directly addressed), a total of 2,280 valid responses were obtained. The sample was controlled for a balanced spread between the sub-regions, high and low season and the national versus foreign tourist market. The most important foreign nationalities were the German, British, French, Dutch and Spanish markets. Respondents tended towards the younger age ranges and higher educational levels.

The main purpose of this chapter is to analyse the rural tourism realities encountered in the three studied regions, giving particular attention to the host–guest relationship that is typically associated with the rural tourism experience and the degree to which it is valued and sought by both hosts and guests. Additionally, the degree to which this relationship extends the home-context to further include the guests' integration into the rural community is analysed. Differences encountered are discussed, in light of the diverse types and degrees of development of the rural tourism business in each region, shaped by distinct legal, social and economic contexts.

The meaning and significance of rural tourism

Rural tourism may be defined very broadly as the entire tourism activity in a rural area (Keane 1992; OECD 1994) or else as a quite specific tourism form or product, closely related to and motivated by features of 'rurality'. An example is 'agri-tourism', which may be considered a specific segment within rural tourism (Wilson et al. 2001). Lane (1994) suggests that rural tourism is that which is: located in rural areas; functionally rural; rural in scale; traditional in character, organically and slowly growing; and controlled by local people. If the last condition is fulfilled, Keane (1992) suggested using the term 'rural community tourism', where tourism development takes place in an integrated and coordinated manner at the local level.

The significance of rural tourism for the development of rural areas may be outstanding, due to potentially significant multiplier effects (Walmsley 2003). Additionally, tourists may increase the areas' attractiveness in the eyes of the local population, enhancing their pride and self-esteem (Kastenholz 2004). Correspondingly, rural tourism, through promoting endogenous development based on natural and cultural heritage, may contribute to the preservation of heritage as well as to the retention of residents in poorly developed rural areas (Lane 1994; Gannon 1994; OECD 1994). That is why rural tourism, if carefully planned, managed and marketed, may significantly enhance economic, social and cultural development (Page and Getz 1997). This potential role of tourism justifies the European Community's efforts to financially support tourism projects in rural areas (Sparrer 2005).

However, tourism should not be considered a panacea to solve all problems of any rural area (Walmsley 2003). The potential of rural tourism to act as a development tool depends on the quality of a region's attractions, services and facilities, as well as on the way these resources are managed, integrated into an overall appealing and distinct rural tourism destination and the way this global product is promoted and made available to the most interested (and interesting) market segments (Kastenholz 2004; Sparrer 2005). These markets' choices are increasingly determined by 'lifestyle-led consumption-oriented' leisure and tourism behaviour, that may be well accommodated in the rural space, commodified as a symbolic setting for a post-modern 'lifestyle-oriented tourism industry' (Walmsley 2003) and provided by 'lifestyle entrepreneurs' (Ateljevic and Doorne 2000).

In this context, the personalised encounter that is provided in rural accommodation units between hosts, as representatives of 'the local people and culture', and guests may play a central role for the quality of the tourist experience (Tucker 2003b). This encounter should be considered the basis of a more complete rural tourism product, to which the concept of the 'commercial home' is particularly applicable. The resulting relationship is frequently sought as a 'means to sharing the hosts' culture, hospitality and local knowledge', although guests may have 'negative feelings of restriction and obligation' from intense social exchanges, while 'hosts themselves may experience a sense of invasion of privacy' (Tucker 2003b: 88). Consequently, the right balance between social exchange and autonomy/privacy is needed, where the commercial dimension might help maintain a certain distance and independence of both parties involved. However, there are different rural tourism realities that should also condition this quality of experience, as shown in the following cases from three European countries.

Concepts of rural tourism in Galicia (Spain), Portugal and Frisia (Germany)

Portugal is not well known as a rural tourist destination and rural tourism, as a legally defined form of accommodation ('turismo em espaço rural' = TER), has only existed there since 1984. EC structural funds, the European LEADER programme and Portuguese Tourism Authorities have significantly contributed to the development of this product.

The Portuguese legislation explicitly refers to some of the features generally considered characteristic of the 'commercial home', defining TER as 'a combination of paid activities and services provided in rural areas, in establishments with family character ... aiming at offering a complete and diversified tourism product in rural areas ... being appropriately integrated in the localities where they are situated, so as to preserve, restore and value the regions' architectural, historic, natural and landscape heritage' (Dec.-Lei n° 54/2002).

TER modalities, in which the 'commercial home' concept is most visible, include Turismo de Habitação (TH) in manor houses or palaces with high-quality architecture, equipment and furniture, which is offered by families living in these buildings; Turismo Rural (TR) offered by families in typical rustic family houses; Agroturismo (AT), which is integrated in a functioning farm and where guests may participate in agriculture; and Country houses (Casas de Campo) which are private rustic houses or huts which may or not be situated in a rural or natural setting.

TER units provide breakfast, as well as other meals if demanded, unless there is a restaurant close by. These meals should be traditional local cuisine and prepared using regional products. A series of information must be made available to guests, such as about services provided, medical facilities, public transportation, but also concerning tourist attractions, traditions and the cultural and natural heritage of the region. All of this underlines the hosts' role in integrating their guests into the wider rural destination and community. An interesting aspect is the fact that legislation requires a clear specification of the frontiers between the private and the public space, in order to reduce ambiguity and tensions inherent in the 'commercial home setting'. Such tensions have been previously identified by Tucker (2003b) in the case of small, family-run commercial homes studied in New Zealand.

Silva (2006) distinguishes between two types of TER accommodation: one more sophisticated, associated to aristocracy, and visible in manor houses and palaces. The other formats, reflecting the majority of supply, correspond to country houses, with traces of regionally typical architecture and decoration. These formats try to reproduce the environment of the richer rural inhabitants, further including a series of ethnographic symbols, idealised as 'authentic' features of a rural way of life whilst being embedded in a comfortable modern accommodation arrangement. Symbolic decor not only represents a general 'rural lifestyle', but is carefully chosen by TER owners and hence reveals their interpretation of this lifestyle as well as their personal preferences when linking rural traditions to what they perceive as a beautiful and comfortable home. This decor thereby signals hosts' emotional engagement, that is still present in their absence (Lynch 2000c).

The TER legislation further suggests that 'complementary activities' are included, based on the provision of equipment permitting outdoors sports such as swimming, tennis and horse riding. Additionally, the owners and managers of these establishments may organise tours, the sale of handicraft or other local products and the organisation of traditional games. However, even if TER is presented as a complete tourism product, the legislator's focus is still on accommodation. This is generally suggested to be of a family nature, with hosts preferably living in the small-scale establishments (maximum 10 beds) together with their guests, i.e. in a 'commercial home' setting, and providing them with local information whereby hosts also serve as 'cultural brokers' (Cohen 1988), delivering the most complete rural tourism product possible.

The officially desired integration of these units in the rural landscape and community reveals a concern about TER units as development tools for rural areas. This emphasis on the integration of the TER unit in the local community is most important for the role owners effectively play as 'cultural brokers', whose relationships with other local agents may help in orienting guests within the local social network.

As in Portugal, rural tourism in Galicia is organised essentially as a publicly subsidised development tool for rural areas. Rural tourism in Galicia is relatively recent. Initiated in the mid-1990s, it was seen as a way to diversify tourism supply in the region. The Rural Tourism Act (1995) aimed at the development of infrastructure in rural areas, using historical and artistic heritage, simultaneously contributing to its preservation. This also enhanced employment, thereby encouraging local people to stay in the area.

The Act defines rural tourism establishments as buildings situated in the rural areas of the Autonomous Region of Galicia, which comply with a series of requirements regarding their construction, age or traditional Galician features. Some also carry out agricultural activities and some provide paid accommodation services. This legislation, which has much in common with the Portuguese, considers the following types of rural tourist accommodation that may fall under the 'commercial home' concept: Group A: provided in manor houses, castles, monasteries, rectories, and houses of exceptional architectural value; Group B: rooms rented out in houses that are located in rural areas and show the traditional features of Galician country houses; and Group C: accommodation on working farms.

In Galicia, rural tourism quickly became an important sector and currently makes up more than 5 per cent of the region's total accommodation supply. However, a supply of almost 500 houses and 5,500 beds show extremely low occupancy rates, leading to the current stagnation of rural tourism in Galicia (Santos and Sparrer 2006). To date, efforts have focused on developing a high-quality accommodation network, overlooking the need to create tourist products that provide additional activities and which may sustain a complete rural tourism system. However, rural accommodation is of a markedly family nature; they are small-scale units (maximum of 12 rooms), offering guests the chance to mix with hosts, and is thereby clearly classifiable as a 'commercial home'.

Unlike the models identified in Portugal and Galicia, rural tourism in Germany tends to be associated with farm holidays, with tourism representing a source of additional income for farmers. Legislation in Germany is not as strict as in Portugal and Spain, being instead based on a policy of subsidies that supports private initiative. One main objective of rural tourism in Germany is to preserve employment in rural areas, not only in agriculture but also in traditional trade. The modality Ferien auf dem Bauernhof (farm holidays) provides accommodation on farms, in apartments and private homes, camping on the farm or sleeping in barns. In addition, this product always includes infrastructure, facilities and catering services (farm-grown produce for breakfast, half and/or full board, etc.). This type of accommodation also tends to be small scale, comprising between 3 and 7 beds. It clearly targets families with children. In East Frisia the term 'commercial home' implies a certain commercialisation of 'rurality' adapting to the tourists' wishes (experiencing farm life, contact with animals, contact with local population, etc.). In these small resort-like establishments, owners often act as recreation managers or tourist guides.

Depending on the degree of emphasis on farming or tourism, some managers focus more on farming, offering only a very basic tourism product. Others make serious efforts to provide a wide range of tourist activities on their farms, such as horse-riding, traditional games, a variety of courses, the sale of farm produce, baby-sitting services, barbecues, etc. The farms also attempt to offer farming activities, although these are occasionally somewhat 'staged', using pseudo sets (animals that can be stroked, a stable with miniature reproductions of the farming world, etc.). However, agriculture remains the principal link between tourism and the rural space. The leisure activities also enhance direct contact between farmers and tourists, as well as with the other guests staying on the farm, sharing experiences and social exchange, and thereby fostering important dimensions of the 'commercial home' concept.

The principal difference between Galician, Portuguese and Frisian rural tourism lies in the fact that, whilst in Galicia and Portugal the emphasis is on the conservation of buildings of architectural value that comply with a set of requirements, in Frisia all accommodation must include some type of farming and focus on a more complete rural tourism product, with aesthetic criteria being less relevant. In all three cases tourism is considered a development tool, increasing the attractiveness of the rural space for both the local residents and tourists.

Generally, establishments are run as a family business, which Getz and Carlsen (2000) identify as a distinctive dimension of rural tourism. This feature may be particularly adequate for creating a 'home' atmosphere. As hosts, managers of rural tourism establishments play a key role providing a personalised 'rural home experience', simultaneously acting as intermediaries between the local culture, the community and tourists.

Visions of the hosts

A mail-survey directed at all legally registered TER owners in 2001 in Portugal (Silva 2006), with a response rate of 24 per cent, showed that owners are typically between 45 and 60 years of age and show higher levels of education (56 per cent). However, 51 per cent have a poor preparation for the tourism sector, being professionally active in other positions such as intellectual and scientific fields. Only 21 per cent referred to an occupation in agriculture. Some of the owners are not original residents from the rural areas where their unit is located, suggesting a phenomenon of 'neo-rurals' moving to these areas, which they tend to idealise.

The heterogeneity of the owners' profile becomes clear when analysing their interests in pursuing the TER business. Ribeiro (2003) divides TER owners in two groups: one motivated by the wish to restore a private, frequently inherited property, with little interest in making profit, the other group considered TER a business, revealing a more pro-active market approach. An exploratory study undertaken by Silvano (2005) in the Natural Park of Montesinho revealed, as the main objectives of engaging in tourism, the restoration of property and the increase of family income. However, when asked about major factors of satisfaction obtained from the activity, less material factors stand out, such as personal realisation, the opportunity of meeting other people from diverse cultural backgrounds and of enlarging one's horizons. This mirrors similar results found for rural tourism providers in New Zealand (Ateljevic and Doorne 2000; Tucker 2003b; Hall, this volume) and Ireland (Mottiar and Laurincikova, this volume). This also highlights a particular relevance of what has been defined as the 'lifestyle entrepreneur' (Morrison et al. 2001) in the rural tourism context. These rural tourism providers may also be classified as 'extrinsic owners', as suggested by Darke and Gurney (2000), who look for personal realisation, with the rural tourism establishment representing a means of expression of self (Lynch 2000c) which is valued by the guest's interest and admiration.

Similar to the Portuguese case, the financial benefits offered by rural tourism as an additional activity weigh heavily in Galicia, although there is also a considerable interest in preserving family heritage through government subsidies. Other motives include the quest for new occupational or personal opportunities and experiences, also sometimes invoked by 'neo-rural' lifestyle entrepreneurs looking for a new way of life (Sparrer 2005).

In Frisia, the principal motivation for those working in agro-tourism is financial, followed by other rather pragmatic considerations such as having sufficient space to rent out rooms and apartments or inheriting the business. Also here, several owners appreciate the opportunity to meet people or refer to a change of profession and way of life. Farm holidays in Frisia are clearly a commercial product that is far removed from the reality of farm life. Additionally, for better selling of this pseudo-idyllic image, owners are forced to invest in maintaining the setting and to take on the extra work involved in caring for the animals held for tourism purposes. Rural tourism managers have learned to build up their farms around their guests' needs and to differentiate their particular tourist potential, since there is a demand for an added value. Consequently there are farms specialising in the family market, accommodating very young children, so that the range of farm holidays on offer leads to a hyper-segmented supply. Within this context it is interesting to analyse the role assigned to farmers through the tourist activity; namely that of recreation managers. The farmers adapt their farms to their guests' expectations, thereby staging farm life. Some farmers include activities that reflect the traditional way of life, offering their guests the chance to learn how to spin yarn, bake bread, make jam, or pick medicinal plants. As a result everyday life tends to be 'museumised' or 'folklorised'. Urry (2002) uses the metaphor of 'rural space as a spectacle', reflecting a post-modern attitude to the countryside. Personalised customer service is an essential part of the business and fundamental to generating customer loyalty. Occasionally, particularly in the high season, this personal contact may prove excessive and the hosts may feel the need to set limits for protecting their privacy and for reducing the work overload produced by customised services (Sparrer 2005).

One major difference between the rural tourism offered in Portugal and Galicia, on the one hand, and Frisia, on the other, is that the owners of the German farms have learned, through years of experience, to sell their lifestyle and landscapes, whilst in the other cases many managers undervalue these resources. Moreover, in Frisia, practically all those offering agro-tourism are or have worked as farmers before, and also frequently assume the role of recreation managers. They are aware that their business success depends on the rural image they project and that the farm setting and its pseudo-decoration constitute the principal reason for sales. In both Portugal and Galicia, only a small part of the rural tourism is agro-tourism, and there is no exact definition of exactly what this concept involves.

In Galician rural tourism a certain trend towards providing a rural setting is visible, with particular attention given to the interior decoration. Houses are decorated with traditional countryside tools which over time have fallen into disuse (such as inglenook fireplaces, bread ovens, rebuilt mills, plus a wide range of traditional objects hung on walls). Yet these establishments are essentially accommodation units located in the rural space that fail to offer activities adapted to a more complete theme of rural tourism. As a result, the owners fail to acquire new functions, their work being essentially limited to the reception of guests, providing them with information, customer service and domestic work (laundry, ironing, cooking, etc.). The situation is similar in Portugal, although here, due to longer experience, initiatives to provide a more complete rural tourism product are more frequent.

Like their counterparts in Galicia and Portugal, the managers of the farms in Frisia act as hosts, as they know that their success depends on the hospitality they provide. However, one may state that Frisia tends more to the 'commercial' side of the 'rural home experience' when compared with the more recent supply available in the Iberian regions. The 'authenticity' of the host–guest interaction might get lost when owners instrumentalise their sentiments towards offering their customers a personalised service. Still, in all regions there is evidence of the real pleasure and true involvement some of the hosts experience when accommodating their guests, revealing dimensions of the activity that go beyond the commercial purpose.

Visions of the guests

According to a survey undertaken amongst tourists visiting rural areas in North Portugal (N = 2,280), motivations of tourists are heterogeneous, although some attributes are generally sought, such as attractive landscape, good climate, proximity to nature, unpolluted environment, hospitality, peace and quiet (Kastenholz 2002, 2004). However, some value more close-ness to a pristine, undisturbed nature, while others seek opportunities for socialising and activities that might be undertaken in a natural context. Others still seek what in the Romantic literature is generally idealised as a rural way of life, revealing a strong interest in traditions, and seeking a rural, calm, scenic and warm atmosphere. It would typically be the last mentioned group, seeking a 'home', that would have the least commercial experience. Tourists are permitted direct access to the 'rural way of life', its traditions and cultural and social particularities, while also being introduced into a broader 'rural tourism community product' made accessible through the hosts. Kastenholz's (2002) study produced evidence for the relevance of the 'people' element within a rural destination image. Even if not all rural tour-ists seek the interaction with locals and integration into a rural lifestyle, there is a specific segment looking for this experience.

Both in Galicia and Frisia (Sparrer 2005) guests often perceive a very good relationship with their hosts, which some classify as friendship. Some tourists spend considerable time with other guests sharing the same interests. Even though the hosts are involved in other tasks (farming, their own family, etc.), they are also present to provide their guests with information, to sell them their home-grown produce and to organise activites. The organised leisure activities, such as barbecues, represent a more structured and less casual way of sharing time. These occasions represent a platform that pro-vides guests with the opportunity to establish contact with the managers and other tourists. From the hosts' point of view, this is a logical means of rationalising their time, since instead of spending time individually with each tourist, they can meet them all together.

Whilst in Frisia the majority of tourists stay on the farms in self-catering apartments, in annexes of the main house, in Galicia and Portugal the tour-ists tend to stay in the same house as their hosts, sharing time at breakfast and, albeit to a lesser extent, at lunch and dinner. Although as a result the tourists perceive a more personalised service and family integration, there is a clear distinction in the roles played by each: whilst the guest is enjoying leisure time, the counterpart is working. It must also be remembered that Galician and Portuguese rural tourism houses offer rather few additional activities, reducing the opportunities for other types of socialising.

In Frisia, agro-tourism targets a clearly defined market segment: families with children. The principal reasons that encourage tourists to stay on the Frisian farms are contact with the farming world, the search for new experiences for their children, contact with nature and animals, and the opportunity for children to play in the countryside, free from the restrictions of urban space. A link with rural space is established through agriculture as a tourist attraction. Tourists are keen to experience life in the countryside and traditional farming, although they also express an interest in the attractions offered by the surrounding countryside and the close by seaside.

Even though participation in farming tends to be passive (such as watching cows being milked, playing with the animals), it does form part of the tourists' daily routine, which is largely spent on the farms. The farms and their pseudo-settings constitute the visitors' contact with the rural space, thereby becoming a tourist resource.

In Galicia a rural holiday results from the desire to be in contact with nature, appreciate landscape, relax and have a change from city life. Another relevant factor is location: the proximity of the Camino de Santiago, of the beach or the city of Santiago de Compostela. From this perspective, the tourist activity is not fully associated with the rural space. When choosing a rural accommodation tourists consider its strategic location and the type of accommodation. They tend to consider rural 'commercial home' establishments as an alternative to hotel-like accommodation, valuing their friendly service, comfort and small size (Sparrer 2005).

Conclusions

The supply of rural tourism was shown as quite diversified in the three cases studied, being sometimes based on operating farms, other times bed and breakfast in family homes, or else exquisite accommodation in manor houses or even castles. In Portugal and Galicia rural tourism is mostly based on country and manor houses and driven by the interest in preserving historically and architecturally relevant heritage, with a major emphasis on accommodation, as opposed to the more complete rural tourism product supplied by farms in Frisia. These differences may be associated with differences in the social, legal and political context. It may, however, also reveal an evolution from a simpler to a more sophisticated, i.e. integrated and experience-focused, concept of rural tourism, as a result of different degrees of business experience and adaptation to the market (the least in Galicia, the most in Frisia). This development of a more integrated tourism product has been identified as a determinant for economic success of rural tourism (Busby and Rendle 2000). However, degrees of commodification and commercialisation of home and rural space, as well as spatial separation between hosts and guests, apparently increase with growing business experience.

Still, similarities do exist in most of the typically small-scale rural establishments providing a tourism experience within a 'commercial home' environment, in which public and private space is shared by hosts and guests, and where the host and frequently the entire family are involved in providing a personalised service and tourism experience. The rural accommodation as the basis of the rural tourism product can correspondingly be clearly identified with the 'commercial home' concept. Ideally, rural tourists seek, and rural tourism suppliers project, a harmonious image of culture and nature that is complemented by a range of services and hospitality. This conjures up values that are associated with private accommodation – namely staying with a family in the countryside – rather than the commercial, standardised and relatively anonymous nature of hotel accommodation.

Both the Portuguese and Galician legislation specify details of the rural tourism establishment, its atmosphere, decoration, functioning and environment that may be considered orientations shaping the commodification of 'home' in a somewhat idealised rural context. There is still, however, much scope for each owner/manager to express his or her personal interpretation of a 'rural home', frequently with the high degree of emotional engagement (Lynch 2000c) of somebody being rather classifiable as a 'lifestyle entrepreneur' rather than a businessman/woman, although both economic and lifestyle motivations are present when deciding to engage in rural tourism.

Associated with the 'rural commercial home' is correspondingly a unique, but not always very professional nor principally profit-driven, way of running the business. This arises from the perspective of suppliers, on the one hand, together with the particular expectation of hospitality and integration into a 'rural' way of life from the point of view of tourists. When living together with the host family, guests naturally interact with hosts far beyond the commercial relationship that characterises hotel stays. Interaction takes place, in the case of Portugal and Galicia, during breakfast or dinner, or around the swimming-pool (if available), whilst in the case of the Frisian farms host-guest interaction occurs when participating in organised recreational activities, such as barbecues, although many other opportunities may arise given the shared spaces in the commercial home. This interaction is a feature frequently sought by those interested in getting to know more about the 'rural way of life'.

Elements that symbolise this rural lifestyle are the possibility of participating in traditional activities, integration into a unique 'rural' landscape, consumption of agricultural products from the working farm, staying in the picturesque, unique setting of a rustic building, but also, and for some above all, personalised relationships and the feeling of being a 'real guest' of 'authentic hosts', sharing daily experiences with people in a small community where everybody knows everybody else. The feeling of 'home' is correspondingly very important for much of the rural tourism experience, where people may feel as though they are coming back to their origin in a symbolic sense. This is associated with a kind of nostalgia for the lost pure relationships between people as well as between people and nature. 'Home', as a social category in the rural context, is further extended to the rural community the host family is part of, and thus in regard to which is expected to act as a 'cultural broker'.

The dreams and ideals some tourists associate with their holidays in rural 'homes', however, do not always correspond to the hosts' realities. In some cases a situation of 'staged authenticity' (MacCannell 1976) solves the potential conflict, as particularly visible in the German farms. The illusion is maintained by keeping the 'real' life spheres of hosts and guests apart, since the hosts also need their space of privacy. In other cases, hosts genuinely enjoy socialising with their guests, seeking contact and joint activities. The 'neo-rural' movement may also be responsible for another type of staged reality, and consequently, the degree to which the tourist motive of becoming truly integrated into a 'rural way of life' is satisfied may be questionable. In any case, the desire exists and the attempt to respond to it may be considered a specific dimension of the 'rural commercial home'. In some cases, such as in the German farms, this additional dimension implies the challenge for tourism providers to engage in a particularly adapted (or staged) form of farm life, as a tourist attraction.

One of the theoretical assumptions of rural tourism is that it should enhance the understanding between local residents and tourists. Except for the particular experiences between hosts and guests, however, a real exchange between rural and urban culture may be questioned, particularly in the Iberian examples analysed, where the integration of the accommodation into its rural environment is modest. The experience on the Frisian farms may also at times reinforce illusions about the rural way of life due to staged rural tourism settings. That said, the potential of living different types of 'home experiences', of having interactions between hosts and guests and experiences of community integration all constitute dimensions of the 'commercial home' experience in the rural context. Much of the quality and 'authenticity' of this experience, though, depends very much on the regional context, the particular establishment, its hosts and the specific interaction sought by the guests.

Part III
Extending the commercial home concept

12 The hospitable Muslim home in urban Malaysia

A sociable site for economic and political action

Patricia Sloane-White

Introduction

The Muslim notion of the hospitable home is based on the Quranic injunction that the Muslim home shall always be open to guests, and that travellers shall never be turned away from food or shelter. In traditional rural life among the Malay-Muslims of Malaysia, the home was a powerful, evocative symbol of sociability, a locus for private and public incorporation and social exchange that brought families and communities into circles of attachment. However, what happens to the meanings of 'home' in a transformed Malaysian setting, as Malays today engage in the 'Asian miracle' of economic development and urbanisation, and are affected by the increasing power of capitalism and politicised national and ethnic identities?

This chapter explores how the Malay-Muslim home in middle-class, urban, contemporary life is used as a site to transact, affirm, exchange and justify new social, economic, and entrepreneurial identities. It demonstrates that the Malay-Muslim idea of 'home' and its imperatives for hosts and guests can be reworked to meet the needs of new economic, political and social roles. It suggests that a modern Malay-Muslim home can have economic utility, but that its utility can be manifested via a traditional cultural idiom. Emerging from a traditional Malay-Muslim definition, a modern home in Malaysia can provide 'earnings' and 'proceeds' through host/guest exchanges. However, in this cultural context it is not *money* that is exchanged between hosts and guests in a commercial home, but 'capital' of another kind: the capital of status, social ambition and political control. As such, I suggest that 'profiting' from a private home can transcend the strictly monetary and obvious commercial realm. It can potentiate both personal reputations and anticipated or future financial returns through 'investments' in *sociability*. In this way, the commercial home paradigm can be extended when analysing what *appear* to be non-capitalistic and even egalitarian and traditional hospitality transactions in a modern, urban Muslim setting. The chapter therefore suggests the ways in which self-interested transactions can be submerged in traditional, ritual and even rural dimensions of 'home' and 'hospitality'.

The Muslim home and feast

On a drive back to Kuala Lumpur from a business meeting in the Malaysian city of Johor, my friend Rokiah (the names in this chapter are changed to protect the anonymity of my respondents) decided to take a detour through Melaka, an historic Malaysian town, to show me the traditional Malay houses for which it is famous. Rokiah was a Malay real-estate entrepreneur whose business ventures I followed closely during four years of anthropological fieldwork on Malay entrepreneurship. 'The Melaka House' (Lim Jee Yuan 1987), decorative, embellished with tiled staircases and wooden balustrades around expansive verandahs, appears frequently in Malaysian tourist brochures as a symbol of Malay rural culture and domestic space. Pointing to the curtains fluttering in the window of a wooden house and the rows of decorative tiles, Rokiah said that 'Malays love their houses. You would never see pretty touches on a dirty Chinese house, where people work and live just to exist.'

Rokiah's comments revealed complex ideas about ethnicity, identity and domestic space in the modern nation of Malaysia. Malays, all of whom are Muslims, make up the majority of the nation's population; they are called *bumiputeras* ('princes of the soil' in Malay, which refers to their claims of indigenity). In 1969, Malay resentment against the Malaysian Chinese, perceived to have monopolised the modern capitalist economy in post-independence Malaysia, erupted into violence. As a consequence, the pro-Malay government put in place a highly interventionist economic and affirmative-action programme directed at creating a capitalist class among the then largely rural Malay-Muslims.

The cohort of professional, middle-class Malay men and women in my study represented the government's policy successes. Ambitious and loyal to the pro-Malay government that had educated them, urbanised them, ensured careers for them in the corporate sector and funded their entrepreneurial ideas, the Malay men and women I knew wanted to demonstrate they had deserved the government's special provisions. Their modern lives had also been deeply affected by the rising power and appeal of Islamic orthodoxy and fundamentalism, and a government that increasingly used Islam and Malay identity as the basis for national identity. In the 1990s and today, Malaysia was rife with ethnic, cultural, economic and religious contestation, with dissension kept under control by its authoritarian pro-Malay state. There was a growing sense that in Malaysia, the Malays were the hosts and the other ethnic groups were the guests. But this is not the way in which the nation, its leaders or its Malay citizenry portray themselves. Instead, in the minds of the Malay men and women – and in the declarations of their Malay leaders – modern Malaysia, like a traditional, Malay house, is a place of great belonging for all.

So, as Rokiah and I drove through Melaka, she pointed out that while traditional houses reflected well the ethnic and religious identity of Malays,

so, too, did the modern Malay house in Kuala Lumpur's middle-class sub-
urbs, where today Malays, Chinese and Indians live in row after row of
identical cement-and-brick structures. It was still easy to tell a Malay house
anywhere, she said. A house was Malay and Muslim, she said, when it was
ever beautiful and welcoming, drawing people into its space, compelling
them to enter. Creating this atmosphere was not about having money or
displaying luxuries, she believed. Your house did not need to be traditional
or rural, like a Melaka house. 'Malay' was a *feeling* your home expressed. It
was, she said, also a feeling that the nation of Malaysia expressed by being
warm and hospitable. This, she said, is 'the Muslim way'. Rokiah knew that
the Prophet Muhammad had said so.

The Muslim house does hold a special place in Islamic belief and practice.
The Quran establishes a link between the domestic house and the divine
house ('Allah's house'), so that the very space within which Muslims live is
sacred (Campo 1991). The Quran states that human dwellings and their fitments are not merely material things within the human realm, but are craf-
ted by and supplied by Allah, providing divinity to even the most mundane
aspects of existence. Just as real houses are characterised as divine space,
paradise, too, in the Quran, is described as an idealised rendering of
domestic space; comprised of rooms and furnished with beds, it is described
as a 'shelter' and a 'house for the blessed'. (Hell for the damned also is
described as a house; it is an 'evil house' and the 'house of eternity' with a
door and beds of fire.) In the Hadith, there is frequent mention of houses.
The Prophet Muhammad clearly stated that the home should be used as a
Muslim place, where it will be illuminated by the light of prayer, ritual and
belief (ibid.: 7–36).

Nevertheless, the beauty and divinity of a Muslim house is not merely
symbolic, it *acts*: It compels and invites. For Muslims, then, there are two
purposes to a house – it establishes spiritual, emotional and physical well-
being for residents, and is a site for sociability with and well-being of guests.
The Prophet enjoined Muslims to use their houses as zones for interaction
between occupants and outsiders. Rokiah alluded to this belief when she said
Malay homes should be welcoming as spaces for hospitality. The Prophet
encouraged Muslims to provide hospitality to Muslims and non-Muslim
alike, and said the means by which Muslim hospitality was best demonstrated was in the shared meal (Buitelaar 1993; Kerlogue 2003; Tapper and
Tapper 1986). As such, in the Muslim world, hosting and accepting meals in
the home is understood to be a good deed, providing both hosts and guests
with religious merit. In the Malay world, the shared meal, or *kenduri*, is thus
called 'the best Islam' (Woodward 1988). In traditional Malay *kampung*s
(villages), houses were specifically designed to receive guests for *kenduri*s
(Hasan-Uddin Khan 1981; Hilton 1956; Provencher 1971).

In the rural past and urban present, Malays held *kenduri*s in their homes
to mark occasions such as circumcisions and engagements, housewarmings,
funerals and weddings, and at key periods in the Muslim calendar, such as

the feast marking the end of Ramadan (*Aidilfitri*, or *Eid*). In traditional settings, feasts were highly inclusive – often the entire community would be
invited. When my urban Malay respondents would describe nostalgically the
*kenduri*s of their childhood, they remembered them as communal celebrations in which everyone played a role, and 'the whole *kampung* came to your
house to help or enjoy'. The sense of inclusion, of shared labour and
expense, and shared interests highlight a ubiquitous Malay theme – that the
feast plays a crucial role in establishing the nature of social attachments
within the locus of the home (cf. Geertz 1960).

The role that feasts play in broadening social ties appears to be a common
feature of what are often referred to as the 'house societies' of Southeast
Asia, where symbols of kinship and domestic belonging are often extended
to the entire community, an idea that was first explored by Claude Lévi-
Strauss (Carsten and Hugh-Jones 1995; Joyce and Gillespie 2000). The traditional Malay house thus became a 'great house' (cf. Gillespie 2000), a setting for an imagined community, in which guests were treated like family,
and the entire village became one through the medium and theme of food
(cf. Sparkes 2003). Southeast Asian 'house society' themes have been
explored in traditional settings, but no in-depth study yet describes how
transformations of 'houses' and 'feasts' in modern, urban Southeast Asian
contexts transform the larger community and even the nation-state into a
'great house'. I contend that by exploring the theme of 'home' in the discourse of Malay political leaders, we can begin to illuminate how metaphors
of belonging and hospitality can be extended far beyond the real home, with
complex social and political implications for hosts and guests. Only then can
we begin to comprehend the Malay 'house' in all its forms as a site for
transactions that provides hosts with 'capital' that transcends monetary
exchange.

The Malay 'open house'

My Malay respondents taught me that Muslim moral and social values are
most potent during Ramadan (fasting month). Fasting or *puasa* is meant to
suppress feelings of desire or *nafsu*, in order to better understand the true
nature of one's humility in relation to Allah. Fasting assures the spiritual
equality of Muslims, for even, as people told me, a king must fast like a poor
man. At the end of Ramadan, at Aidilfitri, one is humbled even more when
asking for forgiveness from those one might have sinned against in the previous year. Yet for all of the solemn meanings granted to Ramadan and
Aidilfitri humility, these, like all Malay rituals, celebrate sociability, established
primarily in the context of food.

In traditional Malay settings, during *puasa*, the door to the house was said
to always be open after sundown, and guests could be assured that merely
wandering in would guarantee a plate of food. The end of *puasa* meant cel-
ebrating with a great feast – this was the *kenduri* in which every house served

guests and all guests returned the hospitality as hosts themselves. At Aidilfitri, Malays visited each village house, eating special foods on the verandah, sharing good wishes. Visiting the childhood homes of my Kuala Lumpur respondents in Malaysia's small towns at Aidilfitri, as we wandered from house to house, eating sweets, visiting at least a dozen houses in an afternoon, I could easily see how feasting turned an entire *kampung* into a 'great house'. Malays call this tradition *rumah terbuka* – the open house. McAllister (1990), in her study of Malay open houses, calls them 'mobile *kenduri*', a communal feast that occurs in many different homes rather than just one, with many different hosts and guests exchanging places.

Today the symbol of the open house has taken on enormous significance in Malaysia. If, in the past, traditional Malay life could be characterised as a 'house society', today, in Malaysia, contemporary life is characterised as 'open-house society'. The official government view is that the Malay 'open house' is a defining feature of Malaysian society. What might have started as a village tradition to celebrate the end of fasting has, in modern settings, become broadly associated with Malaysian national culture, itself a kind of festival to encourage national unity and social exchange across ethnic boundaries.

In the 1990s, at the end of Ramadan, Prime Minister Mahathir Mohamad reminded citizens to use this holiday as a 'celebration of harmony' (*Star* 27 March 1993), to remember their *kampung* roots and 'generous nature by having open houses and inviting their friends and neighbours to join in the celebrations' (*New Straits Times* 27 March 1994). Under Mahathir's successor, Prime Minister Abdullah Badawi, the theme remains: the Prime Minister and top Malay political leaders have open houses at Aidilfitri to which all Malaysian citizens and outsiders are welcome; they enjoin all Malays to do the same. Images of Malay politicians welcoming Chinese, Indian, Malay and European guests appear on the front pages of the newspapers. The centre of Kuala Lumpur is transformed at this time into what is called 'The National Open House', where, in 2004, over 100,000 people ate Malay foods served in tents scattered in the streets. Newspapers reported that 'guests, including foreign tourists and media [were] flown in to witness the ultimate Malaysian identity', and heard a speech by the Deputy Prime Minister that pointed out the Malaysian open-house concept is 'not only unique' in the whole world, but also helps strengthen ties 'between the races' (*New Straits Times* 28 November 2004). Prime Minister Badawi, hosting his own feast in 2004 which reportedly served 200,000 people, said that in Malaysia, while Aidilfitri celebrations are ostensibly 'Muslim holidays', they are really for all the people, 'a national celebration' (*New Straits Times* 16 November 2004). Tracking the media reports from year to year, the 'point' of the 'national' and Prime Minister's open houses seems to be that more and more multi-ethnic guests will be served each year. Newspapers report that Malaysia has become, as a consequence of its festive social and ethnic inclusiveness, 'one big open house' (*New Straits Times* 13 November 2004). It is obvious what is being symbolised at Malaysia's great Malay feasts, namely the village (and nation) as 'family'. Yet these feasts are also sites for Malay social and political control, defining the lines of power and dominance – what Appadurai (1981) calls 'gastro-politics'.

In her study of Malaysian 'festival open houses', Armstrong suggests that the official promotion of such goodwill has actually resulted in a considerable amount of ethnic mixing (1988). In a survey of 50 urban participants, she found that Malays, Chinese and Indians visit each other's homes during ethnic festivals. Generally positive about the way in which these festivals allow Malaysians to momentarily 'suspend' ethnic boundaries, she is optimistic that such visiting advances communication across ethnic lines. My own findings are less optimistic. While the Chinese and Indian co-workers or employees of my Malay respondents might appear briefly at a Malay open house, offer good wishes and then depart, none of my Malay respondents ever went to a Chinese New Year celebration in a Chinese home, fearful of inadvertently consuming pork. Rokiah went to a Deepavali feast of one of her Hindu employees; taking me along, she described how this was the new Malaysian tradition, 'to share religious festivals and feasts', but it was the only time she had entered an Indian house that year. We offered our good wishes, departing after only ten minutes (cf. Sean-Guan Yeoh 2005). At the many dozens of Malay open houses I attended in Kuala Lumpur, the multi-ethnicity valorised by politicians seemed to be merely a symbol for nationhood and really quite beside the point; the 'point' of open-house sociability, as my Malay contacts experienced it, was for Malays, and it was for *networking*.

The open house: a site for Malay social and economic action

To the Malay business person living in Kuala Lumpur, being a guest or a host at elaborate open houses has become a highly competitive and socially validating Malay event. People use these feasts to cultivate network relationships with other Malays, with the goal of increasing economic participation. In the month of fasting and at Aidilfitri, Malay men and women who, interested in establishing business contacts in Kuala Lumpur, can theoretically attend dozens of feasts. My ambitious Malay friends and contacts attended twenty or more such events. Some of the biggest social events of the year in Kuala Lumpur are held during this time. People might be invited to fast-breaking buffets at hotels sponsored by business contacts; to political-party feasts at the convention centre; to private homes of top Malay entrepreneurs or smaller-scale venturers who wish to expand their economic reach; and to corporate dinners sponsored by big *bumiputera* businesses. People who themselves had received invitations to such events freely invited their friends and contacts along, often at the last minute. Frequently, interviewing a Malay business person during the day, I would get an invitation to accompany him or her that night to an 'open house'. I would become the guest of a guest – and was assured that I was always welcome. Just as in the traditional setting, where the door to the house was open to everyone, the same rule is applicable in Kuala Lumpur. The spirit of Muslim hospitality seems to guarantee this. As an anthropologist studying business, I benefited from such hospitality; so, too, did the Malay men and women I knew who wanted to expand their businesses or meet contacts. A few examples from my field-notes should suffice to demonstrate how open-house hospitality worked.

Ishak, one of the entrepreneurs whose business ventures I researched for several years, was invited to many important feasts. With him, I was able to attend an open house sponsored by the Muslim Pilgrimage Fund. At this event, Rokiah, who was Ishak's partner in some of his businesses, came along. Here, she met several people who promised to call on her real-estate expertise for an upcoming office move. Rokiah was an active member of the Malay political party. She invited several of the people she met to attend important politicians' feasts with her the next night.

People were eager to attend the functions that Rokiah had access to, for these were known to be attended by Malays who had good business contacts. Ishak, previously a civil servant, had lots of contacts in government and was often invited to open houses at the homes of important bureaucrats. To these, he brought contacts to whom he promised introductions to top government leaders. Often, in return for such hospitality, the people Rokiah and Ishak met invited them to events they were hosting or to which they had been invited.

For the people in my study who were attempting to establish business contacts through networking, appearing at such events was crucial. Business information passed freely: at one open house I heard about a tender to print tickets for the new toll road; did anyone know a Malay printing firm which they might introduce to the contractor? A husband-and-wife manufacturing team who produced high-end bed linens heard about an international hotel that would be ordering curtains and bedspreads and needed a Malay contact; later, at another event, they met an entrepreneur who might be able to supply them with the fabric this job was likely to require.

My respondents paralleled their experiences at these events to 'kampung' open houses: these modern invitations were meant, as were traditional ones, to be sociable, to offer thanks and share with others. To them, as to all of the entrepreneurial Malays I spoke to during such celebrations, 'doing business' and 'networking' was merely Malay-Muslim social reciprocity and exchange in a modern setting. At such events, they felt they demonstrated what *kenduri* and *rumah terbuka* were always about: houses and guests, the spirit of community, generosity, equality and openness. There was no apparent sense of disjuncture between the food-sharing, home-based feasts recalled from their small-town childhoods and the events they attended in Kuala Lumpur. To them, this was 'home' and 'hospitality' updated for modern, urban life. This obviated the possibility that the participants were merely self-interested *economic* players; representing themselves as social, traditional and ritual participants, they conceived of themselves as acting out the bonds of *social belonging*.

Businesses that evoke Malay homes

Up to now, this chapter has examined how the middle-class, ambitious Malays I knew used real and imagined 'homes' and 'feasts' for political, social, and entrepreneurial purposes. Now, I turn the frame of reference around, to examine the ways in which the actors in my study sometimes conceived of their modern enterprises as 'virtual reality' homes (Lynch and MacWhannell 2000), reconstructing the symbols, fitments and architecture of traditional Malay-Muslim homes into business ideas. In this way, the sociability evoked by the traditional Malay house is being transformed by some Malay entrepreneurs into a business model.

A traditional 'house' in the city

In the 1990s, an expensive restaurant called Sri Melayu opened in Kuala Lumpur. The restaurant was financed and managed by a holding company that includes one of Malaysia's largest merchant banks. Its chairman, Azman Hashim, is frequently described as the top Malay entrepreneur. Sri Melayu, people told me, was especially built at the request of Prime Minister Mahathir to celebrate traditional Malay hospitality in a place that was evocative of village life. It was the first Malay restaurant in Kuala Lumpur to use traditional house-style architecture and traditional methods and design. It had an immense central column, a feature present in every traditional Malay house, around which ceremonies and ritual were focused (Gibbs 1987). It had a 'Melaka Stairway', as seen on the Melaka House. Its roof reflected the style seen in the Malaysian state of Perak. The windows were shuttered, as seen on all traditional Malay wooden houses; long platforms inside the restaurant evoked the verandahs in which Malay hospitality was traditionally offered. In an interview in his office in 1993, Azman Hashim told me that it was a place where 'even the Prime Minister can feel like he is back in the village'. While it was supposed to represent and honour the simple Malay past, what Sri Melayu more accurately evoked was Malay eliteness, for it was built on the scale and embellished with the decor of an *istana* – a palace – and not a house that any village Malay would have lived in.

Sri Melayu was launched with a lavish open house at the end of fasting month. I was invited along by one of my Malay friends. The event was the most eagerly anticipated of that year's holiday. It was attended by politicians, cabinet ministers, Malay business leaders and anyone who could get an invitation. The Deputy Prime Minister was there, sitting on the floor, village style, eating with his hands in the traditional way. After dinner, Azman Hashim gave a speech about how his restaurant was a place to feel 'truly Malay' and incorporate the values of the past into the needs of the modern economic present. He mentioned the importance of food in Malay life, and sharing it in a domestic atmosphere of sociability and generosity. People at the restaurant that night, and in the many nights I ate there with Malay friends over time, were delighted by this Malay house in the city, and believed they could demonstrate there how informal and down-to-earth they still were. In this expensive, opulent place, reminiscent of a Malay palace, it was as if they had come home.

Rumah Hamzeh, a halal *home for Malays*

Sri Melayu appeared at a time when less publicly lauded Malay entrepreneurs than Azman Hashim were similarly experimenting with images and metaphors of the Malay home for a commercial enterprise. For many months, I interviewed two Malay entrepreneurs, Hamzeh and Jamil, who had received a substantial *bumiputera* start-up loan from Bank Pembanguan (the Malaysian Development Bank) to import and market *halal* or Islamically slaughtered beef from Australia for Muslim consumers. Although there was a well-known Malay producer already in the burger business, these entrepreneurs insisted that, unlike his, their business would not rely on any Chinese middlemen or production. Capitalising on the Malay fear that Chinese businesses were likely to cheat them, and, in the case of food, sabotage Muslims' *halal* meat with the substitution of *haram* or forbidden ingredients, Hamzeh and Jamil envisioned overtaking the sales of the existing Malay burger business. As such, Hamzeh Burgers (as they planned to call their company) would be the first 'guaranteed' or *ditanggung halal* processor in Malaysia.

Furthermore, unlike the well-known company, which they claimed employed Chinese workers and distributed burgers to largely Chinese street-vendors, Hamzeh Burgers would be transparent in all of its dealings, ensuring that its suppliers and workers were *bumiputeras*. They had plans to expand rapidly in Malaysia, and then move into the Middle East, where, Jamil said, the market for *halal* beef was enormous. They were excited about their plans, which included creating Rumah Hamzeh (Hamzeh's House), what they called an 'all-Malay, all-*halal*' kind of McDonald's. Rumah Hamzeh would, like McDonald's, be an infinitely expandable fast-food outlet. However, unlike McDonald's, which they described as having 'plastic furnishings and counters behind which workers stood', Hamzeh Burgers would be built along the lines of a traditional Malay house. The atmosphere would be airy and simple, and built with local materials. Curtains would be hung at the windows, Melaka-style. Wooden shutters would block heat and street noise, evoking the calm of a *kampung* house. People could sit on the floor, on mats. In the style of village life, people could eat with their hands – an experience that would be familiar to the Malay locals and enjoyable for the non-Malays and tourists who visited Rumah Hamzeh. (Jamil and Hamzeh acknowledged that consumers of McDonald's food were already comfortable eating with their hands, but that here, it would contribute to the simulacrum of 'home').

Hamzeh and Jamil envisioned a vast consumer base for Rumah Hamzeh. Unsophisticated urban Malays would come because it reminded them of things that were simple and traditional. They thought such Malays probably were 'scared away' from places like McDonald's because of their modern, Western feel, and would flock to Rumah Hamzeh for a more comforting experience in the city. However, rich Malays, business people like themselves, they thought, would come to Rumah Hamzeh, too, because of its association with traditional values, such as home-based hospitality. Here, on the floor, they imagined, Malay business people could relate to each other socially and find common ground as they broadened and conjoined their economic interests. They described Rumah Hamzeh as a place where business people could 'open up' to one another and network, playing off the modern Malay idea that commensality should have an economic purpose. Hamzeh and Jamil discussed franchising Rumah Hamzeh to other Muslim nations. They imagined that the idea of a 'Muslim-style' home for fast food would succeed in such places as Saudi Arabia, Iran and the Gulf States, where they knew Islamist leaders sought to move away from Western business models such as McDonald's. To these entrepreneurs, Rumah Hamzeh would not just be in the business of selling burgers, it would fuse traditional Malay sociability with economic success. Rumah Hamzeh, like Sri Melayu, would, at once, be a traditional, modern, global Malay home for business.

'The home office'

Another group of Malay business people I knew were intrigued by the idea of setting up business centres in Malaysia's growing cities. Rashid, Hamid and Azwan were cousins; and each had a business which catered to other *bumiputra* businesses. Rashid sold office furniture and supplies, Hamid was a distributor for an international computer company, and Azwan supplied corporations with telephone and communication equipment. Hamid, during a trip to America, had seen corporate business centres, where companies could rent desks or small suites, utilise services such as computers, phone systems and fax machines, and rely on a pre-existing staff to assist with clerical duties. As he described this concept to his cousins at a *kenduri* to which I was invited, Rashid and Azwan became very enthusiastic. They believed the idea would have enormous appeal in Malaysia, both for the international companies seeking to start up business there and for local entrepreneurs who were expanding across Malaysia. Rashid was a friend of Rokiah, who, as described earlier, had a commercial real-estate business in Kuala Lumpur. As Rashid, Hamid and Azman began to plan this new venture, they invited Rokiah into their discussions as a potentially valuable partner with knowledge of the real-estate market.

Over the next year, the four met frequently to discuss the idea of setting up business centres in Malaysia. They discussed applying for a *bumiputra* loan from Bank Pembanguan, sure that this government lender would support a Malay-owned business that would serve the needs of other Malaysian businesses. They discussed the resources each centre would need. But as their discussions and planning proceeded, they began to buttress their globally inspired idea with images of localism. For a business centre to work in Malaysia, they surmised, it would have to be 'Malaysianised'. As such, there would be facilities, machines and clerical staff, as well as adept people they characterised as 'business intermediaries' or 'networkers', who could introduce clients to each other. Clients would rent space and resources while the real purpose of the centre would emerge as a kind of sociable environment, where people could drop in to solve business problems and make connections. In one planning session, Rashid hit upon the idea of calling their business centres 'The Home Office'. From that moment forward, their direction was clear: The Home Office would be a professional place, yet a relaxed one. It would be sociable and welcoming. The staff would be cheerful and helpful, always ready to help out with an idea, a resource, or a contact. There would be computers and desks for people who needed them, but in the front, where people would congregate, it would have space like the traditional verandah, where people could sit on the floor and share ideas, just like in a *kampung* house.

The Home Office, they agreed, would be a 'home away from home' for people needing a place to work and meet; it would also be a 'business incubator', a term which was heard with great frequency in Malaysia's business community. Above all, in this 'home office', a modern business with traditional Malay home-style hospitality, sociability and enterprise would mix easily.

Conclusions

This analysis has suggested that the Muslim home in middle-class, urban, Malay life is today used as a site to transact, affirm and exchange new and reworked socio-political identities in a networked economy. As such, I suggest that not only *money* exchanged between hosts and guests defines the nature of the 'commercial home', but in the Malay case, the intangibles of status, social ambition and social control can also be transacted as capital in the home, turning it into a site for political dominance and economic intent. This mobilises the home as an investment, but in a socially and culturally meaningful way that incorporates both traditional Malay-Muslim identity and contemporary obligations of Malayness. In contemporary middle-class Malay life, where financial success is a crucial determinant of ethnically and politically charged economic modernity and status, the Malay-Muslim symbols of 'home', 'hospitality', 'feasts' and 'hosts' have taken on elaborate, highly charged, and novel significance. Blurring the distinctions between hospitality, politics and economics, Malay feasts consolidate complex themes: Major political, nationalistic and corporate events are portrayed in

Malaysia today as extensions of traditional Malay hospitality, such as the 'National Open House', which evokes the Malay 'hospitable home' to suggest ethnic inclusion and national identity on a mass scale.

Not only does the 'house' provide a national icon for inclusion, but its social themes are refashioned by Malay business people into economic action, as they seek to affirm their status and network with contacts, potential clients and joint-venture partners. Thus, using an Islamic and Malay domestic hospitality tradition, Malays are able to employ the traditionally egalitarian symbol of the home for what are primarily status-based economic and social transactions in modern capitalist settings, and claim a culturally valid meaning for increasingly commercialised transactions. As such, not only do modern, middle-class Malay homes and feasts become sites for 'gastro-politics', they are sites for 'gastro-economics' as well.

Clearly, elements of national belonging, ethnic rivalry, social striving and economic ambition are at play in all of the entrepreneurial Malay ventures I researched in Kuala Lumpur. What is striking is how easily and frequently the theme of the traditional 'home' emerges in modern, urban Malay life. It emerges in modern political, religious and ethnic contexts; as a site for economic action, networking and deal-making. The Malay 'home' thus emerges as a powerful, mobilising idea for a business venture, invoking a tradition of hospitality, the quintessence of Malayness, as a metaphor for commerce. The ease and frequency with which the business people I knew applied a house-and-hospitality idiom to their modern ventures suggests that in this setting, a traditional 'house society' – said by anthropologists to be a crucial village institution in much of Southeast Asia – can sometimes be seamlessly refashioned into a modern 'house nation' and a modern 'house economy'. Or, paraphrasing another idea made famous by Levi-Strauss, a house is good for hosting; it is good for politicking; it is good for networking; it is also good for *profiting*.

13 The monastic cloister

A bridge and a barrier between two worlds

Kevin D. O'Gorman and Paul A. Lynch

Introduction

In a theoretical model, religious retreats are placed by Lynch (2005a) within the category of traditional commercial homes, noting that the essence of a commercial home is the use of the home as a vehicle for generating income. This chapter explores the provision of hospitality within Benedictine monastic cloisters in order to contribute to insights on the commercial home, and starts by locating them within the context of literature on religious tourism and the umbrella term 'religious retreat house'.

The literature on religious tourism where 'participants are motivated either in part or exclusively for religious reasons' (Rinschede 1992: 52) has very largely overlooked the importance of the accommodation. The focus has included: classification of forms of religious tourism noting its close interrelationship with holiday and cultural tourism (Murray and Graham 1997; Rinschede 1992); aspects of tourism development, management and environmental protection (Murray and Graham 1997; Rinschede 1992; Shackley 1999); pilgrimage as reinforcing social boundaries and distinctions (Eade and Sallnow 1991); the socially constructed nature of religious spaces (Gatrell and Collins-Kreiner 2006); religious centres (Rinschede 1992). Characteristics of 'religious tourists' have been explored variously noting: an affinity to social and group tourism involving travelling with believers of a similar age (Rinschede 1992); varying age and gender profiles by location and religion (Murray and Graham 1997); debate regarding the various tourist motivations along a pious pilgrim-secular tourist/sacred pilgrimage-secular dimension (Murray and Graham 1997; Nolan and Nolan 1989); and embracing of experiential, existential (pilgrims especially), diversionary, recreational and experimental modes of tourism (Cohen 1979). Of note is discussion concerning conflict and its management between different socio-spatial practices of pilgrims and tourists (Gatrell and Collins-Kreiner 2006); largely, such discussions convey a sense of a distant outsider's perspective and a concern with the macro perspective rather than understanding of organisational micro-dynamics.

One might wish to distinguish between visits to religious sites and stays in religious accommodation. Shackley (1999; 2001) discusses the case of the

St Katherine monastery in Sinai and notes the historical and religious significances of this working site where 25 monks live. An estimated 97,000 visitors per annum have access to a very limited portion of the monastery. Shackley (1999: 547) reports that, as a result of the number of visitors, the monks have difficulty in maintaining their quality of life, and is pessimistic regarding the ability to balance 'God and mammon'. A further study by Shackley (2004) identifies an international religious accommodation market which includes the notions of the religious retreat house. This is defined as: ' ... a small firm that provides catered accommodation and spiritual input for guests (sic) in search of peace and quiet, whether or not this is associated with a religious or monastic experience' (p. 228). These retreat houses include working convents and monasteries and, based on an analysis of Shackley's (2004) description, show several similarities as well as differences in comparison with the traditional commercial home (Table 13.1).

Similarities relate to the dwelling also being a home, business motivations and management methods, and low occupancy, whilst differences relate to the level of product investment, the nature of the accommodation experience and the venture often being loss-making. Noticeably the 'differences' may also be found, although less commonly, in some traditional commercial homes. Shackley (2004) indicates that the religious retreat house accommodation sector is not homogeneous as it embraces a range of accommodation types that do not always include a home dimension, for example religious conference centres. Akin to the commercial home is the description of retreat houses as 'deeply conservative product-led organisations whose constricted operating environments mean ... little opportunity for flexibility ... or innovation' (Shackley 2004: 229). Visitor motivations are

Table 13.1 Similarities and differences of the religious-retreat house described by Shackley (2004) and the traditional commercial home

Features of Religious-retreat House Usually Shared with the Traditional Commercial Home	*Features of Religious-retreat House Usually Differing from the Traditional Commercial Home*
Home dwelling	Spartan accommodation
Serviced accommodation	Rarely en suite
Little or no choice of food	No mod cons in rooms, e.g. television, hairdryer
Weak business motivation of owners	Facilities for disabled
Weak and idiosyncratic management methods	Guests may be required to assist in clearing tables
Low occupancy	Provide a religious or monastic experience
Importance of setting and ambience	Often loss-making
Historic building	Wide range of sizes of accommodation embraced by the term religious-retreat houses not all of a home type

identified as ranging from doing nothing to engagement with religious activities. 'Staff' are people who deal with guest accommodation and the outside world, e.g. the abbot and designated community members. Shackley's description of religious retreat houses is located in the context of a sectoral overview rather than a provider or guest insider perspective of the accommodation experience.

McKenzie and Ryan (2004) describe how, with the help of a lay entrepreneur, a Benedictine monastery in Western Australia has adapted the ethos of hospitality and developed commercial activities in relation to food and wine, taking advantage of an opportunity to align the products to social trends concerning the slow-food movement. A key concern of this community is to preserve and minimise the impact upon the prevailing way of life, in effect to preserve *their* world whilst interacting with the external world. In relation to stays in a Benedictine monastery, Ouellette et al. (2005) surveyed male guest motivations using a preconceived conceptual framework, Attention Restoration Theory (Kaplan 1995), and identified four motivation dimensions: being away, compatibility, i.e. a 'search for an environment … supportive of dealing with difficult and perhaps even painful matters … , beauty and spirituality' (Ouellette et al. 2005: 6). First time 'visitors' (sic) were identified as more likely to have personal problems, and repeat visitors had stronger motivations in respect of beauty and spirituality. Over 90 per cent of the 500+ respondents were aged between 30 and 60 years with a fairly even distribution across age groupings.

Origins of monastic hospitality

St Benedict established the Rule of monastic life (c. 530 AD) that was later to be adopted by most Western monasteries. This foundation became the basis of all Western European religious hospitality. It would influence monastic approaches to caring for the sick (hospitals), the poor (hospices and charities) and the provision of education (the establishment of the first universities), all of which were originally part of the monastic tradition. The Rule, which stressed communal living and physical labour, was also concerned with the needs of the local people and the distribution of alms and food to the poor. During the lifetime of St Benedict, his disciples spread the order throughout Central and Western Europe. As Vogüé (1977) and Regnault (1990) note, the Benedictines were also to have wide influence both within the Roman Catholic Church and later within the secular society. Abbeys were to become typical of Western monasticism. These self-contained communities have within the abbey walls: the abbey church; the dormitory; the refectory, or dining hall and the guesthouse for travellers. The buildings enclose a large courtyard that is usually surrounded by a cloister, or sheltered arcade.

The monks distance themselves from the distractions of the outside world as much as possible; their life is one of solitude and separation that should lead to spiritual enlightenment. By leaving secular society the monks set up an alternative world in which people from the secular world might wish to share (Böckmann 1988). Within St. Benedict's Rule, Western monastic hospitality takes its direction from Chapter 53 which is entitled *'De Hospitibus Suscipiendis'* – 'The Reception of Guests'. This was recognised by Borias (1974) as the key focus for subsequent religious hospitality. During the mediaeval period hospitality offered by monasteries was comprehensive. It included lodging for travellers, accommodation and treatment for the sick, and charitable services for the poor.

The usual period for which hospitality was freely provided was two complete days; and some similar restriction, against the abuse of hospitality, seems to have been prescribed by most of the orders, friars and monks. Lenoir (1856) observes that the prominence of the guest accommodation in all monastic buildings, beginning with the famous plan of St Gall (Switzerland) in the ninth century, attests indirectly to how scrupulously this tradition was respected. However Holzherr (1982) observes that monks have historically not always been completely faithful to Benedict's demand that all guests be accorded full respect. Society was much more sharply stratified in medieval times, and it was virtually impossible to host nobles and peasants in the same manner. A clear example is given by Horn and Born (1979) who demonstrate that the plan of the monastery of Abbot Adalhard (c. 760 AD) shows completely separate guest quarters for rich and poor. This is also highlighted by Thurston (1910) when he records that, in the Rites of Durham, there is an account of the splendour of their guest accommodation and of the hospitality practised therein. Wolter (1880) showed that monasteries were also centres for caring for the sick and the poor and that they had responsibilities for refugees. When there were few urban centres, the monasteries represented the most stable and well-endowed institutions in the countryside. The spread of Western monasticism (primarily based on the Rule of St Benedict for monastic life) together with its influence on religious life generally, and also throughout society, had led to generally accepted and well-understood principles of hospitality. These were later to be adopted and modified within the nation-states as well as by secular organisations as they took over greater responsibilities for the full range of hospitality activities.

Methodology

The researcher's presence and personal perspective has to be acknowledged (Lynch, 2005c). This is relevant both to note taking and interviews in research. As Lynch (2005b: 543) states:

> The interpretation and meaning of research accounts are also affected by the reader's politics of identity, gender, race, age and class, and the construction of these research narratives in turn is influenced by the anticipated audience. Additionally, the reader's ontological and epistemological perspectives impact on interpretation as well as issues of self-perception.

For a period of six years the primary researcher, O'Gorman, whilst under-taking theological studies across Europe, primarily in Spain and Rome, in preparation for ordination into the priesthood, had the opportunity to live frequently in a monastic environment. These experiences and the contacts made throughout that period allowed privileged access in order to gather information. The researcher had maintained regular visits to these mon-asteries for retreat, relaxation and maintenance of friendships. Familiarity with the environment was achieved as well as a level of access that would not otherwise have been available. Familiarity, or 'tacit knowledge' (Lynch 2005b: 542), may mean a tendency to overlook features of behaviours or of an environment well known to the researcher. For example, observations of blessings identified by Bruder (1998) as a high frequency, communicative practice in a monastery with complex multi-dimensional meanings were not noted despite their frequency whereas a first-time visitor might have captured these. The secondary researcher, Lynch, is a 'catholic atheist'.

Information on present-day monastic hospitality summarised in this chapter is based primarily on two monasteries in the United Kingdom, while a total of eight monasteries in Europe were visited. Over a year, two to three visits per monastery were made staying for at least a week. Data collection included: formal and informal guest-participant observations; interviews with resident monks and guests; documentary evidence in the form of spe-cific monastic rules and regulations. Empirical data was gathered by living in the monastic cloister with the monks themselves, sharing their day, their life and their work. Owing to the primary researcher's religious training and per-sonal contacts, he had a privileged status as a guest reflected in access to monks and their social areas. On these occasions, monks were aware that research was being conducted and, during the day, informal observations were made in the refectory, around the cloister and in the chapel; in the evening, there was the opportunity for discussion with other guests. Field notes were made as soon as possible after events, using a mini-recording device and then transcribed in private later that day. The data, analysed using thematic ana-lysis, was structured on Lynch's (2005b) conceptual framework based upon identification of eight elements contributing to the commercial home. This framework is also used to organise the findings: setting; artefacts; discourse; politics of identity; sequences; social control; space; product.

Contemporary monastic hospitality

Setting

Some monasteries receive no more than 100 day visitors a month whereas others can welcome in the region of a million visitors throughout the course of the year. Monasteries are all different, and the hospitality relationship within the modern monastery exists on many levels and locations. For example, there are day visitors, people who stay in a separate guesthouse in the monastery grounds (often women, families and groups) and those that stay in guest rooms within the monastic cloister who are only men.

Most synonymous with the commercial home is the hospitality that the monks offer to the resident male guests who live within the monastic cloister. Therefore the summary of the monastic hospitality being presented is focused on that. The guests are male and live in similar accommodation to the monks, eat in the monastic refectory and normally have open access to the library and to some areas closed to other guests. These male guests have a separate lounge, normally a small kitchen with tea and coffee making facilities and a fridge full of items such as homemade bread and jam, free range eggs and milk.

Artefacts

The bedrooms themselves are clean and basic, but not uncomfortable. On average, within the cloister, the monks can accommodate about a dozen male guests in single room 'cells' containing a single bed, easy chair, desk, chair and light, wardrobe, bedside table and lamp. Sometimes the accommodation offered is en-suite. There is a distinct feeling of austerity in the guests' accommodation whereas the monks' accommodation reflects evidence of longer-term habitation as the space has been personalised with, for example letters, books, computers and family pictures.

The monks and the guests have separate social spaces; it would not be normal for even the cloister guests to have access to the monks' calefactory. This term of Latin origin is one of many indicators used within the monastery to refer to the sitting room, one example of where they distinguish themselves from the outside world by language. In most monasteries silence is observed by the monks throughout the day, whereas guests, in their own social spaces, are free to talk to each other. Thus, whilst the cloister permits greater access to the inner sanctum of the monks, the degree of integration with monks is nevertheless limited by the prevailing rules as well as the social spatial separation.

Although welcoming, the monks give definite suggestions of otherness, not least by wearing their monastic habits; one guest expressed disappointment that they did not find on the back of their bedroom door a habit they could wear for the weekend!

Discourse

Making God the ultimate host, the Rule of Benedict makes it clear that the Abbot is the host responsible for meeting and welcoming the guests. However, there are two other different levels of hosting within the monastery. There is the guest master who has hour-by-hour care of the guests, making sure they are in and seated for communal meals at their place and in their particular place in the church. There are also the other guests who take responsibility for hosting newer guests, showing them where to be at certain times and making them coffee on arrival, washing up after them and in general helping them to relax and feel welcome. Guests asked questions of each other and learned from each others' experiences, serving as mutual sounding boards to check what they should be doing.

Guests are formally welcomed by the Abbot, although this normally takes place after the first meal. On arrival, the guests are greeted by the guest master, often the first monk that many of the guests have ever met. The guest masters were very welcoming but some guests felt that they were holding back. One guest observed that a monk-host spoke in a normal voice but he felt that the monk was not normal. He ascribed to them a status, as it were, of this world but not in the real world. On the other hand, guest masters knew, on the basis of previous guests' comments, of this perception and recognised what their guests were experiencing, but felt that normally the guests were not immediately at ease as they were in a strange environment.

The monks have no real opportunities for incidental interaction with guests and, as the monks proceed through their daily life, there is no impression given that they are interested in interaction. However, any guest wishing to talk to a monk is welcomed and accommodated; interaction with the monks is dependent on the guest seeking it rather than it being offered. Defined thresholds are present beyond the confines of the cloister, especially for one monastery with thousands of day visitors. This was in order to protect the privacy and the peace of the monks, who could quickly become exhibits for garrulous guests. Silence is observed in the Church, refectory and other monastic areas; guests are also encouraged to keep silence in the individual rooms. In some monasteries the monks, with the exception of the Abbot and the guest master, are not permitted to talk to the guests. One monastery had a sign indicating that this does not imply rudeness but was a means of allowing the monks to carry on their daily life.

Politics of identity

There is no such thing as a typical monastic guest. All ages (as long as they are over 18) and walks of life are represented: students exploring a monastic vocation or just looking for time to study or write, people taking a retreat; married men taking time for themselves; professionals looking for an escape from business, etc. However, they do all tend to be from a Christian background, even if they now consider themselves to be agnostic or atheist, and sympathetic to the ethos of the monastery. First-time guest motivations typically included: searching for an escape from the world; exploring a vocation to monastic life; and attempting to deal with life crisis. In this respect, often visitors find that a silent monastery is not the ideal place to deal with life crises as the silence often exacerbates the situation. Further, the monks do not see their role as counsellors, nor indeed the monastery as a place to deal with problems.

The age range of the monks is spread from the young novices in their twenties to the older monks; the majority play a full and active role in the day-to-day running of the monastery. On entering the monastery, the monks make a vow of stability so when they enter a cloister at the age of 20 they can expect to live there for the rest of their life; the monastery is therefore their home.

The monks welcome Roman Catholics, other Christians and indeed all people of goodwill. These are all considered people who are broadly sympathetic to the philosophy of the place, and the monks do not differentiate between them. While the guests are welcomed into the monks' domain, the monks live within an ordered hierarchy and a strictly controlled culture dimension, and they know that their guests do not normally live this way. As long as the guest behaviour does not disturb the life of the monastic community, the monks keep their own counsel. On one occasion when some guests went out in the evening to watch a football match in the local town, the following morning the monks sought out these guests to find out what the score was! The guests were embarrassed that the monks had realised they had gone out, but quickly realised that the monks did not mind, and a greater understanding of their hosts was realised by the guests.

In the bigger monasteries, probably because of the greater physical and social distance present between visitors and monks, the monks are often assumed to be actors there to enhance the tourist experience. One monk recalled being reprimanded by an objectionable day visitor who complained about the monk's lack of name badge. When the monk patiently explained to the tourist that this was actually his way of life, the tourist appeared stunned, amazed and then genuinely moved. In most of the monasteries services are conducted in Latin and intoned in Gregorian Chant. During the day the monks could often find a congregation behaving more like 'an audience at a pantomime'. This does not bother the monks: 'If we reach out and touch even one person's life, that has made a difference. If not we are still serving God.' One guest commented: 'I don't like it when the services are conducted in English, it sounds better in Latin. I know it's silly but I can't help thinking that God hears the prayers better when they are in Latin and there is a lot of incense.'

Resident guests rarely question the monks' sincerity. Time and lived experience within the cloister brings much greater understanding. One guest, who found the lack of conversation at meals difficult at first, said that he found each meal got easier. Every week a monk is given the task of reading throughout the meal. In some monasteries this reading is the only source of news and world affairs that the monks hear. During one of the meals, a guest who had just arrived was surprised that, instead of some religious work, they were listening to an article discussing the blossoming opium trade in Afghanistan and the effects it is having on the West.

The monks believe they are carrying out God's work on earth and that hospitality is an integral part of this work. A visitor to a monastery is therefore not just the guest of the monks but a guest in God's house. Through the behaviour and personal integrity of the monks, everything that the guest experiences is a symbol for how guests should be treated. The hospitality offered to the guests symbolises the hospitality to strangers required under the Benedictine monastic rules laid down by St Benedict which may by inter- preted as locating God as the supreme host. The creation of a shared space for hospitality allows the host and guest to construct a temporary common moral universe. As an example, when a guest is a 20-year-old agnostic stu- dent and the host a 70-year-old monk, they would tend normally to inhabit very different moral universes. Acceptance as a guest in no way suggests equality with the monks or membership of the monastic community.

Sequences

The monks' day is centred around Mass and eight other choral services (often all in Latin) starting as early as 4.00 a.m. and continuing at intervals throughout the day until about 8.30 p.m.; a typical monastic day is outlined in Table 13.2.

All guests are invited to join in the daily religious celebrations. Often they find that prayer in the monastic church is a very profound experience that seems to gain greater significance at daybreak or during twilight and darkness. As one guest commented:

> One of the things I will always remember from my visit is sitting on a church pew at 4.45 a.m. smelling sweet incense and watching the rising sun caress the stained glass windows and project jewelled colours through the smoke onto the church walls; I felt welcomed and relaxed.

Table 13.2 A typical monastic timetable

Time	Activity
4.45am	Rise
5.00am	Vigils and Lauds (Prayers during the night and at dawn)
7.00am	Prime (1st prayer of the day); Pittance (Breakfast); Private Prayer.
8.30am	Mass and Terce (Prayer during the morning)
9.45am	Work, and Classes for Novices
12.45am	Sext (Midday Prayer)
1.00pm	Lunch
2.15pm	None (Afternoon Prayer), followed by work
4.30pm	Tea
4.45pm	Private Prayer
6.30pm	Vespers (Evening Prayer)
7.00pm	Supper, followed by Recreation (can include conversation)
8.30pm	Compline (Prayer before bed)
9.00pm	Retire

Sometimes the guests claim that they feel pressured to conform at first by attending all the services. However, guests are neither forced nor obliged to attend. The monks tend not to even notice if they are there or not and guests are free to come and go as they wish. Attending is considered useful because it removes guests from what they normally do and allows their daily life to be put into perspective. When attending services guests tend to feel included, at ease and often happy, but they also like knowing when the service is going to end.

Within the refectory every male guest is allocated a place at table, normally with a name card placed on top of a napkin. Before the meal is served there are short prayers, often in Latin. The meals are typically simple and wholesome, giving the monks enough calories to keep healthy so that they can continue in their daily work. The majority of meals in the monastery are vegetarian, but on feast days and Sundays, as a celebration, meat is served. On major feast days the monks take particular joy in the high quality of food provided. The guest table is served immediately after the Abbot, as required in the Rule. All the food is served on trays in serving dishes and guests help themselves. Guests have to do nothing but eat during the meal; they are not required even to wash up. Guests often perceive that normal interaction time with the monks would be during the meals. However, despite sharing the same space any interaction is removed by the silence. Some guests commented on feelings of isolation and an obligation to keep their head down and eat quickly, despite being surrounded by some 40 other people.

Social control

One can locate God as in charge in as much as his philosophy as interpreted by St Benedict is represented by the Abbot, the principal host and head of the community, *in loco* owner-manager. The monks, who must live with one another on a day-to-day basis, embody dysfunctional family members. The life of the monastery is governed by the Rule of Benedict, adapted to the modern age. Fifteen hundred years ago when the rule was written there were no public run faculties for the sick or the homeless; now things are different. Various guest masters noted that it is not uncommon for the local police to drop off people with social problems such as drug addiction or homelessness. If they arrive at the monastery, they are given soup and sandwiches and are invited to sleep in a lodging in the grounds just a few minutes away from the monastic cloister and main guesthouse. One guest master advised, it is 'simply not practical to the running of the monastery ... we are not here to be saints; we are monks. That is, the path we have chosen.'.

The Rule of St Benedict is clearly of the utmost importance to the running of the monasteries. It is older and more solid than even the buildings. However, as with the buildings, an element of change has been necessary to ensure the continuing survival of the monastery and its way of life. During the Middle Ages the monasteries had provided detailed and formalised rules for religious hospitality, the care of the sick and the poor, and responsibilities for refugees. However, monasteries no longer need to look after the sick as there are state hospitals, nor should they be expected to look after refugees or those with drug or alcohol problems, as other agencies exist for this purpose.

The monastery reflects a gendered space in that all the monks are male. Although everyone is welcome in the church, female guests are not allowed within the cloister (except for one monastery where female domestic staff were employed). This means that there is no opportunity for women to eat with the monks in the monastic refectory. The three categories of guest accommodation (the cloister, the guesthouse and accommodation for the homeless) are distinguishable by their level of spatial separation as well as apparent social hierarchical separation.

Bells, not the Abbot, control everybody's behaviour; as one monk wryly observed, 'We live in God's house and the bell is the voice of God: it wakes us up in the morning, calls us to prayer, meals and work and then tells us it is time to go to sleep at the end of the day'. With the assistance of paid staff, the monks fulfil the different jobs (cook, cellarer, guest master, gardener, bursar, etc.) within the monastery for periods of at least a year, and all the monks who are able serve each other at table on a weekly rota, with the Abbot serving on Good Friday.

One guest master said, 'There are no ground rules here, do whatever you want, just change the bed and clean the room when you leave'. This of course was not entirely true. Although there were very few written rules within the monastery, guests on the whole knew how to behave. Guests are not expected to help out with the daily duties, although it is very much appreciated. Roughly a quarter of the guests offer to help with daily chores but only a quarter of that number actually do any work.

Space

In the public areas of the monastery there were signs that clearly stated where visitors were not allowed to go; parts of the church, buildings and gardens were restricted. However, different guests have different levels of access. Those who were living in the monastic cloister had privileged access and it is often not clear to others as to why they are going to particular areas and that they had keys (sometimes electronic swipe cards with different levels of access) that allowed them to open doors that were off limits to the day visitors. Limitations in access also meant that many day visitors could pass through the monastery and not even see a monk.

Curiosity often led day visitors to wonder what happened in the cloister, and resident guests were intrigued as to what a monk's cell looked like. As one guest stated: 'I know I am just being nosey but just as I want to open all the old books in the library and try and read the Latin on the pages, I want to open all the doors and see inside too.'

The guests and the monks have a shared environment, but limited shared space; they pray together in separate parts of the church and dine together, in silence, at separate tables in the refectory. Some guests commented that, although they enjoyed joining with the monks at meal times and at prayer, they would also like to have seen them at their daily duties and jobs; they gained great solace and comfort from their interactions with the monks. Another guest stated: 'I've been to many places travelling over the past 20 years ... I've slept in the church of the Nativity at Christmas time, but nowhere compares to these guys ... there is nothing like this place. They are so accommodating.'

Product

As with traditional commercial homes, it is apparent that the lives of the monks as long-term occupants reflect a feature of considerable interest to guests. On the one hand, the monastery serves as a home to the monks. However, the home is particular in terms of its communal nature, distinctive philosophy and order, as well as a degree of openness to the public. On the other hand, the regulation of that home has been adapted not only to conform to the philosophy of place but also, in a relatively seamless fashion, to manage the presence of visitors, including accommodation guests. The monastery cloister accommodation does not fit well within the existing categories of commercial home as proposed by Lynch (2005a). It is therefore suggested that a further category of the communal home is required in recognition of the differences present, including the strength of the underlying philosophy with the consequential behavioural effects, and the relative accessibility by the outside world.

The monks make no charge for staying in the guest monastery. However, common courtesy should dictate that a donation would be appropriate. This is a difficult issue for some of the guests, as the monks do not seem to care about how much is donated. Some monasteries did have signs suggesting donations, always with the caveat that it was optional; deed of covenant envelopes were always available to allow the tax to be claimed back. Donations typically ranged from £20 to £50 per night. A monastery's economic dependency upon the accommodation income varied. Some of the guest masters seemed slightly irritated by people using the monastery as a one night stop off and treating the monks' hospitality as bed and breakfast accommodation; monasteries are also familiar with high-profile figures using their guesthouse in this manner.

Generally, guest masters did not keep detailed statistics of how many people had stayed or the total number of guest nights. Such information may have been interesting but of no real relevance to them. However, in the experience of the field researcher, occupancy levels in the cloisters were usually near 100 per cent. The monasteries operated at a commercial level in other ways, for example: conference facilities; apiaries; brewing and distilling; public commercial restaurants; stained glass window manufacturing; printing and publishing; illumination and illustration; farming and agriculture; and retail.

Most activities were run by paid professional staff who reported to the monastic bursar on their commercial activities. All monasteries were, however, very careful to make sure that these distinct and separate activities did not encroach into the hospitality offered to their guests.

Conclusions

The monastery is extremely complex. There are different layers of the commercial home within the monastery and differing levels of hospitality provision. As has emerged from this analysis, within the monastic cloister the hospitality that is offered to the guest's physical and metaphysical needs is not a simple concept. From the results of this investigation, the dominant themes of modern monastic hospitality are summarised in Table 13.3, which is

Table 13.3 The hospitality conceptual lens applied to monastic hospitality

Theme	Summary of Monastic Hospitality
Setting	The hospitality relationship that the monks have with their resident (male) guests within the monastic cloister is most synonymous with the commercial home. However, other guests can include day visitors, couples and families.
Artefacts	Accommodation furnished in a basic but functional manner, small number of books in the room, but open access to the library.
Discourse	The discourse is primarily framed with religious and hospitality language focused on the domestic hospitality sphere, commercialism is of secondary importance.
Politics of Identity	The monks provide for both the spiritual and temporal needs of the guests. Hosting takes place at various levels with different people (the Abbot, the guest master or other guests) taking the role of host depending on the circumstances. The apparent sincerity and strength of purpose of the monks is manifest and often has a profound effect on the guests.
Sequences	Interaction and full welcome in the daily life of the monastery is as much dependant on the guest seeking it as on it being offered by the monks. The guests can accept or reject the different kinds of hospitality offered.
Social Control	Monastic hospitality is governed by the sixth-century Rule of St Benedict, adapted for the modern age.
Space	Boundaries, delimited by St Benedict 1500 years ago, are necessary for the smooth running of the monastery.
Product	The monastery as well as being the House of God, is also the monks' home. Guests are welcome to visit or stay but not to interfere with it. Commercial activities exist within the monasteries, but the prime purpose of monastic hospitality is not commercial, as hospitality is offered as part of the monastic vocation.

structured around the commercial home conceptual framework created by Lynch (2005b).

Table 13.3 draws out the key features of commercial home hospitality offered within a monastic cloister. The prima-facie purpose of a monastery is not to offer hospitality, but rather to house the monks in a community environment so that they can dedicate their lives and live their vocation to the service of God. The separation of the monks from their guests (and by definition the separation of the monks from the world in general) is not an act of inhospitableness, but is mandated by the Rule and necessary for the monastery to function. Therefore, the ritual reception of guests and the provision of hospitality play an important role by being both the bridge and the barrier between the monastic and secular worlds.

This chapter has added to the existing literature on religious tourism and, in particular, one type of religious retreat house; it has drawn attention to how hospitality can serve as a bridge across the world of a religious community and the outside secular world. It has contributed towards an initial understanding of the nature of one type of religious accommodation where guests usually make a financial contribution towards their stay. However, the provision for guests to stay in the monastic cloister is motivated by their monastic vocation. Whilst there are similarities between a traditional commercial home and the monastic cloister, attention has been drawn to distinctive differences arising from both the communal nature of the institutional home and the philosophical purpose and praxis, suggesting that a further category of 'communal commercial home' is warranted. Further research of this fascinating but complex form of communal home hospitality accommodation is required.

14 The diversification of the commercial home

Evidence from regional Australia

Brian King and Leanne White

Introduction

This chapter examines the commercial home phenomenon in Australia and draws upon the destination region of Daylesford and Hepburn Springs in Victoria to exemplify how changing fashions have led to a diversification of the concept as the destination has recently recaptured the popularity that it enjoyed as a spa destination during the Victorian era. The chapter examines the early development of the guesthouse, incorporating nostalgic associations with migrant cultures including the Swiss-Italians. It charts the subsequent replacement of guesthouses by motels and the recent emergence of a more diverse range of commercial homes. The diversification has occurred in response to the changing demands of domestic and international visitors as well as to the pursuit of home-based tourism opportunities by both locals and by incomers attracted by semi-rural lifestyle. An examination of changing visitor preferences and fluctuating accommodation provision can provide insights into the diversification of the commercial home in areas outside Australia's main urban centres.

The early development of commercial homes in Australia

Whilst Lynch's (2005c) definition of commercial homes as private homes where guests pay to stay and interact with a host is focused on the United Kingdom (UK) experience, this definition has broad applicability to Australia. The introduction of a commercial dimension to the Australian home through the provision of tourist services resembled what had occurred somewhat earlier in the UK. Making strangers welcome within the home, albeit on a user pays basis, is built upon the long-established practice of extending 'hospitality'.

As will be examined in this chapter, however, the emergence of styles of accommodation in Australia exhibits some distinct characteristics, influenced by various domestic and inbound migrations from the UK and beyond. The Australian colonial experience is reflected in the emergence of changing tourist product preferences. Over the course of the nineteenth century, Australia inherited the guesthouse tradition from the UK. Other forms of commercial home such as bed and breakfasts and home-stays in farm and rural settings have developed only recently. With the exception of a brief period of popularity when Melbourne hosted the Olympics in 1956, home-stays in urban areas did not feature in Australian tourism until inbound international visitation took off during the 1980s.

One dimension of the early Australian guesthouse was as a haven from the perceived evils associated with alcohol. In Australia there has been an enduring association between commercial accommodation and the provision of liquor. Davidson and Spearritt (2000: 101) have noted that the traditional separation of public houses and inns was coming to an end in England at around the time of European settlement in Australia and that the two concepts were to remain inseparable in the colonial setting. Of the 'hotels' established alongside the major highways, most also functioned as public houses (pubs). Although Australia never experienced US-style prohibition, the connection between alcohol and accommodation was hotly contested and the commercial home sector was soon caught up in debate about the merit of maintaining a distance between respectable people and alcohol. Furthermore, in nineteenth-century Australia, prevailing gender relations were evident in the way that work was organised within the commercial accommodation sector. During the period following the initial European settlement of Australia in 1788, many publicans were women. The fact that the provision of accommodation and alcohol was closely linked was reflective of a colonial frontier mentality. In due course, the emerging temperance movement argued against female licensees and/or barmaids and discrimination became prevalent during the early twentieth century (Richardson 1999: 64). Concerns about the potential consequences of readily available liquor created a climate of opinion conducive to the provision of commercial accommodation away from pub-style environments. The guesthouse concept offered an alternative to pubs and luxury hotels and particularly appealed to the respectable middle classes. Most guesthouses were 'dry' (did not serve alcohol) and epitomised the spirit of temperance. Within the major tourism destinations, most guesthouses focused on extended stays, were located away from the most frequented precincts and provided women and families with greater privacy than other styles of accommodation.

As was the case in the UK, guesthouses were typically operated by married couples with the woman as the manager and key decision-maker (Walton 1978). In Australia guesthouses were typically small to medium-sized enterprises managed by an owner-operator with cooks and maids providing an informal 'housekeeping' and room service function. Many guesthouse managers stressed homeliness and a sense of community. The typical property layout encouraged encounters with other families in the living areas and even the prospect of forming lifetime friendships.

The interwar period was the heyday of the Australian guesthouse, before a prolonged decline during the post war years which was prompted by technological developments and changing consumer preferences. Reacting to the experience of wartime austerity, travellers were becoming preoccupied with the new and the modern. Increasing car ownership and the prevalence of central heating and air conditioning at home conspired to disadvantage the guesthouse sector relative to alternative accommodation options such as motels. Davidson and Spearritt (2000) noted a decline in the number of guesthouses in Katoomba, New South Wales from 66 in 1930 to just six in 1990. Daylesford and Hepburn Springs also experienced a marked decline.

As the guesthouse sector declined during the post-war period the number of motels proliferated. Like guesthouses, many motels were small businesses operated by a husband and wife team. However, few motels could capture the homeliness of the guesthouse and in many respects the concept was the antithesis of the commercial home. The motel embodied the modernist and functional distinction between commercially provided accommodation and the home. It catered explicitly to the needs of the motorist. The stereotypical motel room window overlooked the car park, but the car was antithetical to domesticity and symbolised transience and personal mobility rather than the type of durable lifelong friendships formed in guesthouses. There was an emphasis on 'self-contained' units and on independence, which offered little scope or incentive for guest interactions. Whilst exceptional husband and wife teams may have conjured up a homely ambience, most motels became largely transactional in character for their owner/operators. The post-war period marked a low point for the commercial home in many areas across Australia, including in Daylesford and Hepburn Springs.

Consumers increasingly sought flexibility in 'planning their day' (Walton 1978: 4) and the remaining guesthouses were progressively supplanted by the bed and breakfast concept. Travellers increasingly viewed set meal times for lunch and dinner as a constraint. Unlike in the UK where bed and breakfast ventures were well established, it was not until the 1990s that the sector appeared explicitly in the accommodation guides produced by Australia's various state and territory tourism commissions. The bed and breakfast sector was stimulated by the expansion of international tourism arrivals after the 1988 Australian Bicentennial celebrations and mainly targeted international guests. The 1994 edition of the *Australian Bed and Breakfast Book* noted that, 'the 400 hosts listed are homeowners who want to share their love of the country with travellers' and offer a 'uniquely Australian experience' (Thomas and Thomas 1994). Such descriptions are consistent with the New Zealand experience where the impetus for many investors in commercial home ventures was to share a part of the 'real New Zealand' with overseas guests (Tucker 2003b). The bed and breakfast sector in Australia and New Zealand was well placed to provide visitors with insights into domesticity as international tourism arrivals expanded.

During the 1980s and 1990s bed and breakfast accommodation expanded into winery regions such as the Hunter Valley in New South Wales, Margaret River in Western Australia and the Barossa Valley in South Australia. These destinations attracted domestic and international tourists and the intimacy and homeliness associated with the bed and breakfast experience complemented the style of personalised service offered at boutique winery cellar doors. The availability of locally produced food and wine in a regional setting offered discerning customers something of the regional tourism experience characteristic of parts of Europe, notably in France and Italy. This connection was to play an important role in the resurgence of the Daylesford and Hepburn Springs area, drawing upon its Victorian heritage with reference to the continental European connection.

Australia's farm and rural tourism sector also expanded during the 1980s and 1990s, drawing upon established European practice and offering 'home-hosting' to a variety of overseas visitor tastes (Craig-Smith et al. 1993). Diversification of the commercial home was evident in winery regions including Daylesford and Hepburn Springs with many family operated wineries offering tastings and cellar door sales. The expansion of the 'home-stay' market accommodated overseas students in home settings, taking advantage of the growth of English language study. This Australia-wide pattern was reflective of established UK practice (Tucker and Lynch 2004) though was less commonplace in Daylesford and Hepburn Springs.

The Daylesford and Hepburn Springs region

With a combined population of 3,500, Daylesford and Hepburn Springs are located three kilometres apart at an altitude of 650 metres and a 90-minute drive from the state capital of Melbourne. The destination is readily accessible for day or weekend trips and attracts around 6,000 tourists each weekend (Ashton and Newton 1999). According to a recent survey on Australia's most frequented short-break destinations undertaken by Publicis Mojo, Daylesford was ranked 11th (Scott 2007). However, as can be seen in Table 14.1 the destination attracts relatively small numbers of overnight international stays compared with Victoria's leading regional destinations. This is indicative that the overwhelming majority of visitors are domestic.

Table 14.1 International visitation in regional Victoria

Destination	
Great Ocean Road	199,000
Phillip Island (penguins)	139,000
Dandenongs/Healesville	101,000
Ballarat/Sovereign Hill	76,000
Yarra Valley	74,000
Mornington Peninsula	59,000
Grampians National Park	48,000
Bendigo	22,000
Victorian snowfields	20,000
Daylesford/Hepburn Springs	14,000

Source: 2005 International Visitors Survey, Tourism Research Australia.

The Daylesford and Hepburn Springs area has about 70 mineral springs – the highest concentration in Australia – and pursues a positioning as the nation's leading spa destination. Capitalising on the renewed 'fashionability' of the concept, the region has recently enhanced its reputation for 'wellness' and 'spa' tourism and is now widely promoted by the Victorian tourism authorities as the state's centre of health-related and spa tourism. Accommodation outlets have actively embraced the concept and some have diversified their service offerings into relaxation, massage and various holistic therapies.

The increasing pursuit of rural lifestyles by urban Australians has stimulated residential development in many accessible inland settings, including Daylesford and Hepburn Springs. Many of the new arrivals have proceeded to open their new homes to paying customers. They appear to have a desire to move away from the suburban lifestyle with its clear differentiation between home and workplace, and towards more integrated semi-rural lifestyles where visitors are welcomed into the home. The pursuit of a different lifestyle inevitably extends beyond the accommodation component and into other dimensions of the 'good life'.

The formation of regional food and wine groups such as Daylesford Macedon Produce has been emblematic of an emerging emphasis on food- and wine-related tourism. This group promotes the various wines produced in the

Figure 14.1 Daylesford – the 'spa centre of Australia'.

surrounding Macedon and Spa Country region as well as locally available products such as cheeses, processed meats, preserves and condiments. Indicative of the connection with global trends, chefs and producers within various Victorian regions, including Daylesford, have participated actively in the international 'Slow Food Movement'. The association with wine, hedonism, conviviality and refined indulgence marks a major shift from the temperance focus of the earlier guesthouses located in regional Victoria, as referred to previously. The provision of 'slow food' is consistent with the idea of the commercial home as an 'authentic' setting where things are done in the 'traditional' way and at a slower pace. However, as will be shown in the next section, authenticity is a contested term in Daylesford and Hepburn Springs.

To explain the emergence of the commercial home in historical context, it is pertinent to recount the experience of the early European arrivals into the region. Hepburn Springs was first settled by Captain John Hepburn in 1838 (Daylesford is named after a town in the English Cotswolds). The population expanded with an influx of miners following the discovery of gold in the 1850s. About 2,000 of the settlers were from Northern Italy and Switzerland and their heritage is still prevalent within the region (Gervasoni 2005). The European migrant connection has been useful for the regional tourism authorities with their food and wine emphasis, drawing upon the various production techniques that migrants brought from their homelands, including the cultivation of olives, grapes and market gardens. The various migrant stories are actively promoted and celebrated, including the establishment of Australia's first pasta factory. This recognition and profile contrasts with the lesser prominence given to the Dja Dja Wurrung indigenous population who inhabited the area prior to white settlement. Whilst some historians have been researching the interactions between settlers and the local tribe, regional promotions have given less prominence to the indigenous dimension than to settler-related heritage. This is indicative that, within the region, 'homeliness' is very Euro-centric and excludes indigenous ideas of domesticity, which have very different connotations in the context of a semi-nomadic society.

During the Victorian era, settlers were attracted by the temperate climate and mineral waters as well as by the prospects of striking gold. The ongoing legacy of the Swiss-Italians embraces the built environment, music, food and wine, and provides an opportunity for the various commercial homes to convey a European-style atmosphere. Following the construction of the rail line in 1880 the Victorian Railways played an important role in promoting what was described as 'Delightful Daylesford' (Davidson and Spearritt 2000: 76). The tourist appeal of the region increased during the early twentieth century when affluent Melbournians arrived in increasing numbers, attracted by the reputed healing powers of the mineral springs. The destination appeal was complex, but did involve an emphasis on familiarity, consistent with the commercial home concept. Tourism development in the area has also exhibited some contradictory elements, indicative that domesticity and familiarity involved a strong element of fabrication. Lake Daylesford, for example, was created in the 1920s and was designed explicitly to enhance the 'European feel' of the town. The Chinese market gardens which had operated on the site were closed to allow the inundation to occur, and native eucalypt trees were replaced with European pines at local parks and the Botanical Gardens, again with a view to providing visitors with familiarity. Whilst not directly an element of the commercial home, the deliberate creation of a sense of familiarity and homeliness helps to reinforce a critical component of the commercial home.

Daylesford and Hepburn Springs entered a period of stagnation during the post-war years, with little investment in the accommodation sector. The resurgence of the area did not occur until the 1980s. The first motoring guide to provide Victorian destinations with a star-rating reported that, ' ... local townspeople are optimistic, that with some restoration, planning and marketing, Daylesford may once more attract the visitor ... ' (Blair 1986: 90). The implication was that mid-1980s Daylesford had tourism potential, but was struggling. Daylesford was awarded a two-star rating (indicating 'recommended' status – the maximum was three stars). This resurgence has subsequently occurred, including the emergence of a flourishing commercial home sector. The setting and the changing demography of the region also provide an important setting for host/guest interactions. In this context, the commercial home is an 'active player in the dissemination of unfolding of scripts' (Di Domenico and Lynch 2007a: 126).

After being out of favour for several decades, spa-related tourism in Victoria experienced a resurgence in the later twentieth century and by 2005 this form of tourism attracted 32,000 international and 80,000 domestic visitors (Tourism Victoria 2005). The size of the market segments from various source countries is indicative of the potential demand for home-style accommodation. The largest of the international markets for spa tourism were Asia (26 per cent); the United Kingdom (19 per cent) and the United States (18 per cent).

Climate and seasonality have helped to shape the tourism dynamics of the region. While the region is popular during Australia's summer months (December to February) there is also substantial visitation during the cooler months. The cold and misty winter weather is featured as part of the charm of the destination, with much of the promotional imagery focusing on food and wine and the idea of homeliness associated with open fires. The long-established 'Cosy Corner Café', for example, promotes the availability of hearty country-style food, as well as more multicultural creations (such as curries) provided in a homely setting. This combination of the traditional/ familiar with the multicultural has helped to broaden the destination appeal. In 2005, Daylesford received international coverage by topping the list of 'funky towns' in the British Airways *High Life* in-flight magazine, providing the destination with a reputation for 'edgy' style, diversity and tolerance. *Australia: The Rough Guide* reports that Daylesford has a 'new age, alternative atmosphere with a very large gay community' (Daly et al. 1999: 852). The *Lonely Planet Guide to Australia* states that the area attracts 'hedonists, spirituality seekers and escapees from the city rat race' and has an interesting blend of 'old-timers and alternative-lifestylers' (Smitz et al. 2004: 535). These traits have provided an important context for the development of the commercial home sector.

There is a contradictory side to the 'funky town' story, however. As tourism has rebounded, Daylesford and Hepburn Springs have experienced profound social and economic change. Incomers have accelerated the gentrification of the area and housing costs have increased, placing financial pressure on lower income residents (Mulligan et al. 2006: 56). Some permanent residents have expressed their dislike of living in streets where many commercial and/or holiday home properties are vacant during weekdays. A recent survey noted that, as visitor numbers have risen, some residents have experienced anonymity and a loss of their normal sense of 'belonging'. Isolation is most prevalent during peak weekend visitation (Mulligan et al. 2006). Although locals are generally welcoming towards tourism, some underlying tensions are evident. Tucker and Lynch (2004) have emphasised the importance of matching host and guest expectations. Whilst the diversity underlying 'funkiness' provides a useful angle for promoters, the attitudes and lifestyle expectations of hosts and guests can be mismatched and even contradictory in commercial home settings.

The rapid transformation of Daylesford and Hepburn Springs from traditional rural settlements to accommodating a diversity of alternative lifestyles has thus created some dissonance in instances where the expectations of hosts and guests differ. Awareness of such tensions may have contributed to the recent efforts to maintain and strengthen the sense of local community. Daylesford Neighbourhood Centre (DNC) offers a range of activities and events including computer courses, cheese making, cottage gardening, blacksmithing and beer making. The DNC also houses the Sweet Justice Women's Community Choir, which provides a women's friendship network. A number of local restaurants also actively promote discounted rates to local residents during off-peak periods. Whilst the various changes are not solely attributable to tourism and reflect wider trends occurring in regional Australia, tourism is undoubtedly playing a key role in shaping the transformation.

The Hepburn Shire Council (HSC) is the local government authority responsible for the administration of Daylesford and Hepburn Springs. The authority-run Daylesford Regional Visitor Information Centre recorded approximately 115,000 visitors in 2005, indicative of the scale of regional visitation (Moses 2006). Visitor information outlets are also located in the smaller townships of Creswick, Trentham and Clunes, which have a more traditional ambience. In pursuing economic diversification the Council aspires to offer the 'premier rural location in temperate Australia for feature film and television series production' with a reputation as a 'film friendly' region for 'commercial and creative filming' (Hepburn Shire Council 2006).

The resurgence of tourism generally, and boutique-style tourism in the home-based environment, has facilitated the Council's efforts to host those involved in film production in commercial home settings. The increased presence of creative visitors and new residents assists the local economy, but challenges traditional attitudes. The influx of 'the creative class' is easier to handle in cities than in such semi-rural settings (Florida 2002). However, some locals may be more receptive to the creative incomers than to pleasure seekers from the city who are less receptive to alternative lifestyles. Again the impetus for change is not solely attributable to tourism, but the increasing appeal of the area as a place to live and to do business is inseparable from the resurgence of tourism.

Indicative of the pursuit of balanced development and sustainability, a Tourism Advisory Council has been formed in Hepburn Springs with a view to assisting the preservation of community lifestyles and capitalising on tourism opportunities (Moses 2005). According to HSC, tourism has become 'one of the key economic forces in the shire' (Moses 2005). The HSC has attempted to improve the professionalism of businesses (including commercial homes) and the area is widely acknowledged as one of the more effectively managed destination regions of Victoria. The establishment of the organisation Daylesford Getaways has provided a useful mechanism for promoting the range of available accommodation with a substantial range of commercial homes featured in *Daylesford and Surrounds Accommodation Guide 2006–07* (Daylesford Getaways 2007). A similar service is offered by the *Daylesford Accommodation Booking Service* and *Daylesford Cottage Directory*.

The provision of water to tourists is a key element of environmental sustainability and resource management in the regional Australian setting. Drought conditions have prevailed across much of South-Eastern Australia over the past decade and since 2002 the regional water authority Central Highlands Water has implemented household water restrictions. By sourcing catchments further afield it has also been planning to increase water availability. In the interim, water consumption is under strict control, with a consequent impact on tourist behaviour. It is ironic that the destination continues to base part of its appeal on the availability of spa-related waters during drought conditions. There is an inherent tension between the needs of residents and visitors for water, though again some of the pressure emanates from outside the tourism sector (notably the demand for irrigation by farmers). Many incomers are environmentally aware and sensitive, though their presence exacerbates water and related challenges.

Regional attractions

The diversity of regional attractions encourages visitors to the destination and influences the commercial home sector. Some attractions are directly associated with spa-related tourism, whilst others are not. The continuing importance of spa- and health-related tourism is evident, but the celebration of food and wine related experiences is symptomatic of the process of diversification. Because much of the food and wine consumed by visitors occurs in domestic settings, it may be argued that the emerging ethos of tourism in the region lends itself to the commercial home alongside the institutions of spa-based tourism. Various local festivals and events also attract visitors into the region and seem to complement the commercial home style accommodation. Many ventures exploit the Swiss-Italian connection, including Lavandula.

As outlined above, much of the regional tourism emphasis is on relaxation, food and wine. This is exemplified by Ellender Estate, where the first vines were planted in the mid-1990s and which specialises in 'ultra cool climate wines'. Visitors are greeted to the 'Leura Glen' property by the Ellender family's pet dogs. This exemplifies the homely atmosphere which is complemented by local food offerings, including wood-fired bread and pizzas. Highlighting the diversity of provision and that not all of the local production aims at sophistication, the nearby Big Shed Wines offers wine varieties such as 'fizzy stuff' and 'sticky stuff'.

Manifestations of the commercial home

Many variants of the commercial home concept are prevalent in Daylesford and Hepburn Springs. Some establishments are 'traditional commercial homes' (Lynch and MacWhannell 2000), consisting of tourism-related businesses

Figure 14.2 Rural artefacts on display at Lavandula – a lavender farm of Swiss-Italian origin.

operated from private homes and involve *in situ* hosting. Households have enjoyed an increasing range of tourism-related commercial opportunities targeted at a variety of customer segments. Providing a parallel with the Daylesford and Hepburn Springs experience, Shaw, Williams and Greenwood (1987) have noted a pattern of inward migration to establish home-based businesses in two resorts in Cornwall, England. They observe that one group of incomers has been attracted by environmental factors and the second group by the opportunity for self-employment related lifestyles. These distinct motives help to explain the absence of a single concept of the home and of the domestic environment amongst incomers. This diversity is inherent in the Daylesford and Hepburn Springs scenario.

The character of the Daylesford and Hepburn Springs area has been substantially influenced by migrants such as the early Swiss-Italian arrivals, but more recently by domestic demographic movements. The phenomenon of city residents (principally from Melbourne) relocating to inland rural locations such as Daylesford and Hepburn Springs has been described as 'Tree Change' (Salt 2006). Many incomers are seeking alternative and slower-paced lifestyles and have established home-based social enterprises or commercial homes. Over a million Australians have left the major cities since 1970 in search of a tree change or its coastal counterpart a 'sea change' (Burnley and Murphy 2004: 3). In a country of only 21 million inhabitants this has been a significant demographic shift. The diversification of the wider regional economy has facilitated diversification within the commercial home sector, with many visitors seeking 'homeliness' as a key ingredient of the destination experience. This may involve staying in accommodation that is clearly defined as a 'commercial home' or finding homeliness in other aspects of the destination experience, such as retail purchases which convey this attribute. Furthermore, marketing of the area often highlights the range and appeal of home-based tourism generally, and bed and breakfast and boutique accommodation establishments, in particular.

The accommodation outlets exhibiting characteristics of commercial homes consistent with Lynch's definition (2004) are guesthouses, boutique hotels, bed and breakfast establishments and farmstays and, to a lesser extent, self-contained accommodation and second homes. The extent to which they conform to the definition depends on the extent to which the properties are genuinely private homes. Even in the case of private homes, the level of host-guest interaction and shared space varies considerably.

Some establishments fit more with Lynch and MacWhannell's (2000) idea of the 'virtual reality commercial home', having a stronger emphasis on the image of the commercial home than on the substance. Masterson has, for example noted that, ' ... most visitors to the area opt to rent a house or unit ... there are hundreds available from quaint in-town cottages to sprawling bush retreats' (Masterson 2007: 27). In many ways this is a trend away from the commercial home as strictly defined. Visitors like many of the ideas associated with the commercial home, though many will ultimately opt for convenience as a way of minimising the commitments and constraints associated with home hosts. Self-contained accommodation involves properties booked for the exclusive use of visitors and often lacks the level of interaction with hosts which is associated with the commercial house definition. This form of accommodation is particularly popular in Daylesford and Hepburn Springs as it allows visitors to plan a self-paced schedule of activities. The names of the various self-contained properties are indicative of the perceived appeal of homeliness. Examples include Possum Cottage on the Lake, Howard's End, Bliss Cottage, 'Diversion', 'Kookaburra Ridge', 'Indulgence', Hilltop Retreat, Linga Longa Cosy Cottages (established 1920), 'The Retreat', Gum Tree Cottage, Impressions of Daylesford and (for a reminder of Europe) Trieste Villas, Italia Nostra Pensione and Tuscany on the Lake. The descriptors are symptomatic of the style of operation with an emphasis including relaxation, health, nostalgia and 'Australiana'.

Though guesthouses are less commonplace than in the early twenty-first century, a number are still in operation, including Mooltan Guesthouse, Hepburn Chalet, Lauristina and Continental House. The formerly iconic guesthouses of Bellinzona and the Springs Retreat have been re-designated as five-star boutique 'resorts' and are now operated by transnational corporations. Because of their substantial room capacity, the latter ventures do not adhere strictly to the commercial home definition. Their promotional material conveys a sense of homeliness to prospective guests, though it is likely that the various parties are aware of the gulf that exists between the ethos of the transnational corporation and the commercial home! As occurred previously in the case of guesthouses, bed and breakfast properties are becoming less commonplace as visitors progressively seek independent meal arrangements. Those remaining include Dudley House, Bibaringa and 65 Main, all of which feature communal recreation and dining areas. This sharing of commercial space with hosts is an important aspect of the commercial home concept.

While most of the area's boutique hotels are too large to justify the commercial home label, it is worth noting that the 30-room boutique Lake House – voted Australia's regional property of the year and Australia's best food and wine experience – has played an important role in setting the stage for the commercial home concept. The husband and wife operating team has been widely recognised for their pivotal role in re-establishing the region for tourism (Lethlean 2007: 3). When Lake House first opened in 1984, the owners sought to make the restaurant and retreat 'a destination' since there was 'no other tourist product' in the vicinity (Ashton and Newton 1999). The Lake House brand has subsequently expanded into the sale of seasonally produced sauces, jams and chutneys in stores such as Harvey Nichols in London and the provision of their own bottled mineral water to guests (Wolf-Tasker 2006a: 2). A number of these products and experiences have an association with 'homeliness'. Co-owner/operator Alla Wolf-Tasker was the recipient of the Age Good Food Guide's Award for professional excellence, and in 2007 was recognised for her work in tourism and hospitality with an Order of Australia.

In keeping with the owner's culinary philosophy, with its emphasis on regional provenance, Lake House menus include a listing of key local producers and growers. Lake House also hosts events such as the '50 Mile Dinner' where all ingredients are sourced from within a 50-mile radius. The dinners celebrate local suppliers, organic produce and sustainable agricultural practices. Indicative of the revival of interest in the traditional health giving properties of the region, Lake House has also introduced 'Wellness Retreat Weeks' (Wolf-Tasker 2006b). Lake House offers yoga, tai chi, forest walks, spa treatments, gourmet cuisine, seminars and cooking demonstrations and such activities are designed to provide participants with a balance for mind, body and spirit. This diversity of provision within a single business is still exceptional within the region, but is reflective of how the economy has expanded the available business opportunities. Whilst the region generally, and Lake House in particular, has embraced many aspects of the commercial home phenomenon, trends such as the search for economies of scale (e.g. increasing room capacity) and the need to accommodate visitor preferences (flexibility of meal provision) have resulted in a stronger emphasis on image than on reality.

Figure 14.3 Wombat Hill Nursery and Cliffy's Emporium are examples of 'homely' local businesses located near the weekly Daylesford Market.

A growing number of tourism micro-businesses operate from home office settings. A notable example is the café and award winning hand-made chocolate outlet Sweet Decadence at Locantro. The premises, which were established in 1911, once housed Locantro's grocery store and were acquired by the current owners in 1999. The confectionary is produced on-site. Examples of the other tourism-related businesses along Daylesford's main thoroughfare are Ex Libris Prints and the Avant Garden bookshop. Cliffy's Emporium, a café/general store which features the produce of over 100 local suppliers and the adjacent Wombat Hill Nursery and Florist are examples of 'homely' local businesses which appeal to both tourists and locals. Some of these businesses operate from home settings, though with a varying focus on the tourist or local market. The latter types of business are more marginal to the commercial home concept, but it is argued here that they do play a critical role in understanding the interface between the domestic domain (the home), the visitor and the wider tourism appeal of the region.

Conclusions

Daylesford and Hepburn Springs are a microcosm of both the early development and more recent diversity of the commercial home in Australia. Provision in the area has expanded progressively from the simple guesthouse format, to diverse businesses operated by both established residents and incomers. These businesses cater to a variety of visitors, exhibiting a spectrum of lifestyle preferences. Some businesses are at best marginal to the commercial home definition as commonly understood, but it is argued here that these properties need to be considered alongside the more conventional commercial home, since they are critical to the emerging destination appeal. Local depictions of homeliness reflect the influence of migrant communities (i.e. non-indigenous to Australia) in the social, cultural and aesthetic landscape. Such ethnic plurality has shaped the development and operation of the commercial home sector, sometimes conveying nostalgia for forms and settings commonly found in Europe.

Like the demographic shifts evident in most Western industrialised nations, Australia in general and Daylesford and Hepburn Springs in particular, have experienced the 'tree change' phenomenon (Burnley and Murphy, 2004). The area is purposely marketed as satisfying a diverse range of resident and visitor interests, with target audiences including straight couples, gays and lesbians, families and retirees, those in search of pampering, gourmands, alternative lifestyle seekers and artists. The diversity of commercial home provision has contributed to Daylesford's reputation as a sought-after 'funky town' for tourists and locals. However, many businesses are trading on the imagery of homeliness and are not commercial homes according to the Lynch definition (2004). It is argued here that the commercial home definition needs to be refined and broadened to accommodate the relationship between 'homeliness' and regional tourism appeal.

Whilst the area's success as a tourist destination owes much to its social diversity, close encounters between hosts and guests in the commercial home setting and beyond increase the likelihood of clashes between conflicting values and attitudes. Given the typical informality of the commercial home sector and the absence of standardised approaches to presentation and the dissemination of information, it is important to understand host and visitor expectations thoroughly. This is particularly important in dynamic destinations such as Daylesford and Hepburn Springs, which are a complex mixture of traditional homeliness, domestic and inbound migrant influences and changing tourist demands. Such an understanding may guide the development of future accommodation provision. This includes the prevalence of the commercial home and its related forms, noting how they have waxed and waned in popularity over progressive decades. It seems likely that diversity will continue to be a tourism strength for the region but the particular mix of provision will still be subject to fluctuating fashions.

15 All at sea

When the commercial home is a sailing boat

Gayle Jennings

Introduction

Commercial home discourses tend to be hegemonically contextualised within fixed land-based settings. This chapter serves to extend the commercial home context to include 'mobile homes' in water-based settings. Such homes are more generally called vessels and are classified as sailing boats/yachts or motorised boats. As vessels, these 'mobile homes' have a variety of domains of use not directly related to the concept of a 'home', for example recreational sailing and other water-based tourism experiences as well as lifestyle pursuits. For some vessels, however, the concept of home 'style of life' (Adler 1935) and/or a 'home' concept are evident. In particular, some vessels exhibit elements of primary 'homes', secondary 'homes', and/or commercial homes.

Additionally, individually and collectively boats as well as harbours may be vicariously and explicitly utilised as home settings and to provide water-based home-scapes. Such commercially oriented and water-based home styles of life have complementarity with dominant domains of usage identified for land-based commercial homes (Lynch and MacWhannell 2000). They also have synergy with some elements of mobile land-based home accommodation albeit that the literature related to the latter is primarily considered from a self-catering perspective (Johns and Lynch 2007). Similarly, owners and/or managers' use of vessels for commercial purposes may be brokered across informal, intermediate and/or formal sectors (Lynch 1998; Lynch et al. 2003; Lynch and Tucker 2003). That being said, the focus of this chapter is sailing boats/yachts and in particular those yachts that are used for long-term ocean cruising.

Long-term ocean cruising is a sub-cultural lifestyle (Jennings 1999, 2005; Macbeth 1985) in which owners of boats sail and live aboard their vessels for extended periods of time crossing oceans of the world. Participants in the subculture are called cruisers and may be further distinguished as captain and crew. The words captain and crew distinguish positionality aboard vessels. Captains assume nautical leadership, management, as well as administrative and sailing roles, responsibilities and duties and delegate the same to crew. Cruising crew, generally, have some familial/relationship-based connection with the captain of a vessel and/or stake in the private ownership of the boat.

When cruisers use their vessels as commercial home enterprises, the cruisers become hosts and their guests are 'contributing' as in 'paying' crew. These guest-crew have no financial or familial/relationship stake in the ownership of the boat as opposed to crew who are hosts. In the course of this chapter, the latter will at times be referred to as host-crew, the former as guest-crew and the term home and boat/yacht will be used interchangeably where there is no ambiguity. The term passenger has not been applied. The term crew intimates participating in the activity of the cruising enterprise itself, whereas being a passenger is associated with being transported and cared for without having to participate in the working operations of the boat, albeit passengers may choose to participate at their leisure but it is not a formal requirement. The difference between crew and passenger articulates boundaries between a commercial cruising home enterprise (crew) and a commercial cruising enterprise (passenger).

Given that the cruisers provide sailing and lifestyle experiences, it is inappropriate to deem them 'sellers' (Slattery 2002) or 'providers of services' (Aramberri 2001). They are hosts. Similarly, the crew are 'guests' rather than 'buyers' (Slattery 2002) or 'consumers' (Aramberri 2001). Elsewhere, Lynch (2005a) has argued similarly with regard to commercial-homes host–guest nomenclature. The uniqueness of the provision of lifestyle experiences aboard yachts is further heightened when the overall context of the yacht is considered. It is a mode of transportation, an accommodation base, leisure and lifestyle pursuit and provider of 'travel experiences'. These experiences are much more than 'just being "there" but with participating, learning and experiencing the "there" they visit' (Pearce 1988: 209), which in cruising circumstances constantly changes as yachts make passages and ports of call.

This chapter focuses on long-term ocean cruisers who take on board 'contributing/paying' crew *in order to* economically support their lifestyle as well as gain additional crew and/or companionship. This focus will serve to extend the framing of commercial home enterprises to incorporate mobile and water-based homes. It will also illuminate the nature of experiences associated with such homes from the perspective of both hosts (owners, captains and family or relationship-based crew) and guests (contributing/paying-crew) so as to understand the nature of their respective experiences. In overview, it will become evident that cruisers' experiences associated with using their yachts as commercial homes are based on social actions framed around *in order to* motives (*Um-zu-Motiv*), that is, future oriented actions, while the guests' experiences are predicated on *because of* motives (*Weil-Motiv*) as well as *in order to* motives. See Schutz (1967) for extended discussion of *Um-zu-Motiv* and *Weil-Motiv*.

All at sea: sailing boats as home

Ethnographic research (Jennings 1999, 2005, 2007a) informing this chapter was carried out with monohull (single-hulled sailing vessels) yachts. Mono-hulled vessels, that is, yachts tend to be compact due to their overall dimensions. For example, a typical forty-foot cruising yacht has an overall length of 12.12 metres (40 feet), a possible width of 3.9 metres (12 feet) at the widest point, headroom (distance between cabin sole – floor and cabin ceiling) of 2.2 metres (6.5 feet). Subsequently, it is not surprising that the following qualifier is made when referring to boats: 'I like the self-sufficiency, the comfort of the boat, it's almost womb like, but it can get cramped' (cruising woman). While most boats are comfortably fitted out, some are more rudimentary, with this being directly linked to the overall cost of the boat, the age of the boat or the period of time since its last overhaul and refit or update, who is cruising aboard the boat, the cruising budget, and the emphasis on the need for comfort over other necessities. Albeit yachts may range from spartanly to luxuriously fitted-out, the greater focus is usually on sailing- and safety-related priorities.

While long-term ocean cruisers may not be considered to have a 'home' in the traditional land-based sense, long-term ocean cruisers certainly have a 'home construct' which is associated with their boats as evidenced in the following reflections: 'You have a permanent home, base, with plenty of facilities, your own water, foods and resources' (cruising man). 'You've got your home with you and it doesn't matter what strange place you are in you are always at home – you know no matter how rough things are, you feel secure in your own place with your own things around you' (cruising woman). In addition to providing a spatial and psychical space that is personalised and private within the changing land and seascapes that cruisers encounter, the boat also provides a space and place which has physiological and affective connections for cruisers as they pursue their lifestyle sailing and travelling aboard their own boats across the oceans of the world. This was evident in the latter cruising woman's comment above and in the following cruising woman's discourse: ' ... when we travel by the boat you keep coming back to your own cocoon, to your own womb, to things you know and get your batteries recharged and you're able to go out [again]'. Similarly, a well-known yachtsperson and yacht designer, Francis Herreshoff, affirmed: 'The cabin of a small yacht is a truly wonderful thing; not only will it shelter you from the tempest, but in the other troubles of life which may be even more disturbing, it is a safe retreat' (Marsh 1990: 62).

These spatial, psychical, physiological and affective connections have synergy with Lynch (2005c) wherein he writes of the home providing spatial and emotional groundings for its residents as well as security, relationships and sites of power conflicts. Further, Lashley's (2000b) social and private domains are evident, as is the commercial domain, which will be noted later in the chapter. In addition to the domains identified by Lynch and Lashley, there are personal-private-psychical and affective domains (Jennings 1999). These were found in cruiser and guest-crew commentaries and are associated with each person's individual (re)interpreted lived life experience as a separate domain emanating from and between social, private and commercial domains.

The preceding commentary about boats/yachts and home resonates with the notion of the 'environmental bubble' discussed by Boorstin (1964) with regard to post(mass)-modern tourists (Jennings 1999). Albeit, in this instance, it is a 'home bubble' aboard a yacht and, as already noted, is also a form of transportation as well as a vessel that offers recreational, leisure, sport and/or tourism pursuits. One cruiser provides insights into the integration of yachts as homes and forms of transport: 'I just thought about it as a mobile home but instead of being on land and pulled behind the car, it's on the water and you sail it. That's what I originally basically looked at it as, a mobile home.' Some of the perceived benefits of this integration of home and transport are: ' ... you have your home with you. It's a cheaper way of travelling and it saves accommodation. You can move at a slow or a very quick pace whichever you do you are not on a set itinerary' (cruising woman). Some cruisers, however, would argue that it is not a cheaper mode of travelling due to the initial capital investment in the boat as well as on-going maintenance costs. These costs can be further exacerbated if cruisers are still maintaining a land-based home. Having a boat as your principal and only home in addition to combining it with travel and transportation was perceived as being cheaper than engaging in other travel modes, accommodation styles and sole land-based home ownership.

Long-term ocean cruising: commercial home comparability and contrastability

Just as the majority of land-based homeowners do not open their homes up or use them for commercial enterprises, the majority of long-term ocean cruisers maintain their yachts as private non-commercial domains due to the nature of their reason or reasons for adopting a cruising lifestyle. One of those reasons was *because of* cruisers' negative reactions to anomic and alienating conditions in their mainstream lives, which cruisers sought to escape *in order to* find freedom in the margins away from rules, regulations and constraining societal structures and organisations. Another reason was associated with need fulfilment, goal seeking *in order to* self-actualise through challenge and adventure. A third reason was related to (*because of*) love, belonging and togetherness; a fourth reason was *in order to* pursue a dream; and, fifth, *in order to* travel. While the majority of cruisers had the financial wherewithal to adopt cruising lifestyles, some were not able to have sufficient to financially support it in a sustained manner. Still others did not have the physical or emotional resource power to cruise alone. These cruisers needed to support their lifestyle by blurring the boundaries between private and commercial domains (see Lashley 2000b). For these cruisers, rather than slow the progress of voyages by having to stop to find work in either the informal, intermediate or formal sectors; a number of cruisers chose to take on board 'guests' *in order to* keep voyaging. Such guests assist with covering costs of voyages and maintenance of the boat as well as providing crew to tackle lonely or taxing passages of some voyages.

Just as some cruisers may work outside the formal sector to increase their 'cruising kitty' (funds to support the cruising lifestyle), the use of the yacht in the commercial domain is primarily associated with the informal economic sector. This is in part *because of* previous anomic and alienating mainstream centre-based experiences of western societies especially with regard to bureaucracy and regulatory practices and processes. Another reason is to mask 'income generation' *because of* cruising permits and entry visas in nations around the world as well as living in the margins of other state systems.

As commercial homes, yachts are micro-enterprises, which tend to operate mostly outside state, national and international hospitality licensing and regulatory processes. Such positioning in the informal sector has complementarity with some land-based counterparts (refer to Lynch 1998; Lynch and Tucker 2003; and Lynch et al. 2003), who report on some land-based commercial homes attempting to avoid bureaucracy or being relegated to the informal sector because of their low commercial activity levels (Lynch 1998). Again, similar to land-based commercial homes (Shaw et al. 1987), part of the economic benefit of such cruising boat/home-commercial enterprises ends up being distributed into adjacent or 'host' communities into which the yachts seek moorings, berths, and anchorage.

Furthermore, provisioning for passages also generates positive benefits for 'host' communities, for example the buying of fruit and vegetables from local markets, which connects buyer and producer/seller, to use Slattery's (2002) terms, and thereby injects 'new' money to circulate within those communities. In some locations, money may be replaced with trade items – fishing hooks, tobacco, soap, washing detergent, flour, rice and sugar. In other instances, there may a significant leakage of revenue. For example, replacing a sail may require sophisticated repairs or expertise above that which exists in some cruising locations resulting in outsourcing of materials and labour. In such circumstances, the commercial home concept of a yacht differs from some of the commentary by Shaw et al. (1987) wherein commercial homes contribute to income staying in local communities. Additionally, unlike fixed land-based commercial homes, the mobility factor of boats distributes economic benefit across a number of host communities and contributes variously within those communities depending on the needs of the boat – provisions, repairs, maintenance, equipment purchases and whether or not materials and services are sourced locally or outside hosting communities.

It is important to note that most of the purchases in visited communities would be made regardless of the yacht being operated as a commercial enterprise or not. While paying-crew may increase the economic contribution, related to provision, souvenir buying and other services to the communities that are visited, generally boat maintenance is an ongoing element of the lifestyle as is provisioning, and the commercial home enterprise does

not change that. Consequently, turnover of commercial businesses as exemplified by Lynch et al. (2003) with regard to small family-run hotels does not
happen with regard to cruising yachts as commercial home enterprises.
People generally do not go cruising to operate their vessels as commercial
enterprises, but rather for the previously mentioned reasons which constitute
a 'style of life' or lifestyle pursuit. Turning the yacht into a commercial home
enterprise is a means that some cruisers use to supplement their cruising
finances and/or share passages by taking on paying-crew *in order to* sustain a
cruising lifestyle.

Subsequently, long-term ocean cruisers who use their boats as commercial
enterprises *in order to* economically support their lifestyle may be classified
as 'lifestyle entrepreneurs' (Buick et al. 2001; Shaw et al. 1987), or as 'social
entrepreneurs' if the support is economically and socially based. As already
stated, using the boat as a commercial home enterprise facilitates ease of
passage making for some ocean cruisers *in order to* continue cruising, and in
addition for some *because of* health and safety reasons: 'I get seasick so I
have a problem with that … and where he is travelling to [next], I don't
like … and that's the next scary part, I'm not going [on that passage]! He'll
have somebody with him. He'll take aboard crew' (cruising woman). The
waters through which the vessel intended travelling are alleged 'pirate'
waters, where boats may be illegally boarded, robbed, scuttled, and captain
and crew physically or mortally harmed. In this instance, and as is sometimes the case with other 'problematic' waters for safety reasons, cruisers
may take on board guest-crew and/or cruise in company (sail loosely in
company with other yachts).

All at sea: hosts and guests

The practices of using cruising yachts as commercial home enterprises is a
contested one, partially emanating from the operations being primarily situated in the informal sector and partially from differences in expectations by
hosts and guests regarding the nature of experiences and responsibilities.
Captains and hosts of cruising yachts which are used as commercial home
enterprises will often draw up crew agreements. Included in these agreements
are the terms and conditions of the cruising experience, the amount, reg-
ularity and nature of use of crew 'contributions' (payment for supporting the
experience). The term 'contribution' has specifically been used to position
the enterprise in the informal sector as a commercial home enterprise with
contributing crew as distinct from a commercial enterprise with paying passengers. However, this difference has been contested. Some guest-crew advocate that they are paying rather than contributing and that the boat has
subsequently been hired or chartered. A counter comment follows:

> You accept that your contribution isn't the price of a charter, or a pas-
> senger fare or for the benefit of the boat or the captain, but represents

your own share of the running costs. ... the deal is only to ask money to pay for the expenses, because it costs money to run a boat, and as long as a crew is going to enjoy a trip, sailing, learning new skills, discovering places, diving, fishing, sleeping on board, using the toilet, the stove, eating, there is absolutely no reason for the owner of the boat to pay for it all. It is not like ... it was a hardship to endure, you are here to enjoy yourself. Whatever you are doing in life, it costs money.

(http://karaka.site.voila.fr/)

Crew agreements also usually cover the vagaries of weather and sailing and potential inability to reach a port by a specific time should 'contributing crew' have onward or return travel arrangements:

I understand and accept that sailing voyages are by their very nature uncertain, and I will not hold the captain or the ship responsible for transportation to the original destination should the ship not reach it.

(http://karaka.site.voila.fr/)

Obviously, this condition separates the transportation role of the cruising commercial home from other transportation providers, which may require a more reliable schedule.

Long-term ocean cruising yachts as commercial homes: issues for hosts and guests

Like their land-based counterparts, yachts when used as commercial homes cross between private and commercial domains (Lynch 2005a). As already noted, yachts support compact lifestyles, wherein a boat's ability to offer a 'home' bubble or retreat can be seriously challenged when everyone is inside at one time. Adding guests and their belongings to the mix can further exacerbate and impact on the 'styles of life' of everyone onboard. Subsequently, when boats are used for commercial home enterprises, the private space of hosts immediately becomes merged with the public and commercial space of the guests. As a consequence, for paying guests coming aboard to 'stay', there are etiquettes, mores, language and nuances that need to be learnt and understood. The transition to boat-based life necessitates the hosts to 'educate' and 'socialise' the guests regarding these. If this is not undertaken effectively then marginalisation of guests from entry into cruising lifestyles and subculture may occur.

Usually, the guest is a 'stranger' (Gudykunst 1983; Simmel 1908/1971, 1950). The host's role is then to assist guests, especially uninitiated ones, to pass through the 'rites of initiation' and to move through 'preliminaries' (separation from own culture) into 'liminaries' (threshold rites of the subculture). Depending on how long the guests stay aboard they may move into 'post liminaries' (aggregation rites) (van Gennep 1975), that is, full participation in the subcultural lifestyle. Consequently and similar to land-based counter-parts, the role of the 'host' is central to the overall experience (Lynch 2005a; Tucker 2003b).

Moving a cruising boat from an essentially private domain into a com-mercial home context, necessitates hosts to have educational and hospitality skills to introduce and educate guests to lifestyle mores, to the overall func-tioning of boats and the skills of sailing and voyaging. Some cruisers have yet to develop and/or refine these skills. Earlier commentary by Bywater (1998) regarding the poor skills level of some commercial home operators in land-based precincts has applicability to a number of commercial home operators in water-based environments.

Long-term ocean cruising yachts as commercial homes: issues for hosts

For those long-term ocean cruisers who choose to turn their boats into commercial enterprises, this is not without consequences. The boat becomes an overlay of ambiguous spaces which are further problematised given the already explained contained-nature of the living and 'working' aboard yachts. For cruisers, the use of the boat as a commercial space results in issues related to social construction and performance of identity shifts. In making such shifts, cruisers simultaneously become 'micro-accommodation providers and operators' with all the attendant roles and responsibilities. This shift, whilst providing financial resources *in order to* continue cruising, re-associates some cruisers with the *because of* bureaucratic functions of mainstream life, which they initially sought to 'escape'. Moreover, for crui-sers private/public/commercial tensions arise from space sharing and the assignment of boat duties. The latter also provides the potential for generat-ing sites of equality and inequality, discrimination, marginalisation, and gender issues for host crew when roles and responsibilities are abrogated to guests with according power differential shifts from host crew to guest crew. Furthermore, to sustain a cruising lifestyle, as already stated, cruisers need to educate and socialise guest crew with regard to observance of rituals, as well as legal and bureaucratic responsibilities. The latter adds an additional responsibility for the captain, who has a formal role with recognised national and international responsibilities, regulations and rules to follow. From an official viewpoint, all responsibility rests with the captain despite signed crew contracts, which means that the captain is responsible for crew, both host-crew and guest-crew.

Long-term ocean cruising yachts as commercial homes: issues for guests

Guest-crew seek a cruising experience *because of* the lifestyle's cheaper transportation costs, slower pace of travel, ability to get into locations not on traditional travel routes, perceptions of adventure and serendipitous encounters with host-captains and host-crew. Guest-crew also seek cruising experiences *in order to* learn to sail, to experience the lifestyle and to see the world using a different travel mode.

For the guest-crew, their issues are related to appropriate cruising lifestyle behaviours and etiquette and, as previously discussed, living aboard a boat. Educating and socialising guest-crew may take time. As a consequence, guests need to experience opportunities to learn in conducive environments as opposed to some (forced) learning, which may occur in less than conducive conditions such as in 'crisis' moments. Furthermore, guests need to understand requisite knowledge and skill bases they will be required to learn in order to fulfil sailing and voyaging duties, otherwise mismatches may generate challenges beyond the skill levels of guests and cause anxiety and fear (Csikszentmihalyi 1997; Jennings 2001). Other issues for guest-crew relate to safety and security issues, which are connected to a captain's competency, a yacht's condition and with the areas through which yachts will travel. Gender issues associated with roles and responsibilities may be administered along stereotypical lines – domestic duties for women and sailing duties for men. Further, aboard boats, resources such as water, energy and space are limited and are generally managed in different ways to land-based practices. Guest-crew need to quickly adapt to these different resource management practices, especially if they have not cruised before. Subsequently, despite guest-crew agreements and briefings by host-captains and host-crew, the actuality of a cruising 'style of life' may result in mismatches between guest-crew expectations and satisfaction. That being said, from a sustainability perspective, a cruising 'style of life' has much to offer commercial home guests, especially, with regard to declining supplies of fossil fuels, peak oil crises, green house emissions, sustainable energy sources; as well as sustaining environments, cultures visited, 'experiences' provided (Jennings 2007b) and lifestyles pursued.

Furthermore, although commercial yacht-homes are small enterprises, they do enable cruisers to provide unique travel and cruising lifestyle 'experiences' (Gilmore and Pine 2002; Pine and Gilmore 1999) for guest-crew, which can be tailored to individuated markets or markets of one (Gilmore and Pine 2000). However, cruising hosts need to monitor the experiences that they provide with regard to core elements of quality tourism experiences, which are associated with personal and social connectivity, experience delivery, combinations of experiences and inter-connectivity of entire tourism experiences (Jennings et al. forthcoming).

Conclusions

The purpose of this chapter was to extend the consideration of commercial home enterprises beyond fixed land-based contexts. In doing so, this chapter focused on the subculture of long-term ocean cruisers who, *in order to* sustain a cruising lifestyle, choose to integrate a commercial home enterprise into their 'style of life'.

Such integration was not without its consequences. For cruisers, the use of the boat as a commercial space resulted in issues related to social construction and performance of identity, home/boat as commercial enterprise, private/ public tensions, sites of equality/inequality, discrimination, marginalisation, gender issues and observance of rituals, as well as legal and bureaucratic responsibilities. For the guest-crew, issues related to appropriate behaviours and etiquette, opportunities to learn in conducive environments, knowledge and skill match or mismatch to challenges, safety and security issues, gender issues associated with roles and responsibilities, resource usage, guest-crew expectations and satisfaction as well as legal requirements and protocols.

While this chapter has served to broaden the concept of 'home', and in particular the 'commercial home', away from land-based precincts, a number of developments are being proposed which further problematise the nature of where 'homes' are situated and in what 'scapes'. For example, at the time of writing this chapter, several ventures were identified, such as a residential cruise line (refer to http://www.residentialcruiseline.com/index.cfm) and cruise-ship apartments (for example, refer to http://www.freedomship.com/). In addition to these developments, there are also virtual-scapes, which have the potential to offer a variety of both e-land-based and e-water-based commercial home experiences. Subsequently, the concept of home and commercial home continues to be (re)constructed and (re)interpreted.

16 Conclusions and research considerations

Paul A. Lynch, Alison J. McIntosh and Hazel Tucker

The chapters in this volume have illustrated the significance of the commercial home enterprise as a distinctive area of study equivalent to that of hotel studies or the study of family or small businesses. Exploration of the commercial home leads to extroversion of the concept beyond hospitality and tourism lenses and labels (notably, the latter are described as unhelpful by McIntosh and Harris in Chapter 7) and necessitates examination and understanding of broader social influences and relationships. This chapter discusses the key themes emerging from the contributions, and includes reflection on distinctive issues involved in researching the commercial home as well as proposing future research considerations. Thus, the chapter is intended to consolidate the variety of contributing chapters in the book as well as to build upon key themes from previous research.

Emergent themes

Analysis of the book's chapters has identified the ten themes below for exploration. The themes are: 1) significance of home; 2) place and space; 3) performance and identity; 4) control; 5) host–guest relationships; 6) lifestyle entrepreneurs; 7) hospitality and society; 8) economic-development tool; 9) commodification; 10) hospitality as a social ethic. It is not the intention to suggest that commercial homes and their guests' experiences are homogeneous – far from it. As described by, for example, Moscardo in Chapter 2, commercial homes operate on a continuum whose purpose may range from simply providing budget accommodation, to enabling access to a particular activity to being a central part of the tourist experience. However, here, a thematic approach is the most practical, although the editors would stress the overlapping and interrelated nature of the themes. As Goulding states in Chapter 8, the commercial home is better seen and understood as an explanatory concept when taken as a whole.

Significance of home

Concepts of home lie at the heart of the commercial home enterprise and are prevalent in different forms. King and White articulate the contested nature of authenticity, eschewed by several of the authors who draw upon the performance metaphor for their analyses, and highlight homeliness as a cultural construct. Significantly, King and White refer to semi-nomadic concepts of domesticity as different from non-nomadic; it might be inferred that spatial anchoring or spatial mobility impinge upon the homeliness/domesticity concepts, although this dimension is played down by Jennings in respect of long-term ocean cruisers. Sloane-White associates traditional concepts of the rural Malay-Muslim home with social belonging, sociality and social exchange, and the theme of tradition and its associations is also explored by King and White in respect of regional tourism marketing practices. There is an apparent juxtaposition of homeostasis and change permeating several of the chapters. On the one hand, the home embodies tradition, historical associations, such as a sense of community and a way of life that lends itself to concepts of nostalgia, but on the other hand, much evidence is given of the changing nature and adaptability of the significance of home interrelated to broader social changes. Sloane-White illustrates the role home plays in identity formation, being a site of transaction, affirmation, justification and exchange of social, economic and entrepreneurial identities. Such identity formation is not simply at the micro- level but at a societal level where, in political discourses, the traditional home concepts of belonging and association embody the nation as a hospitable house, a nation host offering a hospitable paradise. Sloane-White presents most clearly the role of the home as a social networking vehicle that enables greater economic participation within the specific context of contemporary urban Malaysia. Thus, the home becomes a metaphor for commerce as well as social belonging.

O'Gorman and Lynch conceive the home (in whatever form) as a site of negotiation with the outside world whilst simultaneously being a site for attempting to preserve a prevailing way of life, although in turn finding it changed by external 'negotiation'. A similar tension is present in Tucker's chapter. Also, the chapter by Jennings suggests that creation of a home bubble conforms to Boorstin's (1964) 'environmental bubble'. For Jennings, the home is a psychical and affective space and it is perhaps this conceptualisation of space that householders seek to preserve in the face of external negotiation, such as, with paying guests. It would thus be wrong to conceive the private concept of home as immutable. Rather, it is subject to ongoing construction and interpretation. The admission of paying guests acts as a catalyst for change in the home concept as householders seek to adapt to accommodate this external agent through a variety of control mechanisms. Thus, commerciality leads to the migration, the evolution of the home concept, the creation of the commercial home with all its attendant ambiguity and complexity. Ambiguity of the commercial home is found in its various manifestations and associations of paradise and hell, equality and inequality, and in its being a site of discrimination and marginalisation. The commercial home also becomes an arena for the unfolding of new manifestations of gender (see Tucker's chapter). It blurs the boundaries between what is a home and what is a business, between private home and communal home, and between the home as a vehicle for the meeting of kindred spirits, or, conversely, a prison. Such ambiguity underlies host–guest relationships. Hosts may show resistance to the changes effected by hosting and this is illustrated most vividly by McIntosh and Harris and also Goulding, who variously draw attention to the underlying life course of the owner as influencing the construction and operation of the commercial home. Thus, for Goulding, the concept of temporality is explained by the nature of the commercial home, its private ownership and the social and emotional intensity of host–guest relationships within the particular setting.

The significance of the (commercial) home is not confined to the householder or host. As Benmore illustrates, host and also guest perceptions of home influence their behaviours and the varying permutations of behaviours are bound up with the commercial home crossing over social, private and commercial domains. Benmore illustrates the perceptions of the guest as at least partly a process managed by the host, whereas Carmichael and McClinchey argue that host and guest perceptions of the meaning of home are more of an outcome of the host–guest focus upon the physical and social settings. In whatever form, it is apparent that commercial homes form a very important part of the tourism product and this is particularly stressed in relation to rural accommodations. However, despite the identified importance of physical settings, Kastenholz and Sparrer suggest that in the case of farm holidays in Frisia there is a bifurcation between the accommodation product and the reality of farm life, illustrating the differential discourses and performances that may co-exist.

Place and space

Hall conceives spaces of home as including not just the house building, but also the surrounding gardens and countryside. Interestingly, his examination of exurban commercial homes suggests that their public and private space conception gives rise to a new post-preindustrial and post-industrial spatial development; the commercial home space involves internal and, in the specific New Zealand cultural context, external servicescapes connecting hosts and guests which he describes as a transformative space. Hall emphasises the cognitive and sensory responses of the individual to the physical setting. Similarly, Carmichael and McClinchey problematise the complex inter-relationship between the physical and human settings and the temporal, social, cultural, personal and emotional experiential dimensions that affect perceptions and behaviours relating not only to the commercial home but also to the region itself as part of the broader tourism product. However, they ultimately question the relevance of an applied servicescape model; indeed, it may be better to conceive of the commercial home as operating on a continuum from homescape in the smaller establishments through to servicescape in the larger ones.

Place is identified as having multiple meanings which include gendered meanings of the home space. Jennings and Stehlik challenge the concept of place as having an identity that is bound and fixed by time and space. Gendered space figures prominently in the analyses of Jennings and Stehlik, Tucker, and O'Gorman and Lynch. Tucker suggests that there is a gap in the research concerning the gendered nature of hospitality and tourism spaces. Gendered spatial areas emerge clearly, and gender is of particular relevance and importance in the context of the commercial home where home itself has different gendered meanings and construction of gendered identity is bound up with home space(s). The monastery described by O'Gorman and Lynch vividly illustrates gendered space, but the authors point to further spatial dimensions such as social hierarchical separation. Jennings and Stehlik, and also Tucker, illustrate the role of hospitality and tourism as social change agents influencing gendered spatial identity as well as having implications for family relationships. Jennings and Stehlik view spatial identity as mirroring a broader social patriarchal discourse and describe the hosting process as contributing to challenging concepts of space and identity, such that spatial expansion of hosting areas has a deeper symbolic meaning in terms of gendered relationships. Tucker, on the other hand, illustrates how hosting initially shows potential for challenging gendered spatial identity but ultimately cultural gender norms are reaffirmed through spatial separation of hosting from the private home; this latter process provides a novel insight into spatial separation of host and guest in the commercial home which is normally viewed simply in terms of privacy and a commoditised response to visitor throughput. The spatial anchoring of gendered roles in public and private space is clearly demonstrated by Tucker who also sheds light on how gendered identity and behaviours are controlled by being in the public gaze.

Goulding communicates alternative dimensions of the commercial home space through examination of its links to temporality. He illustrates the significance of the host's emotional attachment to space through its symbolic meanings: peace, ownership, free time, privacy, self-occupancy, and also the community embeddedness of the commercial home such that temporality may provide a welcome opportunity for the physical environment to be enhanced.

Performance of identity

The performance of identity is commented upon in several chapters. Kastenholz and Sparrer's chapter suggests farm life is staged in order to meet guest expectations, but also notes a social context where a broader staging of rural life is occurring through the neo-rural movement. Hall identifies a concern of exurbanite hosts to produce an environment that provides illusions of rural authenticity. Implicitly, given his concern with one specific type of commercial home host, the exurbanite, this environment is only one potential type to be found. Hall views the environmental production by the host as co-created with the guest, who shares the spatial representation and values informing its design. It is apparent that in this Goffman-type reading both host and guest are concerned with performing identities on a commercial home stage. Enabling identity performance and discourses affecting the production of hospitableness are artefacts which may be positioned deliberately in order to facilitate discourses supporting performances.

Tucker reveals the impact of gender on identities performed for tourists. In the case of male hosts, performances are linked with broader concepts of place and, interestingly, this mirrors a cultural context where male identities are more in the public gaze. Such male performances are identified as playing to, but also offering resistance to, the identity performed. However, performances by female hosts have greater ambivalence and are less able to resist objectification by the tourist gaze owing to the strength of gendered meanings of the home. Benmore is concerned with the presentation of the commercial home and elaborates differences in the extent to which housework draws upon hosts' emotional labour. Performance is also of particular importance in the context of the Benedictine monasteries described by O'Gorman and Lynch, with clothing's relation to identity-performance being especially noteworthy. Sloane-White illustrates the performance of a nostalgic identity of social belonging, a performance of hospitality as a social ideology, a resurrected social ethic. Pervasive to all the performances is the historical antecedents of the identities being performed, the tapping in to nostalgic discourses played out within the context of the commercial home thereby reinforcing the concept of the home as embodying tradition and upholding of certain cherished values. However, the performances are temporally displaced, in some cases leading to a loss of meaning with consequential effects for the construction and perception of the commercial home product.

McIntosh and Harris focus on the hosting discourse and its idyllic representation as communicated to researchers of the commercial home which they explain as owing to the social practice of hosting as the creation of a form of utopia. They illustrate how a discourse may be used by hosts in order to counteract alternative prevalent discourses, such as, stereotypes of retired people. Thus, the socio-political nature of host discourses is signalled, moving beyond performances as purely for economic benefit.

Control

Control is a central part of the hospitality relationship. In the commercial home a wide range of methods by which the host seeks to control the guest and the hosting experience are described. Various motivations for control strategies are identified including the achievement of greater efficiency and also realising more personal time (McIntosh and Harris), protection of the home and business (Benmore), hosts avoiding inequality in their meetings with tourists (Tucker), maintenance of host lifestyle (O'Gorman and Lynch; Jennings), management of the guest presence (Jennings), management of (bad) behaviour and dirty work (Benmore), and ensuring conformity with bureaucratic and legal guidelines (Jennings). McIntosh and Harris make the point that control strategies may be determined in conjunction with significant others.

Control methods described include: house rules and routines, actively and passively setting limits on capacity to host, use of emotional labour, the creation of spaces for guests enabling host control, spatial separation and social hierarchical spatial separation, education and socialisation of guests through etiquettes, mores, language, nuances, silence, use of bells and differentiation. The Benedictine monastery is of interest owing to the considerable emphasis upon control, perhaps owing to the communal nature of this form of commercial home and that many of the control methods are codified in the Benedictine rules. As is seen most clearly in the monastery and also in Tucker's analysis, hosts may be subject to control as much as guests. Jennings reveals how guests on long-term ocean cruisers who do not comply with the control methods risk marginalisation from the sub-culture and its lifestyle.

Host–guest relationships

The importance of the host–guest relationship is signalled by Kastenholz and Sparrer who identify it as central to the quality of the tourism experience. From a host perspective at least, relationships with guests within the commercial home can have a particular intensity not usually found within larger commercial accommodation. It is suggested that such intense relationships necessitate hosts with particular skills: flexibility, people-oriented, ability to harmoniously balance the home and hosting (McIntosh and Harris). Hall not only points to host-guest relationship management, especially concerning 'backstage' expectations, but also guest-guest interactions. Host motivations for hosting are variously identified as social, psychological and economic, as well as frequently being associated with maintenance or attainment of a desired lifestyle. Indeed, Carmichael and McClinchey view commercial home hosting as contributing to the rural lifestyle. Hosts are described as providing an interface for guests with the regional tourism product (Kastenholz and Sparrer, King and White) whose hospitality and relationship with the home and rural environment symbolises relationships that have largely been lost in time. Hosts' re-creation of such relationships might therefore be perceived as a special skill contributing to the success of the commercial home. Benmore explores the interactive nature of host–guest relationships and its complexity in relation to the commercial, social and private domains where a transactional (as opposed to reciprocal) relationship exists and the host attempts to create a climate of respect through communicating desired social standards, whilst endeavouring to be hospitable to the guests.

Authors who have explored extensions of the commercial home paradigm, notably Jennings, and also O'Gorman and Lynch, provide examples of particular forms of accommodation where guests are expected to participate to varying degrees in the distinctive lifestyles of their hosts. Entering such lifestyles is a key part of the attraction of the accommodation, for example the long-term ocean cruisers described by Jennings: low cost, slow travel, non-traditional travel routes, adventure, serendipitous encounters, learn to sail, to experience lifestyle and see the world through a different form of travel. Other forms of commercial home accommodation (mainly traditional but also virtual reality types), described here, are less prescriptive in terms of the lifestyle on offer, with the possible exception of forms of farm accommodation, although the frequently highly staged nature of the experience works against the enactment of lifestyle. In the case of farm tourism, other associations of commercial homes emerge from the descriptors, such as Kastenholz and Sparrer's description of a rural way of life, a strong interest in traditions, and a particular atmosphere.

Lifestyle entrepreneurs

Commercial home owners are often associated with the label of lifestyle entrepreneurs and this proves a helpful analytical lens for several of the authors here. A question of increasing importance in terms of research into lifestyle entrepreneurs concerns the sort of lifestyle that is supposedly achieved. Examination of commercial home owners allows some light to be shed on this matter, although the lack of homogeneity of commercial home owners means that it is dangerous to generalise in the absence of carefully defined samples.

A starting point is the idea that commercial home owners are socially marginalised (McIntosh and Harris, Mottiar and Laurinickova) operating in relative isolation both sectorally, personally and often geographically. Hosting therefore offers the potential of not only economic benefits that may support a certain improved lifestyle but also social and psychological benefits in addition to, for some hosts, looking after their children from home. Hosting therefore may be entered into in order to facilitate a desired lifestyle and may assist in providing life meaning at a particular lifestage (McIntosh and Harris). Mottiar and Laurincikova provide some evidence of female hosts achieving their starting goals to a fairly large extent and thereby attaining a better lifestyle. The authors also point out that the hosts' benchmark for success is geared around the household rather than the business, so that lifestyle attainment is not being judged in purely economic terms. However, despite achieving particular goals, the act of hosting, as also pointed out by Jennings, and Jennings and Stehlik, creates tensions, particularly in relation to achieving a work–life balance which many might associate with realisation of a desired lifestyle. Indeed, Jennings, and also Jennings and Stehlik, illustrate how hosting to support a lifestyle, owing to its function as a change agent, can jeopardise the lifestyle identity sought as well as giving rise to conflict in family relationships. In the case of long-term ocean cruiser hosts, a problem of hosting is that it re-engages hosts with a bureaucratic world of regulation they may be seeking to escape. Both Jennings and Stehlik, and Tucker illustrate the gendered spatial tensions that

arise from hosting. Kastenholz and Sparrer draw attention to two dichotomous lifestyles – agriculture and tourism – that operate in the context of
the farmstay and it is perhaps a consequence of the struggle for their recon-
ciliation that leads to the staging of farm tourism. The importance of balancing the personal and family lifestyle alongside the hospitality work is a
common tension.

Goulding's argument that lifestyle proprietorship affords temporal flexibility
in commercial homes and provides a basis for flexible, independently constructed trading patterns is important. Alongside the lifestyle goal, Goulding
identifies conditioning factors as well as a broad motivational spectrum as
being influential, thereby adding to theory regarding business operational
behaviours through a more nuanced understanding predicated on not just the
lifestyle entrepreneur lens but the broader characteristics of the commercial
home lens.

Hospitality–society linkage

A recurrent theme is the adaptability of commercial homes to social changes
highlighting the dynamic link between hospitality and society. This link is
the subject of increasing attention as hospitality is used as a means of examining society (Lashley et al. 2007). Thus, Moscardo, through adoption of a systems analysis, locates the commercial home as part of a bigger socio-economic
picture. Sloane-White vividly illustrates the connection between the use of
private home hospitality for career and business purposes and broader socio-
political discourses. Tucker illustrates how tensions centring around gendered
space and hosting are a microcosm of broader cultural performances.

The relationship between the evolution of the commercial home and social
change is explored in some depth by King and White who trace the development of guesthouses in Australia to a commercial accommodation market
positioning in response to social discourses concerning the evils of alcohol.
Thus guesthouses became associated with gentility, the middle class, married
couples and females, and a sense of community. More recent upsurge in the
forms of commercial homes are described as arising from destination popularity with inbound migrants. Commercial homes contribute both as a business
outlet and to the appeal of the region through association with contemporary
discourses such as a slower-paced lifestyle and traditional homeliness. However, the commercial homes' contribution to social change is multi-faceted.
At a local level it contributes to profound socio-economic changes through
mere presence and concentration, through increasing housing costs and
added pressure on lower-income residents, through attracting creative incomers and reducing residents' sense of belonging. Of particular interest in King
and White's account is how commercial homes have moved from being
associated with an alternative sub-group to becoming mainstream. One sees
clearly therefore how the examination of commercial homes can serve as a
lens permitting exploration of their dialectical relationship with society.

An economic development tool

Reflecting the societal linkage, commercial homes are used as a key economic development tool in rural regions (Kastenholz and Sparrer, King and White), frequently as part of a rural tourism 'product' or regional tourism destination promotion. Kastenholz and Sparrer illustrate how the commercial home is identified under legislation as part of an economic development approach that provides employment opportunities, is pro-architectural preservation, facilitates locals to stay in an area, and is integrative to the community and to the landscape. Similarly, King and White associate the diversification of a regional economy with the commercial home sector and with the importance of what the commercial home embodies, i.e. homeliness and being a key part of promoting the regional tourism appeal.

Various tensions arise with the use of the commercial home as an economic development tool, the main one being that of commodification, discussed below. As Jennings argues in the case of long-term ocean cruisers, some commercial home enterprises operate in the informal economic sector, and so the introduction of payment by guests creates its own tensions. These tensions may be managed in various ways, such as through the choice of terminology in the informal economic sector whereby reference may be made to 'contributions' rather than 'payment' and to 'crew' rather than 'guests'. Similarly, 'voluntary donation' is used as a term to refer to payment made by visitors to the Benedictine monastery (O'Gorman and Lynch). Some commercial home hosts may therefore wish to remain outside of legislative and policy spheres of influence and control, and this stance is integral to the nature of the experience they offer. Mottiar and Laurincikova's analysis reveals the hierarchical importance to hosts of first personal, then social and finally professional exchange networks, clearly signalling the difficulties of economic development agencies successfully engaging with a significant proportion of commercial home hosts.

Commodification

Although commercial homes may be associated with offering personalised usually serviced accommodation, a number of the chapters directly or indirectly suggest their increasing commodification (Carmichael and McClinchey, Hall, Jennings and Stehlik, Kastenholz and Sparrer, King and White, Moscardo, Sloane-White). Thus, multiple varieties of commercial home are described. For example, Moscardo suggests commercial homes operate on a continuum with three different forms of accommodation with different price bands. She also suggests that commercial home users may have distinctive profiles but with regional variations, that they seek particular features in travel destinations, and that they participate in distinctive patterns of activity. Such research affirms the distinctive nature of commercial homes whilst recognising their operation across a range of forms of accommodation.

Just as Carmichael and McClinchey point to certain types of commercial home, including older heritage homes, having 'manicured flower gardens', Hall, too, provides examples of hosts managing the sensory experiences of guests in relation to hearing, smell and vision. Further, the commercial home 'servicescape' is developed and managed in order to offset a potential loss of privacy and other issues arising from the sharing of personal and family space. Kastenholz and Sparrer's comparison of international practise is of particular interest in revealing legislative approaches that commodify commercial homes. For example, in Portugal legislation not only codifies types of commercial homes but also suggests clear specification of private and public frontiers in a possible attempt to reduce host–guest tensions that may otherwise arise. Kastenholz and Sparrer locate the commodification of the commercial home as part of a larger picture of commercialising rurality, in part apparently adapting to tourists' wishes. The authors draw attention to the underlying logic of integrating commercial homes into the larger development of the regional tourism product.

King and White describe a similar commodification process, suggesting that many visitors are seeking homeliness as a key part of the specific destination experience. They thus argue for an extension of the commercial home concept based upon an apparent need 'to accommodate the relationship between "homeliness" and regional tourism appeal', citing in particular how homeliness is used as in the promotion of cafés, bookshops, and a café/general store. Sloane-White provides similar examples, such as a restaurant and a home office, where 'actors … sometimes conceived of their modern enterprises as "virtual reality" homes … , reconstructing symbols, fitments and architecture of traditional Malay-Muslim homes into business ideas' (p. 160). So, 'the sociability evoked by the traditional Malay house is being transformed … into a business model' (p. 160). Clearly, King and White's examples above are closest to the virtual reality type of commercial home but, as with Sloane-White's examples, without being a part of the home accommodation sector. What King and White, and Sloane-White's analyses do most clearly, and as echoed also by Kastenholz and Sparrer, is to reveal a process of not only commodification of the commercial home as a physical product but also the commodification of the concept of homeliness across the commercial home and broader service sector. King and White's contribution is interesting in its revealing of a fairly clear commodified commercial home product being promoted as part of a distinctive regional destination tourism strategy. Characteristics of this product include: traditional authentic personalised service, offering local/slow food, having a historical heritage setting, offering homeliness and domesticity but at the same time being associated with hedonism, escapism, an edgy style, diversity, tolerance and creativity.

Echoing a concern at least dating back to one of the seminal studies of a type of commercial home, the British bed and breakfast (Stringer 1981), there is an apparent danger in commodifying the commercial home in that such a process may well damage the type of accommodation experience on offer. Kastenholz and Sparrer express such a concern in relation to the peculiar charm of commercial homes being threatened pointing to a potential loss of authenticity with hosts who 'instrumentalise their sentiments to offering customers [not guests – editors' emphasis] a personalised service' (p. 145). Kastenholz and Sparrer thus point to the seemingly inevitable process of 'commodification and commercialisation of home and rural space, as well as spatial separation between hosts and guests, [that] apparently increase with growing business experience' (p. 147).

The ethic of hospitality

This analysis started with identifying the home at the heart of the commercial home and certainly it represents one half of the heart. The other might be conceived of as the ethic of hospitality (Molz and Gibson 2007) whose various manifestations are found in the commercial home. O'Gorman and Lynch identify the creation of a shared space for hospitality allowing hosts and guests to construct a temporary moral universe. Certainly the role of commercial homes in providing such a hospitality space and bringing people together is noteworthy. At its simplest, then, and perhaps its most idyllic, are hosts who are 'people-oriented individuals looking for wider social contact and the opportunity to share in hearing the travel stories of guests' (McIntosh and Harris, (pp. 99–100). However, the commercial motive complicates the hospitality provision. Benmore addresses this ethical dilemma by asking whether the host–guest relationship should be primarily a hospitable exchange or a commercial transaction. Benmore points to an example of the manifestation of a hospitality conflict whereby the use of emotional labour as part of the admissions vetting process in order to protect the home and business, apparently conflicts with the cultural origins of hospitality traditions. A further hospitality dilemma that has received attention here is that of the problem of commodification of hospitality and the objectification of hosts by the tourist gaze and also its resistance.

O'Gorman and Lynch's contribution highlights rules of hospitality, a social ethic of hospitality that seems pervasive to varying degrees in almost all the chapters here. They argue that everything the monastery guest experiences is a symbol for how guests should be treated under the Benedictine rules; that the ritual reception of guests and the provision of hospitality act as both a bridge and barrier between monastic and secular worlds. Certainly, the sense of reaching out across worlds is a common theme with hospitality both bringing people together but also through its inherent controlling processes acting as a barrier as well in order to civilise the other. For example, hospitality reaches across the inner world of the commercial home host and the outer world represented by the guests, the rural and the urban, the non-affluent and the affluent, the marginalised and the seemingly non-marginalised, the community representative and the visitor, the local and the tourist. The symbolic nature of hospitality is also prevalent: hospitality as an economic vehicle, as a social vehicle, as a mediation of marginalisation and loneliness, as a development tool of social networks and as a re-negotiator of gendered relationships.

Sloane-White joins the two halves of the commercial home heart by suggesting that the modern (Muslim) home can have economic utility manifested via the traditional cultural idiom of hospitality in that it can provide earnings and proceeds through host–guest exchanges. It is not money that is exchanged here but other 'capital': status, social ambition and political control, thus having social and psychological benefits. In the specific context Sloane-White describes, the hosts are electing to invest in sociability, participating in self-interested transactions submerged in traditional, ritual and even rural dimensions of home and hospitality. Such an instrumental use of hospitality, whether for economic, social or psychological benefits, is certainly fundamental to the commercial home accommodation enterprise.

Considerations for further research

In addition to the above key themes, the contributions in this book have raised a number of avenues for further research that will be synthesised here.

Economic development, policies and impacts

The economic and social importance of commercial homes, not only but especially in peripheral and frequently rural locations should not be underestimated. There would be merit in focusing upon the impacts of developing commercial homes within the whole of a region, for example their impacts on economy, employment and the environment, as well as on local produce purchasing patterns and links with specifically 'local' produce development. Additionally, there needs to be further examination of locations where clustering of commercial homes is occurring in order to consider their implications for local economic development, as well as for fostering positive social and community outcomes.

Marketing and destination promotion aspects of the impacts of the commercial home need to be further explored, with particular regard to how commercial homes interact with a destination's image, the range of tourism activities on offer, as well as the potential for commercial homes to play a leading role in the creation of a locale as a tourism destination. There needs to be a focus on the significant role of hosts in contributing towards the destination image, including their articulation with a destination's marketing strategy and, through information provision, their influence on guests' activities in the region.

Lifestyle entrepreneurship

The commercial home as an arena for application of the concept of lifestyle entrepreneurship requires particular consideration. The tensions between the hosts gaining self-fulfilment weighed against the benefits and disadvantages for the family as a whole need to be assessed. Such evaluation should include how children see the role of business in the home and its effects on family life. In addition there should be greater focus on the role of significant others and their contributions towards commercial hosting. Examination is required of the significance of independent variables such as purpose-designed vs. non-purpose-designed hosting accommodation, as well as year-round vs. seasonal hosting, and the implications for hosting and issues such as attitudes to personal space. In relation to the wider community, there needs to be investigation of the implications of the commercial home product in mitigating the negative environmental and social implications of tourism visitation through the commercial home's provision of the positive opportunities for hosts to be in control of the temporal dimensions of tourism activity.

Gender perspectives

Further examination is needed of the gendered production and experience of commercial homes, as well as the implications that running commercial homes has, differentially, for men and for women and their relationship with each other, the family and the community. Further understanding is needed of the ways in which women balance the time given to family and business, and also of how workload is divided between female and male partners in the commercial home business. Another area that merits further investigation is how hosting affects female hosts' interrelationship with their local community and, indeed, their position in relation to the wider society.

Market

This book has advanced our understanding of the visitor profile of the commercial home, which is an area that arguably suffers from the same neglect as the broader commercial home phenomenon. In line with the general thrust of the further research considerations, extensive consideration of the commercial home market should be undertaken.

Host–guest

The intensity of host–guest interaction, together with the point that this interaction is a key part of the commercial home product, comprises a considerable area for further investigation and theorisation. For instance, understanding needs to be deepened concerning the interrelationship of the complex nexus between the role of place, the physical environment, social interactions and control, and host–guest experiences. Whilst the commercial home product, and indeed the guests' perceptions of the destination overall, is very much contingent upon the success of the host–guest relationship, this relationship is often difficult to predict and therefore to manage. Further research into this area could therefore have practical application for training and development interventions focusing on hosts' values, beliefs and attitudes towards hosting in general, as well as issues relating to space, privacy and guest behaviours.

Another area of interest is the extent to which host–guest interaction leads to a sense of well-being and self-worth for both the host and the community through the success of developing relationships with 'strangers' and which often includes development of new and long-term friendships. This focus relates to the ethic of hospitality and how the exchange of hospitality in the commercial home contributes to a wider sense of global community.

Policy and commodification

The adaptability of the commercial home to changing social discourses merits scrutiny, with particular regard to the ways in which the commercial home is evolving in specific social, cultural and political contexts. Particular attention should be given to the product implications arising from the commodification of the commercial home as a result of the surrounding legislation and policy contexts.

Home and hospitality

An important area for further research is the concept of home and homeliness in different non-Euro-centric cultural contexts, for example nomadic societies and developing economies. Moreover, whilst the concept of nostalgia is the subject of wider academic debate, its role in the commercial home as identified in this book has largely been overlooked to date. It is therefore important to further research and theorise the significance or otherwise of home and homeliness for both tourists/guests and for hosts. Further understanding is needed regarding the extent to which contemporary tourists and travellers search for experiences of homeliness and 'tradition' while on the move.

The contributions have led to the development of the typology of commercial homes to include the communal home as well as identifying how the essence of the virtual reality commercial home, which is based around an emulation of the home concept, finds resonance in the product development of retailing outlets. Both of these areas are significant in their own right and merit investigation.

The study of hospitality to date arguably has adopted a narrow cultural perspective. Whilst this book has endeavoured to capture a range of international perspectives, the editors acknowledge the limitations in this range. There is a significant need to address diverse cultural conceptions of hospitality and the contributing roles of the commercial home in a broader cultural context.

Methodological issues

The examination of commercial homes has prioritised the need for researchers to engage in reflexive practices, especially concerning their own position, standpoint and world-views. The researcher needs to consider the ethical responsibility to those being researched when diverse experiences are being shared and discussed. Attention needs to be given to how these diverse experiences are ascribed importance or otherwise in our writing and publishing forms. Reflection is required on the value and significance of the more diverse personal experiences for the advancement of hospitality and tourism theory.

Final thoughts and considerations

The commercial home concept brings the home into the realm of commerce whilst, at the same time, the home remains anchored in its original realm of social belonging and separation from the public world beyond. This book has shown how the commercial home is therefore subject to ongoing negotiation and interpretation, as a space which is continuously re-constructed through new performances that undermine binaries associated with the home, for example public/private, domestic/commercial, stranger/friend. Moreover, as the home is a site of social identity, tradition and belonging, the commercial home becomes a space that encapsulates a microcosm of the social world. As such, the commercial home constitutes a significant research paradigm in its own right.

This book has demonstrated this point through its bringing together of a broad range of international and interdisciplinary perspectives, thereby enabling not only the study of commercial homes in their own right, but also their study in a broader social perspective. This in-depth examination of the commercial home empowers the study of small commercial accommodation and provides a strong conceptual basis for its further investigation and exploration. In so doing, the book has legitimised the study of commercial homes as a mainstream subject of attention and has therefore succeeded in its aim of challenging the primacy of the hotel paradigm.

The book has contributed to a number of significant debates: the ethic of hospitality, lifestyle entrepreneurship, community and economic development, the home construct, gender roles and relationships, and the process of commodification. A major contribution has been to give prominence to this enduring and important but largely neglected socio-economic phenomenon of the home accommodation enterprise. It has made a significant contribution towards unravelling of the domestic/commercial dynamics that become entangled when commercial hospitality is offered in a home setting. A focus on commercial home accommodation has thus been shown to build more consistent patterns of connections between key variables, thereby affording a better way to integrate research findings, and is demonstrative of the power of the commercial home lens.

Bibliography

Adler, A. (1935) 'The fundamental views of Individual Psychology', *International Journal of Individual Psychology*, 1: 5–8.

Aitchison, C. (2000) 'Poststructural feminist theories of representing others: a response to the "crisis in leisure studies" discourse', *Leisure Studies*, 19(3): 127–144.

Aitchison, C. and Reeves, C. (1998) 'Gendered (bed) spaces: the culture and commerce of women only tourism', in C. Aitchison and F. Jordan (eds) *Gender, Space and Identity. Leisure Culture and Commerce*, Brighton: Leisure Studies Association.

Akpinar, N., Talay, İ., Ceylan, C. and Gündüz, S. (2004) 'Rural women and agro-tourism in the context of sustainable rural development: a case study form Turkey', *Kluwer Journal*, 6: 473–486.

Allan, G. and Crow, G. (eds) (1989) *Home and Family: Creating the Domestic Sphere*, London: Macmillan.

Allcock, J. (1995) 'Seasonality', in S. Witt, and L. Moutinho (eds) *Tourism Marketing and Management Handbook*, Hemel Hempstead: Prentice Hall International.

Allen, E., Langowitz, N. and Minniti, M. (2007) *Global Entrepreneurship Monitor 2006. Report on Women and Entrepreneurship*, Babson College and London School of Business.

Alston, M. (1995) *Women on the Land: The Hidden Heart of Rural Australia*, Sydney: University of New South Wales Press.

Ames, E. (1999) *What is Bed and Breakfast*. Online. Available HTTP: http://www.bluemontbb.com/bb/whatis.htm (accessed 17 December 2006).

Andersson, T., Carlsen, J. and Getz, D. (2002) 'Family business goals in the tourism and hospitality sector: case studies and cross-case analysis from Australia, Canada, and Sweden', *Family Business Review*, 15(2): 89–106.

Andrew, B.P. (1997) 'Tourism and the economic development of Cornwall', *Annals of Tourism Research*, 24(3): 721–735.

Andrew, R., Morrison, A. and Baum, T.G. (2001) 'The lifestyle economics of small tourism businesses', *Journal of Travel and Tourism Research*, 1: 16–25.

Appadurai, A. (1981) 'Gastro-politics in Hindu South Asia', *American Ethnologist*, 8(3): 494–511.

Arahi, Y. (1998) Rural tourism in Japan: the regeneration of rural communities. Agnet. Online. Available HTTP: http://www.agnet.org/library/data/eb/eb457/eb457.pdf (accessed 10 July 2007).

Aramberri, J. (2001) 'The host should get lost: paradigms in the tourism theory', *Annals of Tourism Research*, 28: 738–761.

Ardener, S. (ed.) (1981) *Women and Space: Ground Rules and Social Maps*, London: Croom Helm.

Argyle, M., Furnham, A. and Graham, J. (1981) *Social Situations*, Cambridge: Cambridge University Press.

Armstrong, K. (1978) 'Rural Scottish women: politics without power', *Ethnos*, 43(1–2): 51–72.

Armstrong, M.J. (1988) 'Festival open houses: settings for interethnic communication in urban Malaysia', *Human Organization*, 47(2): 127–136.

Ashforth B.E. and Humphrey R.H. (1993) 'Emotional labour in service roles: the influence of identity', *Academy of Management Review*, 18(1): 88–115

Ashton, P. and Newton, G. (1999) *Sleepy Hollow to Boom Town: A Case Study on the Impact of Tourism*, Bendigo: Video Education Australasia.

Ateljevic, J. (2007) 'Small tourism firms and management practices in New Zealand: the center stage macro region', *Tourism Management*, 28(1): 307–316.

Ateljevic, J. and Doorne, S. (2000) 'Staying within the fence: lifestyle Entrepreneurship in tourism', *Journal of Sustainable Tourism*, 8(5): 378–392.

Australian Bureau of Agricultural and Resource Economics, ABARE 2007, '*Australian Farm Survey Results 2004–05 to 2006–07*', Commonwealth of Australia, Canberra.

Bar On, R.R. (1975) *Seasonality in Tourism: A Guide to the Analysis of Seasonality and Trends for Policy Making*, London: Economist Intelligence Unit, Technical Series No.2.

Barnett, S. (2001) 'Manaakitanga: Maori hospitality – a case study of Maori accommodation providers', *Tourism Management*, 22(1): 83–92.

Barrett, M. (1980) *Women's Oppression Today*, London: Verso.

Baum, T.G. and Hagen, L. (1999) 'Responses to seasonality: the experiences of peripheral destinations', *International Journal of Tourism Research*, 1: 299–312.

Beardsworth A. and Keil T. (1997) *Sociology on the Menu*, London: Routledge.

Becken, S., Frampton, C. and Simmons, D. (2001) 'Energy consumption patterns in the accommodation sector – the New Zealand case', *Ecological Economics*, 39: 371–386.

Bed & Breakfast and Farmstay NSW & ACT (BBFNSW) (2006) *Definitions of Bed & Breakfast, Farmstay and other "hosted" accommodation in New South Wales and the ACT.* Online. Available HTTP: http://www.bedandbreakfast.org.au/membership/definitions.html (accessed 18 October 2007).

Bernard, Y. (1991) 'Evolutions of lifestyles and dwelling practices in France', *Journal of Architectural and Planning Research*, 8(3), 192–201.

Bernardes, J. (1987) '"Doing things with words": sociology and "family policy" debates', *Sociological Review*, 35: 697–702.

Bitner, M.J. (1990) 'Evaluating service encounters: the effects of physical surroundings and employee responses', *Journal of Marketing*, 54: 69–82.

—— (1992) 'Servicescapes: the impact of physical surroundings on customers and employees', *Journal of Marketing*, 56(2): 57–72.

Blair, S. (1986) *Blair's Guide to Victoria and Melbourne*, 3rd edn, Melbourne: Globe Press.

Blunt, A. and Rose, G. (eds) (1994) *Writing Women and Space: Colonial and Postcolonial Geographie*, New York: Guildford Press.

Böckmann, A. (1988) 'Xeniteia-Philoxenia als Hilfe zur Interpretation von Regula Benedicti 53 im Zusammenhang mit Kapitel 58 und 66', *Regulae Benedicti Studia*, 14/15: 131–144.

Booms, B.H. and Bitner, M.J. (1982) 'Marketing services by managing the environment', *Cornell Hotel and Restaurant Administration Quarterly*, 23: 35–39.

Boorstin, D. (1964) *The Image: A Guide to Pseudo Events in America*, New York: Harper and Row.

Borias, A. (1974) 'Hospitalité Augustinienne et Bénédictine', *Revue de Histoire de Spiritualité*, 50: 3–16.

Bouquet, M. (1982) 'Production and reproduction of family farms in South-West England', *Sociologia Ruralis*, 22: 227–44.

Bouquet, M. and Winter, M. (eds) (1987) *Who from Their Labours Rest? Conflict and Practice in Rural Tourism*, Aldershot: Avebury.

Bowlby, S., Gregory, S. and McKie, L. (1997) '"Doing home": patriarchy, caring and space', *Women's Studies International Forum*, 20(3): 343–350.

Bowler, I., Clark, G., Crockett, A., Ilbery, B. and Shaw, A. (1996) 'The development of alternative farm enterprises: a study of family labour farms in the Northern Pennines of England', *Journal of Rural Studies*, 12(3): 285–295.

Brandth, B. and Haugen, M.S. (1998) 'Breaking into a masculine discourse: women and farm forestry', *Sociologia Ruralis*, 38(3): 427–442.

—— (2006) 'Emotional work in host–guest relations. Examples from farm tourism', paper presented at the Research Partners' Meeting, 'Crossroads of tourism and work', Kilisjärvi, Finnish Lapland, Paper No.2/06, pp. 21–24.

Breathnach, P., Henry, M., Drea, S. and O'Flaherty, M. (1994) 'Gender in Irish tourism and employment', in V. Kinnaird and D. Hall (eds) *Tourism: A Gender Analysis*, Chichester: John Wiley & Sons.

Brindley, C. (2005) 'Barriers to women achieving their entrepreneurial potential', *International Journal of Entrepreneurial Behaviour and Research*, 11(2): 144–161.

Brotherton B. and Wood R. (2000) 'Hospitality and hospitality management', in C. Lashley and A. Morrison (eds) *In Search of Hospitality*, Oxford: Butterworth-Heinemann.

Brown, B. (1987) 'Recent tourism research in South East Dorset', in G. Shaw and A. Williams (eds) *Tourism and Development: Overviews and Case Studies of the UK and the South West Region*. Working Paper No. 4, Department of Geography, University of Exeter.

Bruder, K. (1998) 'A pragmatics for human relationship with the divine: An examination of the monastic blessing sequence', *Journal of Pragmatics*, 29: 463–491.

Bruegmann, R. (2005) *Sprawl: A Compact History*, Los Angeles: University of California Press.

Bruni, A., Gherardi, S. and Poggio, B. (2004) 'Doing gender, doing entrepreneurship: an ethnographic account of intertwined practices', *Gender, Work and Organization*, 11(4): 406–429.

Brush, C.G. (1992) 'Research on women business owners: past trends, a new perspective and future directions', *Entrepreneurship Theory and Practice*, 16(4): 5–30.

Bryson, B. (1996) *Notes from a Small Island*, Maidenhead: Black Swan.

Buick, I., Halcro, K. and Lynch, P.A. (2001) 'Death of the lifestyle entrepreneur: a study of Scottish hotel proprietors', *Praxis: The Journal of Applied Hospitality Management*, 2(2): 114–125.

Buitelaar, M. (1993) *Fasting and Feasting in Morocco*, Oxford: Berg.

—— (1998) 'Public baths as private places', in K. Ask and M. Tjomsland (eds) *Women and Islamization: Contemporary Dimensions of Discourse on Gender Relations*, Oxford and New York: Berg.

Bunce, M. (1994) *The Countryside Ideal: Anglo-American images of Landscape*, London: Routledge.

Burnley, I. and Murphy, P. (2004) *Sea Change: Movement from Metropolitan to Arcadian Australia*, Sydney: University of New South Wales.

Busby, G. and Rendle, S. (2000) 'The transition from tourism on farms to farm tourism', *Tourism Management*, 21: 635–642.

Butler, J. (1990) *Gender Trouble: Feminism and the Subversion of Identity*, New York: Routledge.

Butler, R.W. (2001) 'Seasonality in tourism: issues and implications', in T.G. Baum, and S. Lundtorp (eds) *Seasonality in Tourism*, Amsterdam: Pergamon.

Butler, R.W., Hall, C.M. and Jenkins, J. (eds) (1998) *Tourism and Recreation in Rural Areas*, Chichester: John Wiley.

Buttner, E.H. and Moore, D.P. (1997) 'Women's organizational exodus to entrepreneurship: self reported motivations and correlates for success', *Journal of Small Business Management*, 35(1), 34–46.

Bywater, M. (1998) 'The guests are sad and desolate. The owner is a sociopath. Welcome back to the Great British hotel', *Observer*, 4 October: 31.

Caballé, A. (1999) 'Farm tourism in Spain: a gender perspective', *GeoJournal*, 48: 245–252.

Cadieux, K.V. (2005) 'Engagement with the land: redemption of the rural residence Fantasy?', in S. Essex, A. Gilg and R. Yarwood (eds) *Rural Change and Sustainability: Agriculture, the Environment and Communities*, Wallingford: CABI.

—— (2006) 'Productive and amenity relationships with 'nature' in exurbia: engagement and disengagement in urban agriculture and the residential forest', unpublished PhD thesis, University of Toronto.

Campo, J.E. (1991) *The Other Sides of Paradise. Explorations into the Religious Meanings of Domestic Spaces in Islam*, Columbia, SC: University of South Carolina Press.

Carmichael, B.A. (2005) 'Understanding the wine tourism experience for winery visitors in the Niagara Region, Ontario, Canada', *Tourism Geographies*, 7(2): 185–204.

Carmichael, B.A. and McClinchey, K.A. (forthcoming) 'Motives, rural images and tourism brokering roles of rural accommodation entrepreneurs in South Western Ontario, Canada', *Tourism Review International*.

Carr, A. (2007) 'Small firms in tourism: international perspectives', *Annals of Tourism Research*, 34(4): 1099–1100.

Carsten, J. and Hugh-Jones, D. (eds) (1995) *About the House: Lévi-Strauss and Beyond*, Cambridge: Cambridge University Press.

Cave Hotel Saksagan. Online. Available HTTP: http://www.turtletour.net/saksagan/ (accessed 7 February 2008).

Chant, S. (1992) 'Tourism in Latin America: perspectives from Mexico and Costa Rica', in D. Harrison (ed.) *Tourism in the less developed countries*, London: Belhaven.

Chaumartin, H. (1946) *Le mal des ardents et le feu Saint-Antoine*, Vienne la Romaine: Les Presses de l'Imprimerie Ternet-Martin.

Chell, E. and Baines, S. (1998) 'Does gender affect business "performance"? A study of microbusinesses in business services in the UK', *Entrepreneurship and Regional Development*, 10(2): 117–135.

Chu, P. (2000) 'The characteristics of Chinese female entrepreneurs: motivation and personality', *Journal of Enterprising Culture*, 8(1): 67–84.

Clark, M. (1995) *Interpersonal Skills for Hospitality Managers*, London: International Thomson Business Press.

Clarke, I. and Schmidt, R.A. (1995) 'Beyond the servicescape: the experience of place', *Journal of Retailing and Consumer Services*, 3: 149–162.

Clarke, J. (1999) 'Marketing structure for farm tourism: beyond the individual provider of rural tourism', *Journal of Sustainable Tourism*, 7(1): 26–47.

Cohen, E. (1979) 'A phenomenology of tourist experiences', *Sociology*, 13: 179–201.

—— (1988) 'Authenticity and commoditization in tourism', *Annals of Tourism Research*, 15(3): 371–386.

—— (1992) 'Pilgrimage centers: concentric and excentric', *Annals of Tourism Research*, 19(1): 33–50.

Collins, D. and Tisdell, C. (2002) 'Age-related lifecycles. Purpose variations', *Annals of Tourism Research*, 29(3): 801–818.

Comer, L. (1974) *Wedlocked Woman*, Leeds: Feminist Books.

Commons, J. and Page, S. (2001) 'Managing seasonality in peripheral tourism regions: the case of Northland, New Zealand', in T.G. Baum and S. Lundtorp (eds) *Seasonality in Tourism*, Oxford: Pergamon.

Cooper-Marcus, C. (1995) *House as a Mirror of Self*, Berkeley, CA: Conari Press.

Craig-Smith, S., Cody, N. and Middleton, S. (1993) *How to be Successful at Home Hosting and Farm Tourism*, Gatton: University of Queensland.

Crang, P. (1997) 'Performing the tourist product', in C. Rojek and J. Urry (eds) *Touring Cultures: Transformations of Travel and Theory*, London: Routledge.

Cromie, S. (1987) 'Motivations of aspiring male and female entrepreneurs', *Journal of Occupational Behaviour*, 7(3): 251–261.

Crow, G. (1989) 'The post-war development of the modern domestic ideal', in G. Allan and G. Crow (eds) *Home and Family: Creating the Domestic Sphere*, London: Macmillan.

Crump, J. (2003) 'Finding a place in the country: exurban and suburban development in Sonoma County, California', *Environment and Behavior*, 35: 187–202.

Csikszentimhalyi, M. (1997) *Living Well: the Psychology of Everyday Life*, London: Phoenix.

Cukier, J., Norris, J. and Wall, G. (1996) 'The involvement of women in the tourism industry of Bali, Indonesia', *Journal of Development Studies*, 33(2): 248–270.

Daly, M., Dehne, A., Leffman, D. and Scott, C. (1999) *Australia: The Rough Guide*, 4th edn, London: Rough Guides Ltd.

Dann, G. and Cohen, E. (1991) 'Sociology and tourism', *Annals of Tourism Research*, 18(1): 155–169.

Darke, J. (1994) 'Women and the meaning of home', in R. Gilroy and R. Woods (eds) *Housing Women*, London: Routledge.

Darke, J. and Gurney, C. (2000) 'Putting up? Gender, hospitality and performance', in C. Lashley and A. Morrison (eds) *In Search of Hospitality: Theoretical Perspectives and Debates*, Oxford: Butterworth-Heinemann.

Dart, J. (2006) 'Home-based work and leisure spaces: settee or work-station', *Leisure Studies*, 25(3): 313–328.

Davidson, J. and Spearritt, P. (2000) *Holiday Business: Tourism in Australia since 1870*, Melbourne: Miegunyah Press.

Davies, E.T. and Gilbert, D.C. (1992) 'A case study of the development of farm tourism in Wales', *Tourism Management*, 13(1): 56–63.

Daylesford Getaways (2007) *Daylesford and Surrounds Accommodation Guide, 2006–07*, Daylesford.

Decrop, A. and Snelders, D. (2005) 'A grounded typology of vacation decision-making', *Tourism Management*, 26: 121–132.

Delaney, C. (1991) *The Seed and the Soil – Gender and Cosmology in Turkish Village Society*, Berkeley and Los Angeles: University of California Press.

Dernoi, L.A. (1981) 'Alternative tourism: towards a new style in North–South relations', *International Journal of Tourism Management*, 2(4): 253–264.

Derrida, J. and Dufourmantelle, A. (2000) *Of Hospitality*, Stanford: Stanford University Press.

DeTienne, D.R. and Chandler, G.N. (2007) 'The role of gender in opportunity identification', *Entrepreneurship Theory and Practice*, 31(3): 365–386.

DGT (2006) *Turismo no Espaço Rural 2005*, Lisboa: DGT.

Di Domenico, M. (2003) *Lifestyle entrepreneurs' in the hospitality sector: guest house owner-occupiers*, unpublished PhD thesis, University of Strathclyde.

Di Domenico, M. and Lynch, P. (2007a) 'Commercial home enterprises: identity, space and setting', in C. Lashley, P. Lynch and A. Morrison (eds) *Hospitality: A Social Lens*, Oxford: Elsevier.

—— (2007b) 'Host/guest encounters in the commercial home', *Leisure Studies*, 26(3): 321–338.

Dimock J.F. (ed.) (1876) *Giraldi Cambrensis Opera*, London: Longman, Green, Longman, and Roberts.

Donovan, R. and Rossiter, J. (1982) 'Store atmosphere: an environmental psychological approach', *Journal of Retailing*, 58: 34–57.

Douglas, M. (1991) 'The idea of a home: a kind of space', *Social Research*, 58(1): 287–307.

Dupuis, A. and Thorns, D.C. (1996) 'Meaning of home for home owners', *Housing Studies*, 11(4): 485–501.

Eade, J. and Sallnow, J. (eds) (1991) *Contesting the Sacred: The Anthropology of Christian Pilgrimages*, London: Routledge.

Ellis, F. (2000) *Rural Livelihoods and Diversity in Developing Countries*, Oxford: Oxford University Press.

England Research (2005) *Rural and Farm Tourism*, London: Visit Britain.

Evans, N.J. and Ilbery, B.W. (1989) 'A conceptual framework for investigating farm-based accommodation and tourism in Britain', *Journal of Rural Studies*, 5(3): 257–266.

—— (1992) 'Advertising and farm-based accommodation: a British case study', *Tourism Management*, 13(4): 415–422.

Fairclough, N. and Kress, G. (1993) *Critical Discourse Analysis*, unpublished manuscript.

Farrell, B.H. and Twining-Ward, L. (2004) 'Reconceptualizing tourism', *Annals of Tourism Research*, 31(2): 274–205.

Fennel, D.A. and Weaver, D.B. (1997) 'Vacation farms and ecotourism in Saskatchewan, Canada', *Journal of Rural Studies*, 13(4): 467–475.

Fesenmaier, D.A. and Gretzel, U. (2004) 'Searching for experience: technology-related trends shaping the future of tourism', in K. Weiermair and C. Mathies (eds) *The Tourism and Leisure Industry: Shaping the Future*, Binghamton: Haworth Press.

Fielden, S.L., Davidson, M.J., Dawe, A.J. and Makin, P.J. (2003) 'Factors inhibiting the economic growth of female owned small businesses in North West England', *Journal of Small Business and Enterprise Development*, 10(2): 152–166.

Finch, J. and Hayes, L. (1994) 'Inheritance, death and the concept of home', *Sociology*, 28(2): 417–433.

Fineman S. (2003) *Understanding Emotion at Work*, London: Sage.

Fitzsimons, P. and O'Gorman C. (2007) *The Global Entrepreneurship Monitor 2006. The Irish Report*, Dublin: Dublin City University.

Fleisher, A. and Tchetchik, A. (2005) 'Does rural tourism benefit from agriculture?', *Tourism Management*, 24: 493–501.

Flognfeldt, T. (1988) 'The employment paradox of seasonal tourism', paper presented at Pre-Congress Meeting of the International Geographical Union, Christchurch, New Zealand, 13–20 August.

—— (2001) 'Consequences of summer tourism in the Jotunheimen Area, Norway', in T.G. Baum and S. Lundtorp (eds) *Seasonality in Tourism*, Amsterdam: Pergamon.

Florida, R. (2002) *The Rise of the Creative Class*, New York: Basic Books.

Frederick, M. (1993) 'Rural tourism and economic development', *Economic Development Quarterly*, 7(2): 215–224.

Freedom ship International (2005) Online. Available HTTP: http://www.freedomship.com/ (accessed 1 August 2007).

Gannon, A. (1994) 'Rural tourism as a factor in rural community economic development for economies in transition', *Journal of Sustainable Tourism*, 2(1/2): 51–60.

Garcia-Ramon, M. D., Canoves, G. and Valdovinos, N. (1995) 'Farm tourism, gender and the environment in Spain', *Annals of Tourism Research*, 22(2): 267–82.

Gatrell, J. and Collins-Kreiner, N. (2006) 'Negotiated space: tourists, pilgrims and the Baha'i terraced gardens in Haifa', *Geoforum*, 37(5): 765–778.

Geertz, C. (1960) *The Religion of Java*, Chicago: University of Chicago Press.

—— (1973) *The Interpretation of Cultures*, New York: Basic Books.

Gervasoni, C. (2005) *Bullboar, Macaroni and Mineral Water: Spa Country's Swiss Italian History*, Hepburn Springs: Hepburn Springs Swiss Italian Festa Inc.

Getz, D. and Carlsen, J. (2000) 'Characteristics and goals of family and owner-operated businesses in the rural tourism and hospitality sectors', *Tourism Management*, 21: 547–560.

—— (2005) 'Family business in tourism: state of the art', *Annals of Tourism Research*, 32(1): 237–258.

Getz, D. and Nilsson, P.A. (2004) 'Responses of family businesses to extreme seasonality in demand: the case of Bornholm, Denmark', *Tourism Management*, 25(1): 17–30.

Getz, D. and Petersen, T. (2005) 'Growth and profit-oriented entrepreneurship among family business owners in the tourism and hospitality industry', *International Journal of Hospitality Management*, 24: 219–242.

Getz, D., Carlsen, J. and Morrison, A. (2004) *The Family Business in Tourism and Hospitality*, London: CABI International.

Gibbs, P. (1987) *Building a Malay House*, Oxford: Oxford University Press.

Gibson, H. (2001) 'Gender in tourism: theoretical perspectives', in Y. Apostolopoulos, S. Sönmez and D. Timothy (eds) *Women as Producers and Consumers of Tourism in Developing Regions*, Westport, CT: Praeger Publishers.

Gibson, H. and Yiannakis, A. (2002) Tourist roles. Needs and the lifecourse', *Annals of Tourism Research*, 29(2), 358–383.

Giddens, A. (1984) *The Constitution of Society: Outline of the Theory of Structuration*, Cambridge: Polity Press.

Gillespie, S. D. (2000) 'Maison and sociétés à maisons', in R.A. Joyce and S.D. Gillespie (eds) *Beyond Kinship: Social and Material Reproduction in House Societies*, Philadelphia: University of Pennsylvania Press.

Gilman, C.P. (1980) 'The home: its work and influence', in E. Malos (ed.) *The Politics of Housework*, London: Allison and Busby.

Gilmore, J.H. and Pine, B.J. (2000) *Markets of One: Creating Customer-Unique Value through Mass Customization*, MASS: Harvard Business School Press.

—— (2002) *The Experience is the Marketing: A Special Report*, Louisville, KY: BrownHerron.

Gladstone, J. and Morris, A. (2000) 'Farm accommodation and agricultural heritage in Orkney', in F. Brown and D. Hall (eds) *Tourism in peripheral regions: case studies*, Clevedon: Channel View.

Goffee, R. and Scase, R. (1985) *Women in Charge: The Experience of Female Entrepreneurs*, London: Allen and Unwin.

Go F.M., Monachello M.L. and Baum T. (1996) *Human Resource Management in the Hospitality Industry*, Chichester: Wiley.

Goffman, E. (1959) *The Presentation of Self in Everyday life*, Middlesex, UK: Penguin.

Gössling, S. and Mattson, S. (2002) 'Farm tourism in Sweden: structure, growth and characteristics', *Scandinavian Journal of Hospitality and Tourism*, 2(1): 17–30.

Goulding, P. (2006) *Conceptualising supply-side seasonality in tourism: a study of the temporal trading behaviours of small tourism businesses in Scotland*, unpublished PhD thesis, University of Strathclyde.

Goulding, P., Baum, T.G. and Morrison, A.J. (2004) 'Seasonal trading and lifestyle motivation: experiences of small tourism businesses in Scotland', *Journal of Quality Assurance in Hospitality and Tourism*, 5(2/3/4): 209–238.

Grant, M., Human, B. and Le Pelley (1997) 'Seasonality', *Insights*, London: BTA/ETB. July, pp. A5-A9.

Grayson, K. (1998) 'Commercial activity at home: managing the private servicescape', in J.F. Sherry Jr. (ed.) *Servicescapes: The Concept of Place in Contemporary Markets*, Lincolnwood, IL: Nike Town Chicago Business Books.

Gudykunst, W.B. (1983) 'Toward a typology of stranger-host relationships.' *International Journal of Intercultural Relations*, 7: 401 – 413.

Guerrier Y. (1999) *Organizational Behaviour in Hotels and Restaurants: An International Perspective*, Chichester: Wiley.

Guerrier Y. and Adib A. (2000) 'Working in the hospitality industry' in C. Lashley and A. Morrison (eds) *In Search of Hospitality*, Oxford: Butterworth-Heinemann.

—— (2003) 'Work at leisure and leisure at work: a study of the emotional labour of tour reps', *Human Relations*, 56(11): 1399–1417.

Guliz, G. and Belk, R.W. (1996) 'I'd like to buy the world a coke: consumptionscapes in the less affluent world', *Journal of Consumer Policy*, 19: 271–304.

Gundry, L. K., Ben-Yoseph, M. and Posig, M. (2002) 'Contemporary perspectives on women's entrepreneurship: a review and strategic recommendation', *Journal of Enterprising Culture*, 10(1), 67–86.

Gurney, C. (1996) *Meanings of Home and Home Ownership: Myths, Histories and Experiences*, unpublished PhD thesis, University of Bristol.

Gustafson, P. (2001) 'Meanings of place: everyday experience and theoretical conceptualizations', *Journal of Environmental Psychology*, 21: 5–16.

Halfacree, K. (1994) 'The importance of "the rural" in the constitution of counterurbanization: evidence from England in the 1980s', *Sociologia Ruralis*, 34: 164–189.

Hall, A.D. (1989) *Metasystems Methodology*, Oxford: Pergamon Press.

Hall, C.M. (2004a) 'Small firms and wine and food tourism in New Zealand: issues of collaboration, clusters and lifestyle', in R. Thomas (ed.) *Small Firms in Tourism: International Perspectives*, Oxford: Elsevier.

—— (2005a) *Tourism: Rethinking the Social Science of Mobility*, Harlow: Pearson.

—— (2005b) 'Reconsidering the geography of tourism and contemporary mobility', *Geographical Review*, 43(2), 125–139.

—— (2005c) *Tourism: Reconsidering the Social Science of Mobility*, Harlow: Pearson.

Hall, C.M. and Müller, D. (eds) (2004) *Tourism, Mobility and Second Homes: Between Elite Landscape and Common Ground*, Clevedon: Channelview Publications.

Hall, C.M. and Rusher, K. (2004) '"Risky lifestyles"? Entrepreneurial characteristics of the New Zealand bed and breakfast sector', in R. Thomas (ed.) *Small Firms in Tourism: International Perspectives*. Oxford: Elsevier.

—— (2005) 'Entrepreneurial characteristics and issues in the small-scale accommodation sector in New Zealand', in E. Jones and C. Haven (eds) *Tourism SMEs, Service Quality and Destination Competitiveness: International Perspectives*, Wallingford: CABI.

Hall, D. (2004b), 'Rural tourism development in southeastern Europe: transition and the search for sustainability', *International Journal of Tourism Research*, 6(3): 165–176.

Harris, L.C. (2002) 'The emotional labour of barristers: an exploration of emotional labour by status professionals', *Journal of Management Studies*, 39: 553–584.

Harris, C. and McIntosh, A. (2007) 'Work–life balance in the commercial home: a study of the personal experiences of home hosts in New Zealand', in CAUTHE: Proceedings of the 17th Annual Conference – Past Achievements, Future Challenges. (Vol. CD-ROM): University of Technology Sydney, 11–14 February 2007.

Hartmann, R. (1986) 'Tourism, seasonality and social change', *Leisure Studies*, 5(1): 25–33.

Harvey, M. J., Hunt, J. and Harris, C.C. (1995) 'Gender and community tourism dependence level', *Annals of Tourism Research*, 22: 349–66.

Hasan-Uddin Khan (1981) 'The Malay house', in *MIMAR 2: Architecture in Development*, Hasan-Uddin Khan (ed.), Singapore: Concept Media.

Heal, F. (1990) *Hospitality in Early Modern England*, Oxford: Clarendon Press.

Helms, M. (1997) 'Women and entrepreneurship: the appealing alternative: business perspective', *Journal of Enterprising Culture*, 10(2): 16–19.

Henry, C. and Kennedy, S. (2002) *In Search of a New Celtic Tiger: Female Entrepreneurship in Ireland*, Dundalk: Centre for Entrepreneurship Research, Dundalk Institute of Technology.

Hepburn Shire Council (2006) '*Tourism Policy*', Daylesford.

Hilton, R. N. (1956) 'The basic Malay house', *Journal of the Malayan Branch of the Royal Asiatic Society*, 29(3): 134–155.

Hirschey, M., Pappas, J. and Whigham, D. (1993) *Managerial Economics: European Edition*, London: The Dryden Press.

Hochschild, A.R. (1979) 'Emotion work, feeling rules, and social structure', *American Journal of Sociology*, 85(3): 551–575.

—— (1983) *The Managed Heart: Commercialisation of Human Feeling*, London: University of California Press.

Hollander, J. (1991) 'The idea of a home: a kind of space', *Social Research*, 58(1): 31–49.

Holloway, J.C. (1998) *The Business of Tourism*, Harlow: Addison Wesley Longman.

Holmengen, H. and Bredvold, R. (2003) 'Motives: the driving forces in achieving pre-ferenced goals in tourism enterprises', in *Quality of Life Reflections*, Arnhem: ATLAS.

Holzherr, G. (1982) *Die Behediktsregel: Eine Anleitung Zu Christlichem Leben*, Benziger, Verlag.

Hoque, K. (2000) *Human Resource Management in the Hotel Industry*, London: Routledge.

Horn, W. and Born, E. (1979) *Plan of St Gall: A Study of the Architecture & Econ-omy of, & Life in a Paradigmatic Carolingian Monastery*, Berkeley: University of California Press.

Hossain, A. (2004) *Bed and Breakfast Visitors in Australia*, Canberra: Bureau of Tourism Research.

Ilbery, B., Bowler, I., Clark, G., Crockett, A. and Shaw, A. (1998) 'Farm-based tourism as an alternative farm enterprise: A case study from the Northern Pennines, England', *Regional Studies*, 32(4): 355–364.

Immerfall, S. (ed.) (1998) *Territoriality in the Globalizing Society: One's Place or None?*, Berlin: Springer Verlag.

Ingram, G. and Sherwood, T. (2002) 'A profile of farm tourism: the South West Tapestry region of Western Australia', *Rural Society* 12(1): 17–26.

Ireland, M. (1993) 'Gender and class relations in tourism employment', *Annals of Tourism Research*, 20: 666–684.

Jackson, J. and Murphy, P. (2006) 'Clusters in regional tourism. an Australian case', *Annals of Tourism Research*, 33(4): 1018–1035.

James, K. (1989) *Women in Rural Australia*, Brisbane: UQP.

—— (2000) 'Agricultural women in Central Queensland and changing modes of production: a preliminary exploration of the issues', *Rural Society*, 10(1): 63–78.

Jennings, G.R. (1999) *From the centre to the margins: an ethnography of long term ocean cruising*, unpublished PhD thesis, Murdoch University, Perth.

—— (2001) 'Flow: having the right skills for the challenge 2001: a tourism odyssey', in *TTRA 32nd Annual Conference Proceedings*, Travel and Tourism Research Association, Fort Myers Florida, pp. 236–246.

—— (2005) 'Caught in the irons: one of the lived experiences of cruising women', *Tourism Research International*, 9(2): 177–193.

—— (2006) 'Quality tourism experiences – an introduction', in G.R. Jennings and N. Nickerson (eds) *Quality Tourism Experiences*, Burlington, MA: Elsevier.

—— (2007a) 'Sailing/Cruising', in G. Jennings (ed.) *Water-based Tourism, Sport, Leisure and Recreation Experiences*, Burlington, MA: Elsevier.

—— (2007b) 'Sustainability of tourism: sport, adventure and recreation in water based environments', in G.R. Jennings (ed.) *Water-based Tourism, Sport, Leisure and Recreation*, London: Elsevier.

Jennings, G.R. and Stehlik, D. (1999) 'The innovators are women: the development of farm tourism in Central Queensland, Australia', paper presented at the 1999 Annual ISTTE conference. One World, One Community, One Mission, Vancouver, Canada, pp. 84–98.

Jennings, G.R., Lee, Y.S., Cater, C., Ayling, A., Ollenburg, C. and Lunny, B. (forth-coming) 'Quality tourism experiences: reviews, reflections, research agendas', *Journal of Hospitality and Leisure Marketing*, Special Issue – Experience Marketing.

Johns, N. and Lynch, P. (2007) 'The self-catering accommodation market: A review of electronic and other sources', *International Journal of Hospitality Management*, 26: 293–309.

Johnston-Walker, R. (1998) 'The accommodation motivations and preferences of international free and independent travellers to New Zealand', in R. Mitchell, B. Ritchie, M. Thyne and A. Carr (eds) *Pacific Rim Tourism: Past, Present, Future*, Dunedin: Centre for Tourism, University of Otago.

—— (1999) 'The accommodation motivations and accommodation usage patterns of international independent pleasure travelers', *Pacific Tourism Review* 3: 143–150.

Jones, G. (2000) 'Experimenting with households and inventing "Home"', *International Social Science Journal*, 52(2): 183–194.

Jordan, J.W. (1980) 'The summer people and the natives: some effects of tourism in a Vermont vacation village', *Annals of Tourism Research*, 7: 34–55.

Joyce, R.A. and Gillespie, S.D. (eds) (2000) *Beyond Kinship: Social and Material Reproduction in House Societies*, Philadelphia: University of Pennsylvania Press.

Julier, G. (2005) 'Urban designscapes and the production of aesthetic consent', *Urban Studies*, 42(5/6): 869–887.

Kandiyoti, D. (2002) 'Introduction: reading the fragments', in D. Kandiyoti and A. Saktanber (eds) *Fragments of Culture: The Everyday of Modern Turkey*, New Jersey: Rutgers University Press.

Kaplan, S. (1995) 'Meditation, restoration and the management of mental fatigue', *Environment and Behavior*, 15: 169–182.

Karaka (n.d.) Online. Available: http://karaka.site.voila.fr (accessed 13 July 2007).

Kastenholz, E. (2002) 'The role and marketing implications of destination images on tourist behavior: the case of Northern Portugal', unpublished Phd thesis, Universidade de Aveiro.

—— (2004) '«Management of demand» as a tool in sustainable tourist destination development', *Journal of Sustainable Tourism*, 12(5): 388–408.

Kaufman, T.J., Weaver, P.A. and Poynter, J. (1996) 'Service attributes of B&B operators', *Cornell Hotel & Restaurant Administration Quarterly*, 37(4): 29–33.

Keane, M. (1992) 'Rural Tourism and Rural Development', in H. Briassoulis and J. van der Straaten (eds) *Tourism and the Environment*, Dodrecht: Kluwer Academic Publishers.

Kelebek Pension. Online. Available HTTP: http://www.kelebekhotel.com (accessed 7 February 2008).

Kerlogue, F. (2003) 'Malay meanings and metaphors in the Jambi Seberang house', in S. Sparkes and S. Howell (eds) *The House in Southeast Asia: a Changing Social, Economic and Political Domain*, London and New York: Routledge Curzon.

Knight, J. (1996) 'Competing hospitalities in Japanese rural tourism', *Annals of Tourism Research*, 23(1): 165–180.

Kotler, P. (1973) 'Atmospherics as a marketing tool', *Journal of Retailing*, 49: 48–64.

Kotler, P., Bowen, J. and Makins, J. (2003) *Marketing for Hospitality and Tourism*, 3rd edn, Upper Saddle River, NJ: Pearson Education Ltd.

Lane, B. (1994) 'What is rural tourism?', *Journal of Sustainable Tourism*, 2: 7–21.

Lang Research (2001) *Interest in Agri-Tourism*, Toronto: Lang Research.

Lanier, P. (2000), 'Bed-and-breakfasts: A maturing industry', *Cornell Hotel & Restaurant Administration Quarterly*, 41(1): 15.

Lashley, C. (2000a) 'Towards a Theoretical Understanding', in C. Lashley and A. Morrison (eds) *In Search of Hospitality*, Oxford: Butterworth Heinemann.

—— (2000b) 'In search of hospitality: towards a theoretical framework', *International Journal of Hospitality Management*, 19(1): 3–15.

Lashley C. and Morrison A. (eds) (2000) *In Search of Hospitality*, Oxford: Butterworth Heinemann.

Lashley, C., Lynch, P.A. and Morrison, A. (eds) (2007) *Hospitality: A Social Lens*, Oxford: Elsevier.

Lawrence, R.J. (1990) 'Public collective and private space: a study of urban housing in Switzerland', in S. Kent (ed.) *Domestic Architecture and the Use of Space*, New York: Cambridge University Press.

Lenoir, A. (1856) *Architecture Monastique*. Paris: Impr. Nationale.

Lethlean, J. (2007) 'Gong a great honour', *The Age* (Epicure supplement), Melbourne, January 30, p. 3.

Levy, D. and Lerch, P. (1991) 'Tourism as a factor in development: implications for gender and work in Barbados', *Gender & Society*, 5(1), 67–85.

Lim Jee Yuan (1987) *The Malay House. Rediscovering Malaysia's Indigenous Shelter System*, Penang, Malaysia: Institut Masyarakat.

Llewellyn, S. and Northcott, D. (2005) 'The average hospital', *Accounting, Organizations and Society*, 30: 555–583.

Long, V. and Kindon, S. (1997) 'Gender and tourism development in Balinese villages', in T. Sinclair (ed.) *Gender, Work and Tourism*, London: Routledge.

Long, V. and Wall, G. (1995) 'Small scale tourism development in Bali', in M. Conlin and T. Baum (eds) *Island Tourism: Management, Principles and Practice*, Sussex: John Wiley and Sons Ltd.

Lovelock, C., Patterson, P.G. and Walker, R.H. (1998) *Services Marketing: Australia and New Zealand*, Sydney: Prentice Hall.

Lowe, A. (1988) 'Small hotel survival – an inductive approach', *International Journal of Hospitality Management*, 7(3), 197–223.

Lubetkin, M. (1999) 'Bed-and-breakfasts: advertising and promotion', *Cornell Hotel & Restaurant Administration Quarterly*, 40(4): 84–90.

Lundtorp, S., Rassing, C.R. and Wanhill, S. (2001) 'Off-season is no season: the case of Bornholm', in T.G. Baum and S. Lundtorp (eds) *Seasonality in Tourism*, Amsterdam: Pergamon.

Lynch, P. (1998) 'Female microentrepreneurs in the host family sector: key Motivations and socio-economic variables', *International Journal of Hospitality Management*, 17(3): 319–342.

—— (1999) 'Host attitudes towards guests in the home stay sector', *Tourism and Hospitality Research*, 1(2): 119–144.

—— (2000a) 'Setting and it's significance in the homestay sector explorations', in A. Roper and Y. Guerrier (eds) *A Decade of Hospitality Management Research*, Oxford: Butterworth Heinemann.

—— (2000b) 'Networking in the homestay sector', *The Service Industries Journal*, 20 (3), 95–116.

—— (2000c) 'Homing in on home hospitality', *The Hospitality Review*, 2(2), 48–54.

—— (2003) 'Hospitality, space and social control in the homestay sector', unpublished PhD thesis, Queen Margaret University, Edinburgh.

—— (2004) 'Home sweet home: the significance of the home setting in hospitality', in *Proceedings of the Council of Australian Tourism and Higher Education Annual Research Conference*, Brisbane, Australia.

—— (2005a) 'Reflections on the home setting in hospitality', *Journal of Hospitality and Tourism Management*, 12(1): 37–49.

—— (2005b) 'Sociological impressionism in a hospitality context', *Annals of Tourism Research*, 32(3): 527–548.

—— (2005c) 'The commercial home enterprise and host: a United Kingdom perspective', *International Journal of Hospitality Management*, 24(4): 533–553.

Lynch, P. and Tucker, H. (2003) 'Quality homes, quality people: the challenge of quality grading and assurance in small accommodation enterprises', in R. Thomas (ed.) *Small Firms in Tourism – International Perspectives*, Oxford: Elsevier.

Lynch, P. and MacWhannell, D. (2000) 'Home and commercialised hospitality', in C. Lashley and A. Morrison (eds) *In Search of Hospitality: Theoretical Perspectives and Debates*, Oxford: Butterworth-Heinemann.

Lynch, P., Di Domenico, M. and Sweeney, M. (2007) 'Resident hosts and mobile strangers: temporary exchanges within the topography of the commercial home', in J. G. Molz and S. Gibson (eds) *Mobilizing Hospitality: The Ethics of Social Relations in a Mobile World*, Aldershot: Ashgate.

Lynch, P., Halcro, K., Buick, I., Johns, N. and Gillham, M. (2003) 'An investigation into networking by owner-managers of small hotels in the Scottish borders', unpublished study, Queen Margaret University College, Edinburgh.

Maani, K.E. and Cavana, R.Y. (2000) *Systems Thinking and Modelling*, Auckland: Prentice Hall.

Macbeth, J. (1985) *Ocean Cruising a study of affirmative deviance*, unpublished PhD thesis, Murdoch University, Perth.

MacCannell, D. (1973) 'Staged authenticity: on arrangements of social space in tourist settings', *American Journal of Sociology*, 79(3), 589–603.

—— (1976) *The Tourist: A New Theory of the Leisure Class*, New York: Schoken Books.

Madigan, R., Munro, M. and Smith, S.J. (1990) 'Gender and the meaning of home', *International Journal of Urban and Regional research*, 14(4): 625–647.

Magellan (2005) Online. Available HTTP: http://www.residentialcruiseline.com/index.cfm (accessed 1 August 2007).

Mallett, S. (2003) *Conceiving Cultures: Reproducing People and Places on Nuakata, Papua New Guinea*, Michigan: University of Michigan Press.

—— (2004) 'Understanding home: a critical review of the literature', *Sociological Review*, 52(1): 62–89.

Mann, S. (1997) 'Emotional labour in organizations', *Leadership and Organization Development Journal*, 18(1): 4–12.

—— (2004) '"People-work": emotion management, stress and coping', *British Journal of Guidance and Counselling*, 32(2): 205–221.

Manzo, L.C. (2003) 'Beyond house and haven: toward a vision of emotional relationships with places', *Journal of Environmental Psychology*, 23: 47–61.

Marlow, S. and Patton, D. (2005) 'All credit to men? entrepreneurship, finance, and gender', *Entrepreneurship Theory and Practice*, 29(6), 717–735.

Marsh, N. (1990) 'Hall of fame: L. Francis Herreshoff, yacht designer and philosopher', *Cruising World*, January, p. 62.

Massey, D. (1994) *Space, Place and Gender*, Minnesota: University of Minnesota Press.

—— (1995) 'Places and their pasts', *History Workshop Journal*, 39: 182–192.

—— (1996) 'Masculinity, dualisms and high technology', in N. Duncan (ed.) *Body Space*, London: Routledge.

Masterson, A. (2007) 'Put a spring in your step', *The Age* (travel supplement), Melbourne, 25 August, pp. 26–27.

McAllister, C. (1990) 'Women and feasting: ritual exchange, capitalism and Islamic revival in Negeri Sembilan, Malaysia', *Research in Economic Anthropology*, 12: 23–51.

McGehee, N.G. and Kim, K. (2004) 'Motivation for agri-tourism entrepreneurship', *Journal of Travel Research*, 43: 161–170.

McGehee, N.G., Kim, K. and Jennings, G.R. (2007) 'Gender and motivation for agri-tourism entrepreneurship , *Tourism Management*, 28: 280–289.

McGregor, J. and Tweed, D. (2002) 'Profiling a new generation of female small business owners in new zealand: networking, mentoring and growth', *Gender, Work and Organization*, 9(4), 420–438.

McIntosh, A. and Campbell, T. (2001) 'Willing workers on organic farms (WWOOF): a neglected aspect of farm tourism in New Zealand', *Journal of Sustainable Tourism*, 9(2): 111–127.

McIntosh, A.J. and Siggs, A. (2005) 'An exploration of the experiential nature of boutique accommodation', *Journal of Travel Research*, 44: 75–81.

McKenzie, F. and Ryan, M. (2004) 'Monastic traditions: lessons for wine tourism communities', in J. Carlsen and S. Charters (eds) International Wine Tourism Research, *Conference Proceedings of the International Wine Tourism Conference*, Margaret River, 2–5 May, Vineyard Publications, Perth.

Medwed, M. (2000) *Host Family*, London: Victor Gollancz, London.

Menzies, T.V., Diochon, M. and Gasse, Y. (2004) 'Examining venture-related myths concerning women entrepreneurs', *Journal of Developmental Entrepreneurship*, 9(2), 89–143.

Mills, S. (2005) *Gender and Colonial Space*, Manchester and New York: Manchester University Press.

Mirchandani, K. (2000) '"The best of both worlds" and "cutting my own throat": contradictory images of home-based work', *Qualitative Sociology*, 23(2), 159–182.

Molz, J.G. and Gibson, S. (2007) (eds) *Mobilizing Hospitality: The Ethics of Social Relations in a Mobile World*, Aldershot: Ashgate.

Moore, G. (1990) 'Structural determinants of men's and women's personal networks', *American Sociological Review*, 55: 726–735.

Moore, J. (2000) 'Placing home in context', *Journal of Environmental Psychology*, 20: 207–217.

Morgan, N. and Pritchard, A. (1998) *Tourism Promotion and Power: Creating Images, Creating Identities*, Chichester: John Wiley and Sons Ltd.

Morris J.A. and Feldman, D.C. (1996) 'The dimensions, antecedents, and consequences of emotional labor', *Academy of Management Review*, 21(4): 986–1010.

Morrison, A.J. (1998a) 'Small firm statistics: a hotel sector focus', *The Services Industries Journal*, 18(10): 132–142.

—— (1998b) 'The tourist accommodation sector in Scotland', in R. MacLellan and R. Smith (eds) *Tourism in Scotland*, London: International Thomson Business Press.

—— (2002) 'Small hospitality businesses: enduring or endangered?', *Journal of Hospitality and Tourism Management*, 9(1): 1–11.

—— (2006) 'A contextualisation of entrepreneurship', *International Journal of Entrepreneurial Behaviour & Research*, 12(4): 198–209.

Morrison, A.J. and Conway, F. (2007) 'The status of the small hotel firm', *The Services Industries Journal*, 27(1): 47–58.

Morrison, A. J. and Teixeira, R. (2004) 'Small firm performance in the context of agent and structure: a cross cultural comparison in the tourist accommodation sector', in R. Thomas (ed.) *Small Firms in Tourism: International Perspectives*, Oxford: Elsevier.

Morrison, A.J., Baum, T. and Andrew, R. (2001) 'The lifestyle economics of small tourism businesses', *Journal of Travel and Tourism Research*, 1: 16–25.

Morrison, A.J., Rimmington, M. and Williams, C. (1999) *Entrepreneurship in the Hospitality, Tourism and Leisure Industries*, Oxford: Elsevier.

Morrison, A.M., Pearce, P., Moscardo, G., Nadkarni, N. and O'Leary, J. (1996) 'Specialist accommodation: definition, markets served, and roles in tourism development', *Journal of Travel Research*, 35(1): 18–26.

Moscardo, G., Saltzer, R., Norris, A. and McCoy A. (2004) 'Changing patterns of regional tourism: implications for tourism on the Great Barrier Reef', *Journal of Tourism Studies*, 15(1): 34–50.

Moses, S. (2005) 'Tourism: how to make it work for everyone', (media release), Hepburn Shire Council, Daylesford.

—— (2006) 'Visitors to spa country on the increase', (media release), Hepburn Shire Council, Daylesford.

Mottiar, Z. (2007) 'Inter-firm relations of lifestyle entrepreneurs: Westport Ireland', *International Journal of Entrepreneurship Special Issue on Tourism*, 8(1), 67–74.

Mottiar, Z. and Tucker, H. (2007) 'Webs of power: multi-firm ownership among tourism firms in Courtown, Ireland and Kusadasi, Turkey', *Current Issues*, 10(4), 279–295.

Mulligan, M., Humphrey, K., James, P., Scanlon, C., Smith, P. and Welch, N. (2006) *Creating Community: Celebrations, Arts and Wellbeing Within and Across Local Communities*, Melbourne: The Globalism Institute, RMIT University.

Munro, M. and Madigan, R. (1999) 'Negotiating space in the family home', in I. Cieraad (ed.) *At Home: An Anthropology of Domestic Space*, Syracuse: Syracuse University Press.

Murray, M. and Graham, B. (1997) E*xploring the Dialectics of Route-Based Tourism: The Camino de Santiago*, Tourism Management, 18(8): 513–524.

Namasivayam, K. and Matilla, N. (2007) 'Accounting for the joint effects of servicescape and service exchange on customer's satisfaction evaluations', *Journal of Hospitality and Tourism Research*, 31(1): 3–18.

New Straits Times. 'Hari Raya Cheer', 27 March 1994, p. 1.

—— 'A feast for 200,000', 13 November 2004, p. 2.

—— 'Malaysians celebrate', 16 November 2004, p. 4.

—— 'Thousands at open house', 28 November 2004, 5.

Newman, A.J. (2007) 'Uncovering dimensionality in the servicescape: towards legibility', *The Services Industry Journal*, 27(1): 15–28.

Ngaima, S.K. (2002) 'Principles of social systems', *Futurics*, 26(1/2): 37–47.

Nolan, M. and Nolan, S. (1989) *Christian Pilgrimage in Modern Western Europe*, London, NC: The University of North Carolina Press.

North West Farm Tourism Initiative (2004) *Evaluation Baseline Study*, Cumbria.

Nowicka, M. (2007) 'Mobile locations: construction of home in a group of mobile transnational professionals', *Global Networks*, 7(1): 69–86.

Noy, C. (2004) 'The trip really changed me: backpackers' narratives of self-change', *Annals of Tourism Research*, 31: 78–102.

Nummedal, M. and Hall, C.M. (2006) 'Local food in tourism: an investigation of the New Zealand South Island's bed and breakfast sector's use and perception of local food', *Tourism Review International*, 9(4): 365–378.

Nuntsu, N., Tassiopoulos, D. and Haydam, N. (2004) 'The bed and breakfast market of Buffalo City (BC), South Africa: present status, constraints and success factors', *Tourism Management*, 25: 515–522.

O'Dell, T. (2005) 'Experiencescapes: blurring borders and testing connections', in T. O'Dell and P. Billing (eds) *Experiencescapes: Tourism, Culture and Economy*, Copenhagen: Copenhagen Business School Press.

O'Gorman, K.D. (2007) 'Dimensions of hospitality: exploring ancient and classical origins' in C. Lashley, P. Lynch and A. Morrison (eds) *Hospitality A Social Lens*, Oxford: Elsevier.

Oakley, A. (1974) *The Sociology of Housework*, Bath: Pitman Press.

OECD (1994) 'Les Stratégies du tourisme et le développement rural', in *Politiques du tourisme et tourisme internacional'dans les pays de l'OCDE 1991–1992*, OECD: Paris: 13–79.

Oh, H., Fiore, A.M. and Jeoung, M. (2007) 'Measuring experience economy concepts: tourism applications', *Journal of Travel Research*, 46: 119–132.

Oldham, G., Creemers, G. and Rebeck, T. (2000) 'An economic evaluation of tourism: a case study of accommodation facilities in southern Maputaland', *Development South Africa*, 17(2): 175–188.

Ollenburg, C. and Buckley, R. (2007) 'Stated economic and social motivations of farm tourism operators', *Journal of Travel Research*, 45(4): 444–452.

Oppermann, M. (1998) 'Farm tourism in New Zealand', in R. Butler, C.M. Hall and J. Jenkins (eds) *Tourism and Recreation in Rural Areas*, Chichester: Wiley.

Ouellette, P., Kaplan, R. and Kaplan, S. (2005) 'The monastery as a restorative environment', *Journal of Environmental Psychology*, 25(2): 175–188.

Page, S.J. and Getz, D. (1997) 'The business of rural tourism: international perspectives', in S.J. Page and D. Getz (eds) *The Business of Rural Tourism: International Perspectives*, London: International Thomson Business Press.

Paterson, R. (2002) *'The invisible farmers – women in agriculture'*, Australian Bureau of Statistics, 1384.6 – Statistics – Tasmania, 2002. Online. Available HTTP: http://www.abs.gov.au/Ausstats/abs@.nsf/90a12181d877a6a6ca2568b5007b861c/dd316da6a444df9eca256c320024784b!OpenDocument (accessed 10 December 2006).

Peacock, M. (1993) 'A question of size', *International Journal of Contemporary Hospitality Management*, 5(4):29–32.

Pearce, P.L. (1988) *The Ulysses Factor: Evaluating Visitors in Tourist Settings*, New York: Springer-Verlag.

—— (1990) 'Farm tourism in New Zealand: a social situations analysis', *Annals of Tourism Research*, 17(3): 337–352.

Pearce, P.L. and Moscardo, G. (1992) *The Boutique/Specialist Accommodation Sector: Perceived Government Needs and Policy Initiatives*, Townsville, Queensland: James Cook University.

Pearce, P.L., Moscardo, G. and Ross, G. (1996) *Understanding and Managing the Tourism Community Relationship*, London: Elsevier.

Perkins, H.C. and Thorns, D.C. (1999) 'House and home and their interaction with changes in New Zealand's urban system, households and family structures', *Housing, Theory and Society*, 16: 124–135.

Phillips, L. and Jorgensen, M.W. (2004) *Discourse Analysis as Theory and Method*, London: Sage.

Phizacklea, A. and Wolkowitz, C. (1995) *Home-working Women: Gender, Racism and Class at Work*, London: Sage.

Pine II, B.J., and Gilmore, J.H. (1998) 'Welcome to the experience economy', *Harvard Business Review*, 76(4): 97–105.

—— (1999) *The Experience Economy: Work is Theatre and Every Business is a Stage*, Boston, MA: Harvard Business School Press.

Provencher, R. (1971) *Two Malay Worlds: Interaction in Urban and Rural Settings*, Berkeley: Center for South and Southeast Asian Studies, University of California.

Prugl, E. (2004) 'Gender orders in German agriculture: from the patriarchal welfare state to liberal environmentalism', *Sociologia Ruralis*, 44(4): 349–372.

Quek, P. (1997) *Little inns big business*. Online. Available HTTP: http://www.hotel-online.com/Trends/PKF?Special/LittleInns_Sept1997.html (accessed 17 December 2006).

Rainwater, I. (1966) 'Fear and house-as-haven in the lower class', *American Institute of Planners Journal*, 32: 23–31.

Rapport, N. and Dawson, A. (1998) *Migrants of Identity: Perspections of Home in a World of Movement*, Oxford: Berg.

Regnault, L. (1990) *La Vie Quotidienne de Pères du Désert en Egypte au IVe Siècle*, Paris: Hachette.

Reimer, A. and Kuehn, R. (2005) 'The impact of servicescape on quality perception', *European Journal of Marketing*, 39(7/8): 785–808.

Renzulli, L. A., Aldrich, H. and Moody, J. (2000) 'Family matters: gender, networks, and entrepreneurial outcomes', *Social Forces*, 79(2), 523–546.

Ribeiro, M. (2003) 'Espacos rurais como espacos turísticos: reflexoes em torno da construcao da oferta de turismo em espaco rural, em Portugal', in Portela and Caldas (eds) *Portugal Chao*, Oeiras: Celta.

Richards, W. (2006) 'Causes for seasonal fluctuation and its effects on the tourist industry and managing seasonalities – case studies and best practices', in *Proceedings from the ETIN and European Parliament Seasonality Conference*, Brussels, 8 June 2006.

Richardson, J. (1999) *A History of Australian Travel and Tourism*, Melbourne: Hospitality Press.

Rinschede, G. (1992) 'Forms of religious tourism', *Annals of Tourism Research*, 19: 51–67.

Ritzer, G. (1993) *The McDonaldization of Society*, London: Pine Forge Press.

—— 'Inhospitable Hospitality', in C. Lashley, P. Lynch and A. Morrison (eds) *Hospitality: A Social Lens*, Oxford: Elsevier.

Robinson, M. and Lynch, P. (2006) 'The power of hospitality: a sociolinguistic analysis', in C. Lashley, P. Lynch and A. Morrison (eds) *Hospitality: A Social Lens*, Elsevier: Oxford.

Rogerson, C.M. (2004) 'Transforming the South African tourism industry: the emerging black-owned bed and breakfast economy', *GeoJournal*, 60(3): 273–281.

Rosaldo, M. Z. and Lamphere, L. (eds) (1974) *Women, Culture, and Society*, Stanford, Calif.: Stanford University Press.

Rose, G. (1993) *Feminism and Geography. The Limits of Geographical Knowledge*. Minneapolis: University of Minneapolis Press.

Rubery, J. (2005) 'Reflections on gender mainstreaming: an example of feminist economics in action?', *Feminist Economics*, 11(3), 1–26.

Rupena-Osolink, M. (1983/84) 'The role of farm women in rural pluriactivity: experience in Yugoslavia', *Sociologia Ruralis*, 23–24: 89–94.

Rybczynski, W. (1986) *Home: A Short History of an idea*, New York, NY: Penguin Books.

Sachs, C. (1983) *The Invisible Farmers: Women in Agricultural Production*, Totawa, New Jersey: Rowan and Allanheld.

Saegert, S. (1985) 'The role of housing in the experience of the dwelling', in I. Altman and C.M. Werner (eds) *Human Behaviour and Environments: Advances in Theory and Research, Volume 8: Home Environments.* New York: Plenium Press.

Sakach, D.E. (2004) *Bed & Breakfast and Country Inns*, American Historic Inns.

Salt, B. (2006) *The Big Picture*, Melbourne: Hardie Grant Books.

Samarasuriya, S. (1982) *Who Needs Tourism? Employment for Women in the Holiday industry of Sudugama, Sri Lanka*, Colombo: Research Project for Women and Development.

Sant Cassia, P. (1999) 'Tradition, tourism and memory in Malta', *Journal of the Royal Anthropological Institute*, 5: 247–263.

Santos, X. and Sparrer, M. (2006) 'Galicia', in: AECIT: *La actividad turística española en 2005*, Madrid: Ramón Areces: 459 – 472.

Saunders, P. (1990) *A Nation of Home Owners*, London: Unwin Hyman.

Schutz, A. (1967) *The Phenomenology of the Social World*, trans. G. Walsh and F. Lehnert, Chicago, IL: Northwestern University Press.

Schwaniger, M. (1989) 'Strategic management in tourism', in S. Witt, and L. Moutinho (eds) *Tourism Marketing and Management Handbook*, New York: Prentice-Hall.

Scott, D. (2007) 'Melbourne comes out on top in short breaks poll', *The Age* (Travel supplement), Melbourne, 28 April, p. 3.

Scott, J. (1997) 'Chances and choices: women and tourism in Northern Cyprus', in T. Sinclair (ed.) *Gender, Work and Tourism*, London: Routledge.

Sean-Guan Yeoh (2005) 'House, kampung, and tamun: spatial hegemony and the politics and poetics of space in urban Malaysia', *Crossroads*, 17(2): 128–158.

Seekings, J. (1989) 'Components of tourism', in S. Witt and L. Moutinho (eds) *Tourism Marketing and Management Handbook*, New York: Prentice-Hall.

Seeley, J., Sim, R. and Loosley, E. (1956) *Crestwood Heights: A Study of the Culture of Suburban Life*, Toronto: Toronto University Press.

Selwyn, T. (2000) 'An anthropology of hospitality', in C. Lashley and A. Morrison (eds) *In Search of Hospitality*, Oxford: Butterworth-Heinemann.

—— (1996) 'Introduction', in T. Selwyn (ed.) *The Tourist Image: Myths and Myth Making in Tourism*, New York and London: John Wiley and Sons Ltd.

Seymour, D. and Sandiford, P. (2005) 'Learning emotion rules in service organiza-tions: socialization and training in the UK public-house sector', *Work, Employment and Society*, 19(3): 547–564.

Shackley, M. (1993) 'Guest farms in Namibia: an emerging accommodation sector in Africa's hottest destination', *International Journal of Hospitality Management*, 12(3): 253–265.

—— (1999) 'Tourism development and environmental protection in southern Sinai', *Tourism Management*, 20: 543–548.

—— (2001) *Managing Sacred Sites*, London: Thomson.

—— (2004) 'Accommodating the spiritual tourist: the case of religious retreat houses', in R. Thomas (ed.) *Small Firms in Tourism: International Perspectives*, London: Elsevier.

Sharpley, R. and Vass, A. (2006) 'Tourism farming and diversification: an attitudinal study', *Tourism Management*, 27: 1040–1052.

Shaw, G. and Williams, A.M. (2002) *Critical Issues in Tourism: A Geographical Perspective*, 2nd edn, Oxford: Blackwell Publishing.

Shaw, G., Williams, A. and Greenwood, J. (1987) 'Comparative studies in local economies: the Cornish case', *Built Environment*, 13(2): 73 – 84.

Sherry, J.F., Jr. (ed.) (1998a) *Servicescapes: The Concept of Place in Contemporary Markets*, Lincolnwood, IL: Nike Town Chicago Business Books.

—— (1998b) 'The soul of the company store: Nike Town Chicago and the emplaced brandscape', in J.F. Sherry Jr. (ed.) *Servicescapes: The Concept of Place in Contemporary Markets*, Lincolnwood, IL: Nike Town Chicago Business Books.

Shortall, S. (1992) 'Power analysis and farm wives, an empirical study of the power relationships affecting women on Irish farms', *Sociologia Ruralis*, 32(4): 431–451.

Sibley, D. (1995) *Geographies of Exclusion*, Routledge: London.

Siiskonen, P. (1996) *Overview of the Socio-economic Position of Rural Women in Selected Central and Eastern European Countries*, Rome Food and Agriculture Organization of the United Nations.

Silva, L. (2006) 'O turismo em espaço rural: um estudo da oferta e dos promotores', CIES *e-working paper* n° 16/2006, ISCTE: Lisboa.

Silvano, M. J. (2005) 'O turismo rural como factor de desenvolvimento sustentável na perspectiva dos impactos criados nos promotores do alojamento turístico. O caso do Parque Natural de Montesinho', unpublished Master's thesis: Universidade de Aveiro.

Simmel, G. (1908/1971) 'The stranger,' in D.N. Levine (ed.) *George Simmel on individuality and social forms, selected writings*, Chicago: University of Chicago Press.

—— (1950) *The Sociology of George Simmel*, trans. K.H. Wolff, Glencoe, IL: Free Press.

—— (1983) 'Soziologie des Raumes' in H.J. Dahme and O. Rammstedt (eds) *Georg Simmel. Schriften zur Soziologie. Eine Auswahl*, Frankfurt a.M.: Suhrkamp.

Simpson, R. and Altman, Y. (2000) 'The time bounded glass ceiling and young women managers: career progress and career success – evidence from the UK', *Journal of European Industrial Training*, 24(4), 190–198.

Singh, V., Vinnicombe, S. and James, K. (2006) 'Constructing a professional identity: how young female managers use role models', *Women in Management Review*, 21(1), 67–81.

Sixsmith, J. (1986) 'The meaning of home: a exploratory study of environmental experience', *Journal of Environmental Psychology*, 6: 281–298.

Slattery, P. (2002) 'Finding the hospitality industry', *Journal of Hospitality, Leisure, Sport and Tourism Education*, 1(1): 19–28.

Smailes, P.J. (2002) 'From rural dilution to multifunctional countryside: Some pointers to the future for South Australia', *Australian Geographer*, 33(1): 79–95.

Smith, W.A. (2003) 'Does B & B management agree with the basic ideas behind experience management strategy?', *Journal of Business & Management*, 9(3): 233–247.

Smith-Hunter, A.E. and Boyd, R.L. (2004) 'Applying theories of entrepreneurship to a comparative analysis of white and minority women business owners', *Women in Management Review*, 19(1), 18–28.

Smitz, P., Ashworth, S. and Bain, C. (2004) *Australia*, 12th edn, Footscray: Lonely Planet Publications.

Sönmez, S. (2001) 'Tourism behind the veil of Islam: women and development in the Middle East', in Y. Apostolopoulos, S. Sönmez and D. Timothy (eds) *Women as Producers and Consumers of Tourism in Developing Regions*, Westport, CT: Praeger Publishers.

Sparkes, S. (2003) 'Introduction: the changing domain of the house in Southeast Asia', in S. Sparkes and S. Howell (eds) *The House in Southeast Asia: a Changing Social, Economic and Political Domain*, London and New York: Routledge Curzon.

Sparrer, M. (2005) *El turismo en espacio rural como una estrategia de desarrollo. Una comparación a nivel europeo*, unpublished PhD thesis, Universidade de Santiago de Compostela.

Star. 'Prime Minister urges festival harmony', 27 March 1993, p. 1.

Stehlik, D., Lawrence, G. and Gray, I. (1999) *Australian farm families' experience of the drought of the 1990s. A sociological investigation*, Canberra: Report to the Rural Industries Research and Development Corporation.

Stringer, P. F. (1981) 'Hosts and guests: the bed and breakfast phenomenon', *Annals of Tourism Research*, 8(3): 357–376.

Sullivan, C. (2000) 'Space and the intersection of work and family in homeworking households', *Community, Work and Family*, 3(2): 185–204.

Sullivan, C. and Lewis, S. (2001) 'Home-based telework, gender, and the synchronization of work and family: perspectives of teleworkers and their co-residents', *Gender, Work and Organization*, 8(2): 124–145.

Sweeney, M. and Lynch, P.A. (2008) 'Towards a typology of commercial homes', *Proceedings of 16th Annual Council for Hospitality Management Education Hospitality Research Conference*, University of Strathclyde.

System Three (2000) *Scottish Accommodation Occupancy Surveys 1999: Final Report*, Edinburgh: System Three (Prepared for Scottish Tourist Board).

Tapper, R. and Tapper, N. (1986) '"Eat this, it'll do you a power of good": Food and commensality among Durrani Pashtuns', *American Ethnologist*, 12(1): 62–79.

Telfer, E. (1996) *Food for Thought: Philosophy and Food*, London: Routledge.

—— (2000) 'The philosophy of hospitableness' in C. Lashley and A. Morrison (eds) *In Search of Hospitality*, Oxford: Butterworth-Heinemann.

Thomas, J. and Thomas, J. (1994) *The Australian Bed and Breakfast Book*, Brookvale: Moonshine Press.

Thomas, R. (1998) 'An introduction to the study of small tourism and hospitality firms', in R. Thomas (ed.) *The Management of Small Tourism and Hospitality Firms*, London: Cassell.

Thompson, C.J. and Arsel, Z. (2004) 'The Starbucks brandscape and consumers (anti-corporate) experiences of glocalization', *Journal of Consumer Research*, 31(3): 631–642.

Thurston, H. (1910) 'Hospitality', *The Catholic Encyclopedia*, 7: 484–85.

TNS Travel and Tourism (2005) *Scottish Accommodation Occupancy Survey 2004: Methodological Report*, Edinburgh: TNS (Prepared for VisitScotland).

Tombs, A. and McColl-Kennedy, J.R. (2003) 'Social-servicescape conceptual model', *Marketing Theory*, 3: 447–475.

Tourism Australia (2007) *Agri-tourism*, Online. Available HTTP: http://www.tourism.australia.com/Marketing.asp?lang=EN&sub=0437&al=2560 (accessed 25 November 2007).

Tourism Queensland (2002) *Farmstay Tourism*, Brisbane: Tourism Queensland.

Tourism Victoria (2005) *Spa Tourism Market Profile*, Melbourne: Tourism Victoria.

Tucker, H. (2001) 'Tourists and troglodytes: negotiating tradition for sustainable cultural tourism', *Annals of Tourism Research*, 28(4): 868–891.

—— (2002) 'Welcome to Flintstones-land: contesting place and identity in Göreme, Central Turkey', in S.Coleman and M.Crang (eds) *Tourism: Between Place and Performance*, Oxford: Berghahn Books.

—— (2003a) *Living with Tourism: Negotiating Identities in a Turkish Village*, London: Routledge.

—— (2003b) 'The host–guest relationship and its implications in rural tourism', in D.L. Roberts and M. Mitchell (eds) *New Directions in Rural Tourism*, Aldershot: Ashgate.

—— (2005) 'Narratives of place and self: differing experiences of package coach tours in New Zealand', *Tourist Studies*, 5(3): 267–282.

—— (2007) 'Undoing shame: tourism and women's work in Turkey', in *Journal of Tourism and Cultural Change*, 5(2): 87–105.

—— (2009) 'Recognising emotion and its postcolonial potentiality', in *Tourism Geographies*, 11(4).

Tucker, H. and Keen, D. (2005) *Hosting Guests in Rural New Zealand: A Social Analysis of the Bed and Breakfast and Homestay Sector*, Dunedin: Department of Tourism, University of Otago.

Tucker, H. and Lynch, P. (2004) 'Host–guest dating: the potential of improving the customer experience through host-guest psychological matching', *Journal of Quality Assurance in Hospitality and Tourism*, 5 (2/3/4): 11–32.

Tyrväinen, L., Silvennoinen, H., Nousiainen, I. and Tahvanainen, L. (2001) 'Rural tourism in Finland: tourists' expectation of landscape and environment', *Scandinavian Journal of Hospitality and Tourism*, 1(2): 133–149.

Urry, J. (1990) *The Tourist Gaze: Leisure and Travel in Contemporary Societies*, London: Sage.

—— (2002) *The Tourist Gaze*, London: Sage Publications.

Valentine, G. (1997) 'A safe place to grow up? Parenting, perceptions of children's safety and the rural idyll', *Journal of Rural Studies*, 13(2):137–148.

Vallen, G. and Rande, W. (1997) 'Bed and breakfasts in Arizona', *Cornell Hotel & Restaurant Administration Quarterly*, 38(4): 62–75.

van Eeden, J. (2007) 'Gendered tourism space: a south african perspective', in A. Pritchard, N. Morgan, I. Ateljevic and C. Harris (eds) *Tourism and Gender: Embodiment, Sensuality and Experience*, Wallingford: CAB International.

van Gennep, A. (1975) *Rites of Passage*, London: Routledge & Kegan.

van Manen, M. (1990) *Researching Lived Experience, Human Science for an Action Sensitive Pedagogy*, The State University of New York, London, Ontario, Canada.

VisitScotland (2002) *Note on the Accommodation Stock in Scotland, 2001*, Edinburgh: VisitScotland.

Vogüé, A. (1977) *La Règle de saint Benoît, VII, Commentaire Doctrinal et* Spiritual, Paris: Les editions du Cerf.

Wakefield, K.L. and Blodgett, J.G. (1994) 'The importance of servicescapes in leisure service settings', *Journal of Services Marketing*, 8(3), 66–76.

—— (1996) 'The effect of the servicescape on customers' behavioral intentions in leisure service settings', *Journal of Services Marketing*, 10(6): 45–61.

—— (1999) 'Consumer response to intangible and tangible service factors', *Psychology and Marketing*, 16(1): 51–68.

Walker, B. and Salt, D. (2006) *Resilience Thinking – Sustaining Ecosystems and People in a Changing World*, Washington, DC: Island Press.

Walmsley, D. J. (2003) 'Rural tourism: a case of lifestyle-led opportunities', *Australian Geographer*, 34: 61–72.

Walton, J.K. (1978) *The Blackpool Landlady – A Social History*, Manchester: Manchester University Press.

Wardhaugh, J. (1999) 'The unaccommodated woman: home, homelessness and identity', *Sociological Review*, 47(1): 91–109.

Warren, J. (1998) *Rural Tourism in New Zealand*, Wellington: Centre for Research, Evaluation and Social Assessment.

Wearing, S. (2001) *Volunteer Tourism: Experiences That Make a Difference*, New York: CABI.

Weaver, D. and Fennell, D.A. (1997) 'The vacation farm sector in Saskatchewan: as profile of operations', *Tourism Management*, 18(6): 357–365.

Weiler, S. and Bernasek, A. (2001) 'Dodging the glass ceiling? Networks and the new wave of women entrepreneurs', *The Social Science*, 38: 85–103.

White, N.R. and White, P.B. (2004) 'Travel as transition, identity and place', *Annals of Tourism Research*, 31(1): 200–218.

Whyte, W. (1948) *Human Relations in the Restaurant Industry and Communications in the Food Service Industry*, School of Hotel Administration, Cornell University.

Wilkinson, P.F. and Prativi, W. (1995) 'Gender and tourism in an Indonesian village', *Annals of Tourism Research*, 22(2): 283–299.

Williams, C. (2003) 'Sky service: the demands of emotional labour in the airline industry', *Gender, Work and Organization*, 10(5): 513–550.

Williams, A.M. and Hall, C.M. (2000) 'Tourism and migration: new relationships between production and consumption', *Tourism Geographies*, 2(1): 5–27.

—— (2002) 'Tourism, migration, circulation and mobility: the contingencies of time and place', in C.M. Hall and A.M. Williams (eds) *Tourism and Migration: New Relationships Between Consumption and Production*, Dortrecht: Kluwer.

Williams, A.M., Shaw, G. and Greenwood, J. (1989) 'From tourist to tourism entrepreneur, from consumption to production. Evidence from Cornwall, England', *Environment and Planning A*, 21: 1639–1653.

Williams, C. and Buswell, J. (2003) *Service Quality in Leisure and Tourism*, Wallingford Oxon: CABI Publishing.

Willits, F.K., Bealer, R.C. and Timbers, V.L. (1990) 'Popular images of rurality: data from a Pennsylvania survey', *Rural Sociology*, 55 (4): 559–578.

Wilson, S., Fesenmaier, D., Fesenmaier, J. and van Es, J.C. (2001) 'Factors for success in rural tourism success', *Journal of Travel Research*, 40: 132–138.

Wodak, R. and Meyer, M. (2001) *Methods of Critical Discourse Analysis*, London: Sage.

Wolf-Tasker, A. (2006a) *Lake House: A Culinary Journey in Country Australia*, Prahran: Hardie Grant Books.

Wolf-Tasker, A. (2006b) *Lake House* (seasonal newsletter), Daylesford: Lake House.

Wolter, M. (1880) *Praecipua Ordinis Monastici Elementa*, Brugis: Desclée.

Wood, R. (1994) 'Hotel culture and social control', *Annals of Tourism Research*, 21(1): 65–80.

Woodward, M. R. (1988) '"The Slametan": textual knowledge and ritual performance in Central Javanese Islam', *History of Religions*, 28(2): 54–89.

Index

accommodation xiv, xv, 1, 21, 30, 147–48; budget 27, 28, 31, 32, 37, 131, 196; marginalised forms 21; patterns of accommodation use 27–28; site 16, 73–74, 75, 76–77, 80–83; *see also* bed and breakfast; commercial home; farmstay; guesthouse; hotel; motel; servicescape

Africa: commercial home 26; Namibia 36; South Africa 36

anthropology 9, 10, 129, 154, 159, 164

Asia 185; *see also* cave-homes of Göreme; Malay-Muslim home

Australia 20, 90, 179–93; agriculture 50; alcohol 180, 211; Asia 185; Australiana 190; authenticity 184, 205; bed and breakfast 15, 26–27, 180, 181–82, 189, 190; boutique hotels 187, 189, 190; car 181; Central Queensland region 16, 51–59; Chinese market gardens 185; climate 184, 185; commercial home 20, 26, 179, 184, 187, 188–93, 211, 213 (development 179–82, 184, 186, 192, 193, 211; diversity 20, 182, 188–89, 192, 193); commodification 213; creative class 187; Daylesford 179, 181, 182–93; Daylesford Visitor Information Centre 186; demographics 185, 189, 192; diversity, diversification 185, 186, 188, 189, 193, 212, 213; domestic/international tourism 179, 180, 181, 182, 185; domesticity 181, 184–85, 192, 205; ethnic plurality 20, 192; Europe 20, 180, 182, 184, 185, 190, 192; family business 108; Far North Queensland region 25, 26–30; farm tourism 16, 50–59, 182; farmstay

26–27, 50–59, 180, 189; festivals and events 188, 191; film 186–87; food and wine 182, 183–84, 185, 188, 190, 191; friendship 180, 181; funky 185, 186, 192; gender issues 180; gourmet cuisine 191; guest/host interaction 185, 186, 189–90, 193, 209; guesthouse 179, 180–81, 189, 190, 192, 211; health 183, 187–88, 190, 191; Hepburn, Captain John 184; Hepburn Shire Council 186–87; Hepburn Springs 179, 181, 182–93; home-based tourism 179, 182, 187, 189; homeliness 20, 180, 181–82, 184, 185, 188, 189, 190, 192, 193, 205, 211, 212, 213; home-stay 180, 182; hospitality 179; host 181, 186, 209; hotel 27, 180; Indigenous Australians 184; Jennings, Gayle 16, 50–59, 207, 210; Katoomba 181; King, Brian 20, 179–93, 209, 211, 212, 213; Lake Daylesford 185; Lake House 190–91; landscape 192; lifestyle 20, 179, 183, 186, 187, 192; marketing 185, 189, 205; meals 181, 190, 191; micro-businesses 192, 213; migration 20, 179, 180, 184, 189, 192, 193, 211; mineral springs 183, 184; Moscardo, Gianna 15, 25, 26–30; motel 179, 181; New South Wales 181; New Zealand 181; Northern Italy 179, 184, 188, 189; nostalgia 20, 179, 190, 192; railway 184; regional 182, 183–84, 186, 187, 188, 189, 191, 192, 205, 212; relaxation 183, 188, 190; resorts 190; resurgence 185, 187; rural tourism 179, 182, 183; sea change 60, 189; seasonality 185; self-contained accommodation 181, 189, 190; Slow

246   *Index*